HELLAS

A Short History of Ancient Greece

A STATUE OF THE SIXTH CENTURY

HELLAS

A SHORT HISTORY
OF ANCIENT GREECE

C. E. ROBINSON

BEACON PRESS   BOSTON

With the exception of plates I, III, V, IX, XIII,
XIV, and the illustration on the title page, all
illustrations are the work of the author.

Translations, except where otherwise noted,
are by the author.

Plates I, IX and XIV are reproduced from photographs
by Nelly's Studio, New York.

Contents

Contents

List of Illustrations

FULL PAGE PLATES

ILLUSTRATIONS IN THE TEXT

A map of Ancient Greece, and a Chronological Table follow this list of illustrations.

ANCIENT GREECE

Scale of Miles

10 0   50   100

⊙ *Members of Athenian Empire*

Amphipolis

Pella

MACEDON   ⊙   ⊙

Methone   CHALCIDICE

Pydna   *Olynthus*

Potidaea

Mt.Olympus✳   ⊙ ⊙

A   E   G

THESSALY

CORCYRA   E·U·B·O

I   *Thermopylae*

O   PHOCIS

N   *Naupactus* *Delphi*   BOEOTIA

Ithaca   *Thebes*

I   *Plataea* *Decelea*

A   *Megara* *Eleusis*

CORINTH   ATHENS

Olympia   *Mycenae*

Mantinea ARGOS

ARCADIA

Megalopolis

Mt.Ithome✳

MESSENIA SPARTA

Pylos

Melos

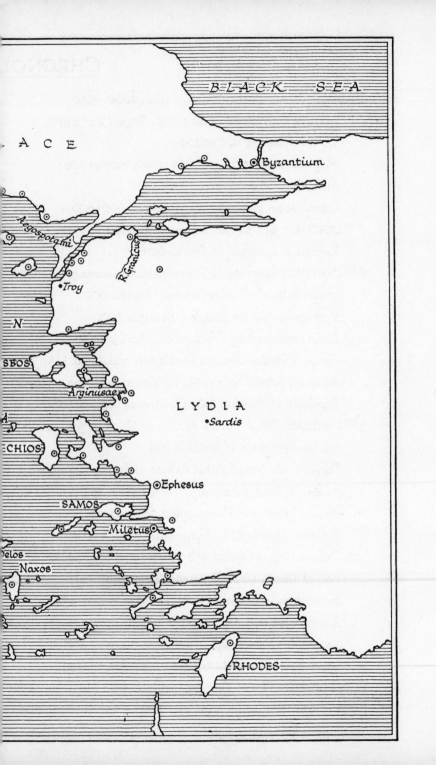

BLACK SEA

Byzantium

THRACE

Aegospotami

R. Granicus

Troy

LEMNOS

LESBOS

Arginusae

LYDIA
Sardis

CHIOS

Ephesus

SAMOS

Miletus

Delos

Naxos

RHODES

PREHISTORIC. Minoan Civilisation 4000-1250.

    Achaens enter Peloponnese c.1250. Trojan War c.1180.

    Dorian Invasion 1100-1000.

    Migrations to Asia Minor 1150-1000. Homer 900?

    Main City-States formed 900-750.

    Colonisation of Black Sea, Sicily, etc., 800-600.

7TH CENTURY. Sparta quells Messenian revolt 630.

    Reforms of Lycurgus at Sparta 610?

6TH CENTURY. Sparta wins Peloponnesian supremacy 590-20.

    Ionian Culture:- Thales flor. 590: Sappho 600:

    Pythagoras 540 (in Italy): Heraclitus 500.

    Ionia conquered by Croesus of Lydia (560-46).

    Cyrus of Persia captures Sardis 546 and Ionia 543.

    Athens:- Solon's Reform 594: Pisistratus' tyranny 546-27:

    Expulsion of Hippias 510: Cleisthenes' Reform 508.

5TH CENTURY. After Darius' débâcle in Scythia 514, Ionia

    revolts 499: sack of Miletus 494.

    Darius sends army against Athens: defeated at Marathon 49

    Athenian fleet enlarged by Themistocles 482.

    Xerxes' Invasion: Thermopylae, Salamis 480.

    Plataea, Mycale 479: Eurymedon 466?

    Delian League formed 478: secessions begin 467.

    Fall of Cimon 462: Pericles in power 461.

    Expedition in Egypt 459-4: Treasury moved 454.

    Aegina captured 457: Land Empire won 457.

    Peace with Persia 448: Parthenon built by 438.

    Land Empire lost 447: Peace with Sparta 445.

Peloponnesian War:- Corcyra incident 433: Megarian decree

First Phase:- Attica invaded 431: Plague 430-29: Pericles dies

TABLE

Lesbos revolts 428-7: Pylos taken 425:
attack on Boeotia 424: Brasidas in Chalcidice 424:
Brasidas and Cleon killed 422: Peace of Nicias 421.
cond Phase :-Athens and Argos ally against Sparta: Mantinea 418.
Sicilian expedition 415: Syracuse attacked 414: defeat 413.
Spartans occupy Decelea 413: Lesbos, etc. revolt 412.
Revolution of Four Hundred 411: Alcibiades' recall 411.
Spartan fleet defeated near Byzantium 411.
Lysander wins Cyrus' aid 408: Alcibiades deposed 406.
Athenian victory at Arginusae: admirals executed 406.
Battle of Aegospotami 405: Athens surrenders 404.
Thirty Tyrants expelled 403: Lysander recalled 402.
Cyrus leads 10,000 Greeks against Persian king 401.
H CENTURY. Agesilaus' campaign in Asia Minor 396-94.
Corinthian War begins 395: Conon and Persian fleet
defeat Spartans 394: Persian king dictates Peace 386.
Thebes captured by Sparta 382: freed by patriots 379.
Thebes and Athens fight Sparta 378: Peace Congress 371.
Sparta attacks Thebes, Leuctra, 371. Epaminondas
invades Peloponnese 370, 369, 365: killed at Mantinea 362.
hilip of Macedon 359-36: takes Amphipolis, Pydna, etc. 357-3.
Phocians seize Delphi 356: Philip checked at Thermopylae 352.
Philip takes Olynthus 348: fooling Athenian envoys, sacks Phocis 346.
Amphictyons enlist Philip's aid 339: Chaeronea 338.
lexander's accession 336: victory over Persians at Granicus 334.
routs Darius at Issus 333: takes Tyre 332:
winters in Egypt 332: victory at Arbela 331:
takes Babylon, Susa, etc. 331: Expedition to Samarcand,
India, etc. 329-5: death 323.

FOREWORD

"In Greek history," says Mr. Robinson, "little that happened mattered much; it is what the Greeks thought that counted." It has counted so much, indeed, that no one of us can enter into his European cultural inheritance without some knowledge of what the Greeks thought. Study of the Greeks transcends antiquarianism: their experience is permanently relevant and perennially capable of providing illumination and direction for our own spiritual problems.

It is upon this illumination that Mr. Robinson has focused his book; his aim is to present the aspects of Greek history that are of abiding and direct interest to the thoughtful modern. In the sense that a span requiring six stout volumes of the Cambridge Ancient History is here dealt with in fewer than two hundred pages, this is a popularization; but it is a popularization of the right sort, done by a mature scholar whose more technical work compels respect for his general interpretations.

The analogies and examples in this book are mainly British because the author is an Englishman. He uses (and very aptly) words like "Gestapo" and "Quisling" because he wrote it in 1946. And there is a sense of exultation in democracy because democracy had just won a difficult war against its enemies. The original title was *Zito Hellas: A Popular History of Ancient Greece*. "Zito Hellas" means "Long live Greece!"

MOSES HADAS

INTRODUCTION

"Nothing moves in the world," it has been said, "which is not Greek in origin." "Yes, but," the critic replies, "the lesson has been learnt long since: whatever matters in Classical Culture is by now absorbed into the life-blood of our civilization; further study of it seems superfluous." This is wholly to misconceive the function and influence of the Classical spirit. Throughout the centuries Greek thought has displayed an unfailing capacity to kindle thought in others, and there is scarcely a turning-point in Western history at which its explosive force has not been at work. First it broke through the cramping walls of the small Greek states which bred it, and diffused itself into the larger atmosphere of Alexander's Empire, transforming the whole life and outlook of the Near East. Next it penetrated the mind of Rome, shattering the narrow conservatism of the Republican regime, animating with its cultural ideals the men who governed the Empire, and finally laying the intellectual foundations of the Christian Church. At the Renaissance it scattered the mists of mediæval obscurantism and opened all manner of new horizons for individual initiative. Lastly, it inspired the philosophic ideas which underlay the French Revolution and thus helped to launch the Common Man on his fumbling, painful and still unfinished search for a better world-order. For this is the way of the Greek spirit. It destroys, but it destroys to rebuild; and the constructive impulse, whether its origin be acknowledged or no, is still operative among us to-day. The more we are able therefore to understand the principles of its working, the better for ourselves and posterity.

In all spheres of life—religious, artistic, educational and the rest— stagnation of the human spirit sets in when Means are mistaken for Ends, when ritualism, for example, is made a substitute for worship, when technical skill takes precedence over the search for beauty, or when pedantry obscures the true appreciation of literature. No age can escape the temptation; but in a scientific age the temptation is perhaps strongest of all. The opportunities which Science holds out are so dazzling that it seems fatally easy to think them desirable in themselves. Yet obviously it is the use to which they are put that determines their value. The very same means which, if rightly used, may carry us into Utopia, might equally land us in the nightmare robotism of some Brave New World. "Look to the End," said the ancient philosophers; and by that one word they implied the prime motive force, the final objective and the ideal consummation of human existence. "View life in its entirety, not piece-meal," was their message then—and is now.

The Greeks never shared our own instinctive distrust of ideas; and more than with most peoples their practice reflected their thought. By and large, right or wrong, they observed their own standard of values; and consciously or unconsciously they distinguished between Means and Ends. An instance or two must suffice.

They were an acquisitive folk; but wealth, once gained, they regarded (in the words of their own greatest statesman) as "a means to creative activity," or, as we might say, to a fuller and more civilized life.

They were a busy folk too; but they knew that "a pennyworth of ease is worth a penny"; and an existence of indiscriminate hustle would never have appealed to them.

They were athletic, none more so; but their spare time was devoted to the exercise of mind, perhaps even more than of body, so that their word leisure or "scholê" took on the meaning of "school." Certainly about the priority of intellectual over physical values the more thoughtful among them were never in doubt. If a choice had to be made between writing a great poem or inventing a new drug, your modern men might hesitate; the Greek would not.

One last illustration: and for the rest the reader must draw his own conclusions from the subsequent chapters of this book. No people believed more wholeheartedly in order and planning; indeed, it was the secret of nearly all they achieved. But they believed in liberty still more; and the idea that any free-born individual should become a mere cog in organization's wheel would have shocked all true Greeks to the core.

Among their many picturesque legends of the Underworld, two are peculiarly illuminating. One related how a certain criminal called Sisyphus was there everlastingly doomed to keep pushing a great boulder uphill, and how, every time the top was reached, it rolled back again to the bottom. The other told of the Danaid maidens whose equally futile task it was to pour water into a sieve. In other words, the Ancient Greeks' notion of eternal punishment was perpetual frustration—a Means without an End.

HELLAS

A Short History of Ancient Greece

CHAPTER I

DARKNESS AND LIGHT

I

"When a cat dies in a house, its inmates shave their eyebrows; when a dog dies, they shave body and head all over." So Herodotus the Greek historian observed when visiting Egypt; and it is hardly surprising that he thought it a queer sort of country. He saw much in it, of course, to admire, and, like all Greeks, he was deeply impressed by the "Wisdom" of its inhabitants. What puzzled him was that their everyday habits seemed to be the exact opposite of what he was used to at home. "In Egypt," he says, "women go to market; men stay at the loom. Women carry loads on their shoulders, men on their heads. Their meals are eaten in the street; their 'toilette' done indoors. Dough is mixed with the feet, mortar with the hands. And in writing or counting they work from right to left, perversely insisting that it is the Greeks who go left-wards, and they who go to the right." Trifling divergences of custom we should say and leave it at that. But to Herodotus it was sheer topsy-turvydom; and in point of fact, if we look below the surface, his instinct was correct. For the contrast between Egyptian and Greek was far greater than even he guessed. It went very deep indeed.

Now there is no denying that Egypt possessed a great civilization—the most brilliant civilization which had so far existed in the West. She produced the engineers who planned the construction of the Pyramids, the architects who built the gigantic temples still standing by the banks of the Nile, astronomers who devised a calendar of astonishing accuracy, doctors who understood a great deal about human anatomy, and mathematicians who had gone further in arithmetic and geometry than all the rest of mankind put together. Greek science itself, as we shall presently see, was to owe a very real debt to these technical and professional triumphs.

But technical triumphs are no indication of true civilization; men may invent aeroplanes and motor cars, and men may also use them like devils. So there is another side to the picture. Despite all the material splendour of their achievement, the "Wisdom" of the Egyptians—the whole structure of their religious and philosophic thought—was built on the craziest foundation. The Sphinx with its lion's body and human head

13

remains to us as a symbol of their fantastic conceptions. For it was thus that they imagined their gods. Their mythological lore was full of similar monstrosities compounded of bird and animal forms in strange combinations. Of their bull-god Apis—the prototype of the Israelites' Golden Calf—Herodotus has left us a description. "In Cambyses' reign," he says, "the god Apis appeared in Egypt. He is the calf of a cow which can never calve again; and when struck by lightning she then conceives Apis. He is identified by the following markings—a black coat with a white square on the forehead and the figure of an eagle on the back; his tail-hairs are double and there is a scarab on his tongue. When he appears, the Egyptians all put on their best clothes and make merry."

Such superstitious nonsense may sound harmless enough, but beneath it lay a creed which stunted the mental growth of the entire race. The ruling Pharaoh, so it was believed, was a Divine being. After his death and mummification he became a national god, and thus assumed his place as Director of the Universe. During his lifetime, it followed that as supreme head of the state he could dictate the beliefs and behaviour of all his subjects. Under Pharaoh's rule no room was left for the free exercise of human reason; and a system which confused science with magic and philosophy with superstition could not but lead to spiritual stagnation. The Hebrew prophet knew what he was talking about when he scornfully proclaimed "The strength of Egypt is to sit still."

The priesthood was all-powerful. Conserving the traditions and prescribing the ritual which governed the people's daily lives, they held all the "keys of knowledge." It was from the priests that Herodotus acquired his information about the history and geography of the land; and one story he tells—to all appearances against himself—is worth quoting. He was enquiring, he says, about the source of the Nile; and in a certain temple he got what he wanted from the priest in charge of the sacred records. Between two distant cities, he was told, were a pair of conical hills and in the middle of these a bottomless spring out of which the great river flowed. The name of one hill, his informant assured him, was Crophi, and the name of the other Mophi. But here the traveller's eye must have twinkled. This was really too good to be true; and with characteristic suspicion he inserts the proviso, "I rather fancy he was pulling my leg."

Here, however, we may hazard a guess that Herodotus was deceived, for nobody could have believed what an Egyptian priest believed and yet retained a sense of humour. And in this trivial incident it is not perhaps too fanciful to discern the contrast between two different types

14

of mind—on the one hand the mind of the Egyptian, conventional, conservative, and ready to accept whatever absurdity tradition might dictate; on the other hand, the mind of the sceptical inquisitive Greek who would accept nothing at its face value, who sought by all the means in his power to arrive at the truth, and whose historic task it was to remodel human life in the light of his new knowledge. In that contrast lies the real significance of Greek civilization.

2

Like ourselves, the people of Ancient Greece were of mongrel breed, a fusion of two racial stocks. The one came down from the North, a Greek-speaking folk who (as did the Anglo-Saxons in Britain) imposed their speech on the country. The other was an indigenous race of some-what mixed stock. Of their language nothing more than a few stray words survived; but already before the immigrants' arrival we know that they had developed a very remarkable culture.

Evidences of this ancient pre-Greek culture are widespread round the Aegean. In the Peloponnese particularly—or, as it is now called, the Morea—many remains have come to light. Of these the most impressive may be seen at Mycenæ in the north-east below Corinth. Here still stand the ruins of a great hill-citadel. Its fortifications are built of huge boulders, roughly piled in tiers without mortar. On one side of them is an imposing gateway, flanked by protecting walls and supporting on its gigantic lintel a magnificent bas-relief of two rampant lions. Inside the fortress can be traced the foundations of the royal palace; and nearby Dr. Schlie-mann, the pioneer of excavation in Greece, dug up the royal graves. Masks of beaten gold had been placed on the faces of the dead and other golden ornaments buried beside them. The natives were great craftsmen. They excelled in inlaid metalwork, and their superb painted pottery has been found in many parts of the country.

The cradle of this culture lay, however, not on the mainland, but in the island of Crete. Centrally placed on the Mediterranean trade-routes, Crete had long been in contact with even earlier civilizations. It had certainly been influenced, perhaps even colonized, by Egypt. The enormous wealth of its monarchs was won by commerce. The Aegean, so legend said, was swept by their navies. Almost certainly they dominated Mycenæ and other mainland settlements; and we know from archæo-logical finds that their merchants plied for traffic in every quarter of the Middle Seas. Trinkets made in the island even found their way as far as Britain.

When at the beginning of this century Sir Arthur Evans embarked on the excavation of Crete, the splendour of his discoveries took even archæologists by surprise. At Cnossos he unearthed the royal palace. It was a vast edifice piled tier by tier up a hillside. It contained broad stone staircases leading to long stone galleries. In the storerooms were jars each large enough to hold one of Ali Baba's forty thieves. There was an efficient drainage system constructed with earthenware pipes and superior to anything known in Europe before the eighteenth century. Here and there the walls had been painted with gay scenes from contemporary life. But most sumptuous of all was the royal throne-room, originally supported upon massive columns of timber and adorned with a frieze of griffen-like monsters. Decorative art in the West has seldom, if ever, reached a higher pitch, and the bold rhythmical patterns with which Cretan pottery was painted—varied often with fishes and flowers, more rarely with human figures—might excite the envy of any designer.[1]

Such writing as has survived at Crete has never been deciphered.[2] In any case it is thought to consist of mere traders' inventories. So of the history and habits of either island or mainland, nothing certain is known. But of their religion at any rate something may be conjectured partly from archæological finds and partly from later survivals.

In many lands of the Mediterranean basin, the powers of fertility had long been an object of worship. When primitive peoples first discovered that sex was the origin of birth, they not unnaturally came to regard such a life-giving force as divine. The source of vegetable-growth was equally venerated; and along with these cults often went the cult of the dead, whose spirits, it was thought, could influence earthly life from the shadowy abyss of the underworld. In Crete, we have reason to believe, most if not all of these various cults existed. The statue of a fertility goddess has been dug up (unless experts are mistaken); and closely associated with her were two creatures of sinister import, the snake and the owl. In Crete, too, as in many parts of the world, the bull was regarded with reverence. Of its cult nothing certain is known, but paintings have been found which show human beings tossed headlong by the animal's horns, and there was an old Greek legend that once every year a tribute of youths and maidens was offered up to a monster half-human and half-bull who dwelt in the recesses of an intricate labyrinth. There can, in fact, be little doubt that human sacrifice was a ritual of the gloomy creed which prevailed among the indigenous folk of both Crete and mainland Greece. Such then was the dark background of mystery,

[1] Cretan culture has come to be known as "Minoan," after the name of its legendary King Minos.
[2] In 1954 Ventris deciphered Minoan script as representing Greek language.

16

A Lady of Mycenæan times: reconstruction of a wall-decoration at Tiryns.[1]

[1] Compare illustrations on pages 129 and 175.

superstition and horror against which the immigrants from the north were one day to build a new and sunnier edifice of rational thought and more genuinely civilized life. But now it is time to turn and consider how these Greek-speaking immigrants first came to the country.

3

Far away in the Balkans and beyond, there was all this while proceeding one of those great migratory movements which have periodically altered the face of the Western World. This time it was our own racial ancestors who were on the move—members of that prolific and populous family which (starting, we may guess, from the shores of the Baltic) spread out in many directions and came eventually to repeople a large part of Europe. Wherever the members of the family went, they carried their speech with them. Among the central swamps and forests of the continent it became the German language—later to be brought by Anglo-Saxons to these shores. In Italy it became the language of the Romans. Another of its variants was Greek; and, most singular of all, it was taken across the Himalayas into India, and there it has been preserved in the Sanskrit or Sacred Script in which were written the very ancient religious hymns still treasured by Hindu Brahmins.

In each of its new homes this Indo-European speech, as it is called, underwent some natural modification, but not sufficient to obscure its identity; and scores of words [1] might be cited to prove the common origin of these widely scattered peoples—peoples who, as we know, were destined in the fulness of time to change the whole course of human civilization.

Among the first members of this great family to arrive in the Greek peninsula were a group known as Achæans. Some of these elected to stay in its upper half among the broad plains of Thessaly. Other Achæans pushed further south and entered the Peloponnese. Whether they came as hired mercenaries or simply by peaceful penetration we cannot tell; but in any case these Greek-speaking peoples settled down to adopt the customs and culture of the indigenous population; and, being men of forceful character, it was not long before they made themselves masters in the land. For about 1200 B.C.—scarcely a century after their first arrival—an Achæan was reigning on the throne of Mycenæ. We even know his name. He was Agamemnon, the man who led an Achæan host against the Asiatic city of Troy near the mouth of the Dardanelles.

[1] A few instances may be given: Greek patêr; Latin pater; English father. Greek agr-os; Latin ag-er; Eng. acre; Grk. treis; Lat. tres; Eng. three; Grk. geran-os; Eng. crane; Grk. thur-a; Eng. door; and Grk. pher-o; Latin fero; Eng. bear.

By now the ferment of migration was gathering strength. Not long after Agamemnon's day some Thessalian Achæans again crossed the Aegean and settled along the coast where the way had already been cleared for them by the destruction of Troy. What prompted their departure from Europe was no doubt the restless pressure of other Greek-speaking tribes already arriving out of the north. And about 1100 B.C. fresh hordes of these swept down over the whole peninsula. Some settled in its upper half, others crossed the narrow waters of the Corinthian Gulf and invaded the Peloponnese. These newcomers—Dorians they called themselves—were men of fiercer spirit than their Achæan forerunners. They sacked Mycenæ and burnt it; and their occupation of the country—slow process though this must have been—made a violent break in its history. The old habits of peaceful intercourse, on which the native culture had been built, were now broken down. The traditions of craftsmanship gradually decayed. Trade was arrested; and in the course of time the great civilization, growth of two thousand years and more of patient effort, was irretrievably destroyed.

But not its memory. This was carried by a further wave of emigrants to the eastern side of the Aegean; and there in new soil the old seed took root and bore a fresh blossom of intellectual and artistic genius which remains one of the wonders of the world.

These emigrants were mixed bands of Achæans and of the old indigenous race, and they hailed from Attica. Thanks to the comparative infertility of its soil, this district had escaped the inroads of Dorian destruction; but into it refugees from the terror had crowded for safety; and, as its space was insufficient for all, an overflow of landless folk took ship eastward for the Asia Minor seaboard. Here they found a gap still vacant between the previous settlements made to northward by Achæans from Thessaly and to southward by Dorian adventurers from the Peloponnese. So in this central strip of the coastline—henceforth to be known as Ionia—the Attic emigrants made their home, and, strange to say, they prospered exceedingly. Before many years were out, they were building up a civilization—the first civilization recognizable as essentially Greek—which was destined to stand out as a unique landmark in the history of human progress. The fact is that these spiritual heirs of the old indigenous culture proved themselves also intellectually to be the most precocious members of the whole Greek family; and, the two strains thus blending, the first fruits of their union were not long to be delayed. For here were produced, at some date between 900 and 700 B.C., two of the greatest literary masterpieces of all time—the Iliad and Odyssey of Homer.

The origin and authorship of these two poems are an unsolved mystery.

But one thing at least we may accept. Soon after the Trojan War minstrels began to celebrate that notable Achæan exploit. Their lays—and Troy was not their only theme—were handed down from generation to generation of minstrels. Then eventually they were carried over to Asia Minor along with the emigrants, perhaps in the first instance by the Thessalian Achæans. And later on in Ionia—though not before 900 B.C.—they grew into a great saga of narrative poetry of which the Iliad and Odyssey alone survive. Whether those two poems were, as the ancients believed, the work of a blind bard named Homer, or whether they took shape gradually by passing through the hands of a series of poets, it is impossible to say. Yet to give unity to an epic fifteen thousand lines long must at one stage or another have required the master-hand of some outstanding genius; and, although it is unlikely that Iliad and Odyssey were the same author's workmanship, it will be more convenient henceforth to treat them both as Homer's.

The theme of the Iliad is the war against Ilion or Troy. Paris, son of the Trojan King Priam, had eloped with Helen, the beautiful wife of Menelaus, Agamemnon's brother. Under the latter's leadership an Achæan host, drawn partly from the Peloponnese and partly from Thessaly, set sail for Troy to recover her. For years they fought outside the city. Then—and here the Iliad opens—Achilles, the greatest of Achæan warriors, took offence at some slight and sulked in his tent. Without him the war went ill for his fellows; and at length under strong persuasion he lent his arms to his bosom friend Patroclus. Patroclus was slain by the Trojan champion Hector; and Achilles wild with grief went forth to take revenge. Three times round the walls of Troy he hunted the fleeing Hector, then brought him to battle and killed him. Finally— though this is not told in the Iliad—the Greeks took the city by a ruse. Making a great wooden horse, they left it near the walls and feigned departure. The unsuspecting Trojan dragged the monster inside; but in the dead of night Greeks, concealed in its belly, slipped out and opened the gates. Their comrades poured in, and Troy went up in flames.

The Odyssey tells of the homeward voyage of Odysseus or Ulysses, a Greek prince who had sailed to Troy from an island off Western Greece called Ithaca. His adventures in the palace of the witch-queen Circe whose spells turned his companions to swine; his hairbreadth escapes from Scylla and Charybdis, two sea-monsters of the Messina Straits; his capture by a one-eyed giant, the Cyclops Polyphemus, whom he first made drunk and then blinded with a red-hot stake; his final return to Ithaca where he slaughtered the insolent suitors of his faithful wife Penelope—all this makes a narrative beside which most travellers' stories pale. The Odyssey is written in a lighter vein than the Iliad, and has not the same tragic grandeur. But it contains greater variety and gives a more detailed picture of everyday life in the Heroic Age.

Homer is telling—let us remember—of times which he himself had not witnessed. The culture he describes is the culture of "Golden Mycenæ" in the days before the Dorians came to sack it. Much that he has to tell tallies closely with what has been discovered both there and elsewhere on the Greek mainland—even down to such details as the decorations of a palace or the shape of a drinking cup. The society he depicts was an aristocratic society. His story is the story of kings and chieftains who rode into battle behind "high-stepping steeds" while the common folk marched on foot, or who feasted and drank in their splendid halls while their underlings served them at table or the plough.

To call them aristocrats, however, may give a false impression. They were simple folk enough, living much the life of a mediæval lord of the Manor, strolling to the harvest-field to watch the reaping, hunting wild boars on the hills, gossiping on terms of easy familiarity with their retainers or even their slaves. One of them is described in extreme old age tending his orchard trees in tattered gloves and gaiters.

But there is none the less great dignity about these men. They possessed a strong sense of *noblesse oblige*. Their code of behaviour was high. Fathers taught it to their sons and the sons' greatest shame was to fall short of their fathers. Warriors first and foremost, their chief pride was in arms. "If I must die," says one of them, "let it not be without a blow struck and glory won and some great deed for men who come after to tell of." Their manners were courteous. They showed a quick tact to note if offence were given or to smooth a ruffled temper. They were hospitable to a fault. No stranger but was sure of a place at their board or a bed in their verandah. The parting guest was sped with the gift of a golden goblet or some weapon of war. Towards women they behaved with consideration and even sympathy—in this differing greatly from the Greeks of historical times among whom a woman's influence was slight and her status unenviable.

In the Odyssey there is one beautiful episode which so well illustrates the delicacy and refinement of Achæan manners that it seems worth quoting here—if only in abbreviated paraphrase.

Odysseus after shipwreck and an incredible feat of swimming had reached the land of Phæacia, and in utter exhaustion had sunk to sleep on the shore. Here by chance came the King's daughter Nausicaa accompanied by her maids and bringing the household linen to wash in an estuary. After a picnic meal they played "catch," and their ball falling in the water the maids put up a scream. This woke Odysseus, and he came towards them foul with brine from the sea and holding a branch of foliage to cover his nakedness. Nausicaa alone stood her ground; and he addressed her as follows:

"I cast myself on your mercy, lady queen. Whether you are goddess or mortal woman I know not. But, if mortal, how happy must your parents be, and how proud your brothers to see so fair a young thing take the floor at the dancing. In all my life I never saw man or woman to match you. You put me in mind how once in Delos by Apollo's altar I noticed a young palm-tree growing. Never did I set eyes on tree springing up so fine and straight, and I gazed on it long and wonderingly. And now I feel the same awe and reverence when I look upon you; and I am too deeply abashed to approach you or clasp your knees in entreaty. Twenty days I have been in the deep, till yesterday I escaped here to land. But now have pity on me, lady queen. Show me the way to your city and lend me some wrap from the linen to clothe myself. May the gods give you your heart's desire, a man to wed and a home and harmony to bless it. For there is no better thing than this, when a man and wife keep house together in harmony of spirit, to the sorrow of their foes and the joy of their friends and in their own two hearts, above all, the happiness ringing."

Odysseus bathed and washed the brine from his body and put on the clothes she gave him. Then the goddess Athena changed him so that he was fresh and young again; and when he came out on the shore gleaming with beauty and grace, the girl was amazed and said to her maids:

"It was surely heaven's will that brought this man to Phæacia. A moment ago he was foul to look on, and now he is godlike indeed. Well content would I be to have a husband like him and that he should dwell in our land and never leave us."

And then, turning quickly from the sentimental to the practical (a rare touch of psychology), she added: "But now, give him food and drink."

So it was the old story of love at first sight, told perhaps for the first time and never surely with a more tender restraint. Odysseus seems not to have noticed it. Later, before he left, Nausicaa said her good-bye. "God be with you, my friend, and when you reach home, then think sometimes of me; for you owe me your life"; and he answered (a little heartlessly perhaps), "God send I may indeed reach my land in a happy home-coming; and be sure, my lass, that once there I shall ever make my thanksgiving to the good angel who saved me."

But life in those days was no soft life. War after all was an Achæan's main business; and the Iliad is as full of the thunder of battle as is the Odyssey of adventure by sea. Here is struck, as we have said, a deeper note. "It is the mightiest story of the mightiest men. It is also the greatest dirge for the brave men who are doomed to die young; and the sentiments and thoughts which such glorious deeds evoke are expressed with a majesty and simplicity which have no parallel in the literature of the world." [1] The mightiest men—but very human too, men capable of foul as well as of glorious deeds. When Hector, lying in dust at the feet of his conqueror, craves that his body may at least be spared mutilation, Achilles answers with a savagery which almost takes the breath away: "Dog, would to heaven I had it in me to carve up your flesh and eat it raw, so surely as none shall save you from the mauling of the beasts."

The Achæan heroes were indeed men of violent and sometimes unrestrained passions. But then so too were their descendants. Let there be no mistake about the Greeks. They were vehement in their hatreds and vehement in their loves; and fond as they were of repeating the adage, "Mêden agân" or "Nothing in excess," it was not because they admired mediocrity, but because, knowing their own danger of running to extremes, they recognized the more clearly the need for self-mastery. Their whole history is the tale of a struggle for the supremacy of reason over the instincts of barbarism.

It was the continuous endeavour of the "prophets" of Greece (if "prophets" we may call them) to inculcate these precepts of reasonableness and self-control. Homer—the earliest and most influential of them all—set the model of conduct and character for the race. Not that he ever actually preached. His sentiments are always conveyed through the mouths of his heroes. Thus, even the voice of Achilles is heard lamenting his own folly. "Would strife might die among gods and among men and anger that drives even the wise to vexation, mounting like smoke in the heart of a man with a sweetness as of slow-dripping honey." By such-like touches worked with consummate artistry into the narrative, Homer built up his message. Taking the traditional code of aristocratic behaviour, and idealizing it (much as Malory in his Morte d'Arthur idealized the chivalric code of his age), Homer evolved the conception of what, for lack of a better word, we must call the Greek "Gentleman."

Such a conception can scarcely have been the work of a single brain—a strong argument for ascribing the poems to a series of authors. And still more is this true in the field of religious ideas. For here, too, the Homeric epics mark an advance which is even more striking. The Greeks were convinced polytheists; and though they certainly brought their own deities with them on entering the land (Zeus lord of the sky and Phœbus Apollo the sun-god were two of them), yet they must have been ready

[1] Quoted from Maurice Baring's "Have you anything to declare?"

to acknowledge the gods of the indigenous native and even to identify their own gods with theirs. Thus Hera, Zeus' wife, was known to Homer as "Ox-headed" or "Ox-eyed," Athena, Zeus' daughter, as "Owl-eyed" —clear evidence of some amalgamation of cults. Snakes, too, were kept in many Greek shrines quite late on in history. Human sacrifice was still known to Homer; for Agamemnon himself was compelled to slay his daughter. And, though the deification of sex was no longer paraded, it still found an echo in the many legends telling of Zeus' amours with mortal men's wives and in the grossness which accompanied some of the Greeks' agriculural rites.

But despite such survivals the Homeric poems reveal a complete transformation of men's idea of the deity. Now the gods dwell no longer in a shadowy underworld,[1] but in serene sunshine above the snow-capped peaks of Mount Olympus beyond Thessaly. They are no longer monstrosities like the Minotaur or the Sphinx, but human in appearance and human in character, with the frailties as well as the virtues of mankind. Each has his own personality and his proper function; Phœbus the sun-god becomes the healer of disease, Athena the patron of crafts, and so on. They interest themselves greatly in the affairs of men. Nothing could happen on earth but they had a finger in it—was it not by Athena's magic that Nausicaa fell in love with Odysseus. They are swift to punish the oath-breaker or to reward the pious, to visit Nemesis on the proud or avenge the victim of wrong. Fate alone they could not control; not even Zeus himself might intervene to save a man whose time was come.

The influence of religion on Greek life must not, however, be exaggerated. In it, as in the life of all early peoples, there was a vast deal of ritual and a vast deal of superstitition. But little moral edification could be gained from the contemplation of a deity like Zeus; and it was characteristic of Homer and the later Greek "prophets" that they looked manward rather than godward for their ethical ideals. Nor are the heroes of the Iliad and the Odyssey mere puppets in the hands of the unseen powers. By their courage or cowardice, their pride or their piety, they are felt in some sense to be shaping the issues of their lives. Homer the artist saw deeper than Homer the theologian; and it was perhaps his supreme achievement that he recognized the human individual to be, if not indeed the "master of his fate," yet at the very least the "captain of his soul."

The place which the poems held in the national mind finds no parallel in secular literature. They were to the Greeks much what the Old Testament was to the Jews. They were recited at their great religious festivals. Children were brought up on them. Schoolboys learnt them by heart.

[1] This Underworld was henceforward reserved for the souls of dead mortals.

Adults quoted them as we might quote the Bible; and even philosophers appealed to them as though to an authoritative source. Nor was this any mere adulation of a literary masterpiece. In Ionia, with the creation of these poems, had been born a new sense of human dignity and human destiny. The old order was passing away. The gloom of Crete had been dissipated. Egyptian absurdities had been left behind. The Greeks had still a long way to travel and superstition died slow. But already they had turned away from the darkness and set their face towards the sunlight. It would be hard indeed to think of Achilles or Hector grovelling to a scareb-marked calf. Still less can we imagine the "wily Odysseus" obeying an order to shave his eyebrows because a cat had died or to fasten golden bracelets on the front paws of a sacred crocodile.

CHAPTER II

FARMER, TOWNSMAN AND MARINER

1. THE CITY STATE

Some memories of the great emigrations, the composition of the Homeric poems, and a few semi-historical legends—this is all there is to show for the three hundred years which followed the Dorian Invasion. Darkness and chaos settle down on the land; and when Greece emerges at last into the light of recorded history, the period of resettlement is over and the national life has begun to assume the pattern of which the succeeding chapters of this book will trace the development.

Tacitus, the Roman writer of the first century A.D., has given a description of the Germany of his day. There the political unit was still the tribe— a group of kindred. At its head was a king, commander of the host. Under him were a number of chieftains, representatives of leading families; and these met in council to tender him advice—the equivalent of the "Witangemot" in Anglo-Saxon England. From time to time over issues of major importance, the common folk were collected in an assembly or "moot," either to give assent to the Council's decisions by clashing their shields or alternatively to express disapproval by hooting.

What Tacitus observed among the primitive Germans, was also true of the primitive Greeks. Among them, too, when they came to settle for good, the same three elements existed—King, aristocratic Council, and popular Assembly. In some states these three elements persisted well into historical times; but in all the power of the King sooner or later declined, given place at first to Aristocracy and in some cases eventually to Democracy.

By its geographical configuration Greece falls into natural divisions. Among the mountains which cover a large part of the peninsula, are numerous small valleys or plains, not more on an average than twenty miles long and less than a dozen miles wide. Cut off from each other by the intervening hills, these valleys were to prove an ideal breeding-ground for political development. But the process of consolidation into what we ourselves should call states, was a matter of time. At first several tribes perhaps would settle in a single valley, portioning out the available land, the best portions to King and nobles, but a small plot at least to each commoner. The immediate task was the struggle for existence. Sustenance had to be found for a growing community, and for a long period there was little time or energy for much else.

In Greece as in all countries before the Industrial Revolution, the vast majority of men were always farmers or peasants. The plainland, though in parts pretty fertile, was strictly limited in extent; and once the foothills were reached, rock came close to the surface; so that every scrap of soil must be carefully husbanded by terracing and continuous toil. Summer droughts parched it; winter storms, which send torrents streaming down the slopes, scoured it away. Some scanty grazing could be had on the mountains. Sheep were kept for their wool; goats and more rarely cows for their milk. An animal was too precious to be killed for the table; and meat was seldom eaten except on festal occasions when a part of the flesh had first been sacrificed to some god. Corn grown in the plains provided the main staple of diet, though bread was often seasoned with pickled fish. Olive-trees, whose soft grey-green foliage still shimmers over the Greek countryside, furnished oil—then a most precious commodity fulfilling the functions of paraffin, butter and soap. Everywhere, too, the vine was grown. As in most parts of the continent to-day, wine mixed with water was the national drink. In days when sugar-cane and sugar-beet were unknown, honey served their purpose.

But agriculture, as we have said, was a struggle against odds. Plough-oxen would die in winter for lack of fodder. Harvests would fail from drought; and the spectre of famine was never far distant. "Bad in winter, cruel in summer, never good," was the verdict of the rustic poet Hesiod on village life in the eighth century B.C.

Yet if the Greeks had never been anything but farmers, Greek History would not be studied to-day. Town-life, even during the chaos of the Dark Age, had never altogether disappeared. The author of the Homeric poems knew of it not only by hearsay. The vivid pictures he gives of it are evidence that he had seen it for himself. He tells, for instance, of one city inhabited by sea-going folk. "Round it was a high wall and the way to it ran across a narrow spit with a fair haven on this side and that; and beside the road were beached the rowing-vessels; each man had his slip. Beyond, surrounding the sea-god's fair shrine, lay the place of assembly, walled with large boulders dragged thither." In another passage he describes the scenes carved on the metal surface of a shield. "In one quarter," he says, "was a city; and in the city a marriage-festival was going on. Brides were being led by torchlight through the streets; and the wedding-hymn rang loudly to the tune of psaltries and pipes, while in their porches the women looked on admiringly. Elsewhere the folk had gathered in the market-place, and there a quarrel had arisen over the blood-money due for a murdered man. One party publicly declared he would pay, the other would not have it that way, and both wished to lay the matter before an umpire. The people, held back by the heralds, shouted support to this party or that. Nearby on a sacred circle of polished stones sat the elders. Each in turn took a bâton from the hands of the heralds and went forward to deliver his verdict; and in the middle of all lay two golden talents to be given to whoever were adjudged to have made the fairest decision."

In this scene may be perceived the germ of a new and promising growth towards a better-ordered, more politically conscious society. And in many Greek valleys, before the Dark Age was over, a township, such as Homer depicts, was already coming to be the centre of the people's life. At Athens, for example, in the plain of Attica the nucleus of such a town had certainly grown up under the great rock-citadel, later known as the Acropolis. Thucydides, the fifth century Historian, has recorded the first step, and a very momentous step, in its political development. "Originally," he says, "there were many townships in Attica, each administering its own affairs and often at war with its neighbour. But Theseus (a legendary monarch as it might be our own King Arthur) united all the inhabitants of Attica, establishing at Athens one central Council and a common Town-hall. Though they continued to live on the land, Theseus compelled them to resort to the new metropolis and all were duly inscribed on her citizen-roll." From such an act of union sprang what is known to history as the "City State." The City State, then, was a political unit embracing an area equivalent to a small English county; and by virtue of membership therein, as Thucydides implies, every free-born inhabitant of that area enjoyed the advantages of centralized government and came increasingly, as we shall see, to take a personal hand in it.

New ideas demand a new usage of words; and it is highly significant that "Polis" the Greek word for "city" was henceforth used for the "state." From the word is derived, of course, our own word "politics." And, more important, from the new synthesis of meaning was to spring our own conception of the State. That conception was not to be found in the previous civilizations of antiquity. No "politics" in our sense were possible under the absolute monarchs of Egypt or Mesopotamia. No genuine idea of "citizenship" is traceable among the Old Testament Jews. Their kings sent men to death like irresponsible despots; and when the Hebrew prophet denounced social wrongs, he appealed to the justice of Jehovah, not to the Rights of Man. It was not, in fact, until the Greek experiment was made that the whole life of a scattered populace was thus knit together in a constitutional system—a system which was at once the guarantee of the individual's civic liberties and also the focus of his civic loyalties and obligations.

Whoever said that men first came together in cities to find Justice, was not wide of the mark. What value was set upon Justice even among the primitive Greeks is shown by the previously-quoted passage from Homer. The populace held strong views about the rights and wrongs of the quarrel. Both parties desired a fair ruling; and two golden talents was not thought too high a price for obtaining one. In the centralized court of the Polis Justice would be still more jealously guarded. The aristocratic judges would be more closely watched; and a stronger public opinion would be focussed on their decisions. Every citizen, rich or poor, well-born or commoner, was now legally on an equal footing. Fair play was to be the ever-growing demand of the masses; and there could be no worse outrage in the eyes of a true Greek than condemnation without proper trial. The privilege of arguing his case and standing up for his right was breath of life to him; and as a member of the Polis he was assured of that privilege. Justice, in short, was not least of the reasons why the new political union appealed to him, and why he came to take a conscious pride in his membership of the wider community.

But then, as now, town-life had other attractions. These grew with time, and more and more folk, in Attica at least, must have moved in to live at the capital. The Greeks were nothing if not sociable. They enjoyed the stir and bustle of the city, the processions and pageants, the dancings and choir-singings, and, when these too became the fashion, the dramatic entertainments. In the market higgling for purchases gave zest to the daily round. It brought a chance too of meeting friends. The Greeks were great talkers, voluble, argumentative and excitable. They loved nothing better than to foregather for a gossip. The warmth of a smith's forge made it a popular rendezvous, and the barber's shop rivalled it. In such ways, and many others, urbanization, as one of their philosophers said, enabled men to live a fuller and better life.

The date which tradition assigned to the unification of Attica was absurdly remote; but it can hardly have occurred later than 700 B.C. In some parts of Greece, where the country was wilder and the people more backward, such unification was longer in coming; in certain districts it never came at all. But in the principal plains or valleys City States were formed pretty early.[1] Thus between Athens and the Isthmus there was Megara; on the Isthmus itself Corinth, south of Corinth near the old site

[1] In none, however, was the process of unification so complete as in Attica, and local townships were frequently not absorbed. Athens in a large measure owed her greatness to her uniquely centralized government.

of Mycenæ was Argos, and lower down in the Peloponnese Sparta. In upper Greece and bordering on Attica, Boeotia produced several cities of which Thebes was the chief. And besides all these, there were many others too insignificant for mention. So, by the time when history proper begins, Greece was already divided up into a score or more of independent City States, some larger, some smaller, but all intensely jealous of their neighbours and ready on the smallest provocation to go to war with them. As may equally be seen in the history of North Italy during the early Renaissance, local patriotism and local rivalries are apt to be strongest when the political units of a society are small.

2

Whether town-life or country-life usually does more to breed a spirit of adventure, there can be no doubt about the Greeks. They were perhaps the most adventurous people in history. Living as most of them did within sight of the coast, they had the sea in their blood, and the popularity of the Odyssey testifies to their love of maritime enterprise. From Homer, too, a good deal may be gleaned about their methods of navigation. Hoisting their solitary sail to a following wind or, if that failed them, falling back on the oar, they would creep along, whenever possible, within sight of land (for in those compassless days the open sea was a nightmare). When they wished to sleep and eat, they would haul their ship ashore. No doubt, like Odysseus' crew, they argued endlessly with the skipper, and no doubt they grumbled as much. The Odyssey, indeed, is full of the weariness of the rowers and the desperate hazards of current or storm. But, when navigation became more skilful and ships more seaworthy, the Greeks enjoyed their cruises over the "wine-dark" waters of the sunny Aegean. One of them—an olden-time Masefield—has left a record of his own enjoyment:

> O set me in the poop with a pallet for my bed
> and the sea-spray drumming on the leather overhead;
> mill-stones for fire-place where the flames flicker through
> and the stew-pot's a-bubble and the cook minds the stew;
> ship's plank for table with a sail thrown across
> and boatswain's merry whistle and a game of "Pitch and Toss"
> for I love my fellow-men and I'd have the same again
> as I had it not so many days ago.

But the Aegean was not enough to content Greek mariners. From the earliest times they pushed boldly further afield—northwards into the Black Sea (the "Euxine" or "Hospitable" as with euphemistic superstition they called it) southwards to Libya, eastwards to Egypt, and westwards not only to Sicily and Italy but as far as Spain and Southern France. It seems tolerably certain that Greeks were the first of Mediterranean navigators to reach our own island; and Homer even knew sailors' tales of the land of the Midnight Sun, "where herdsman calls to herdsman as the one drives in; and the other, as he drives forth, answers back. There a man who slept not, might earn a double wage, by shepherding and

A Greek ship with sail furled to the yard-arm. (Taken from a vase-painting.)

tending cattle turn about; so narrowly are divided the ways of the Day and the Night."

Trade was, of course, the original purpose, as it was also the increasing result of this audacious exploration. But it had another and very remarkable consequence. As we have already seen, the chief problem confronting the young Greek communities was how to provide for a growing population. Emigration to Asia Minor had provided no more than a temporary solution. The population still grew. Arable land was limited, and there were more mouths than its resources could feed. There remained but two alternatives to emigrate or to starve. So from about 800 B.C. onwards began a deliberate policy of colonization. It was no random enterprise of hunger-stricken refugees. It was planned and well-organized, and there could be no better proof that the governing-class of the new City States took their responsibilities seriously. The magnitude and scope of the movement was incredible. A single Ionian city, Miletus, sent out no fewer than eighty colonies. The islanders of Euboea on the European side of the Aegean showed an almost equal vigour. Other states, such as Corinth, for example, also played an important part. The result was that in the course of a century and a half—between 750 and 600 B.C.—not merely were the shores of the Black Sea and the Northern Aegean colonized liberally, but Sicily and the southern part of Italy were also dotted by Greek coastal settlements. Even as far west as the South of France a colony was planted at Marseilles.

These colonies carried with them the political institutions of home. Each became an independent City State. They seldom had formal relations with the parent-city; they paid her no tribute. Apart from sentimental ties of common customs and occasional reunions for joint religious rites, they acknowledged no allegiance. They resented her interference, and only on rare occasions of special peril did they appeal for her armed assistance.[1]

Like the City States of the motherland, the colonies depended at first on their agriculture, but trade soon developed; and this indeed was the original purpose of some settlements, notably those made by Miletus. Geographical conditions favoured an exchange of commodities. Round the Black Sea, for instance, where corn grew well, the vine and olive did not; so in return for wine and oil,[2] the colonists shipped grain home to Greece. Athens as we shall see, with her growing population, came more and more to rely on this source of supply. Such exchange was greatly assisted by the issue of coined currencies. This innovation came from Lydia, an inland kingdom of Asia Minor. But once the Greeks learnt it, its use spread rapidly and replaced the old-fashioned method of barter. So commerce flourished as never before; and the Aegean and the Southern Adriatic must have been the scene of a busy traffic which served to knit together in friendly intercourse the scores of small City States of which the Greek world was now composed.

---

[1] Corinth alone kept some real control over her colonies; in one case at least she habitually sent out governors.

[2] Hence the fine collections of Greek pottery in Russian Museums.

Yet, sharing though they did a common religion, a common language, common political habits, and—with a certain qualification—a common outlook on life, the members of the Greek world were no nearer to unity. Their love of independence outweighed all advantages of political fusion. Quarrels between individual states or groups of states were incessant, and throughout her history internecine war remained the curse of the country. If ever a people committed racial suicide, it was the Greeks.

CHAPTER III

BODY AND MIND

A strictly uniform outlook on life, we have implied, was scarcely to be expected of Greeks; their personalities were too strong. We may, however, discriminate between two broad groups of them, each roughly homogeneous in type and each representing one or other of the two original racial stocks. In one group were the folk of Attica and its offshoot the Ionians, both claiming descent from the old indigenous natives. The other group were descended from the Dorian invaders—Spartans, Argives, Corinthians and other Peloponnesian peoples. The racial distinction between the two groups may not in reality have gone very deep; for other elements, the Achæan, for example, must have intermingled with both. Still the Greeks themselves believed in the distinction, and on the strength of it a conscious antagonism developed between the two groups. How strongly their types were contrasted will be shown in this chapter.

1. SPARTA

Pre-eminent among the Peloponnesian group were the Spartans; and in them the Dorian type assumed its most extreme form. By comparison with Ionians most Dorians were unintellectual; the Spartans—for reasons later to be discussed—were downright anti-intellectual. Most Dorians inclined towards conservatism; the Spartans—for the same reasons—were ultra-conservative. Thus, long after most Greek states had discarded it, they still clung to the monarchy—a dual monarchy at that, representative of some early fusion of two tribal groups. Again, in the Spartan Assembly, the vote was still taken by a ridiculously primitive method; the opposing sides both shouted and the louder shout won. More powerful, however, than either Monarchy or Assembly was the aristocratic Council; and here, too, the same conservative instinct insisted that the Council should represent the wisdom of age; no member might be less than sixty years old. The sole innovation in the Spartan constitution concerned the executive. In war-time the two kings as commanders-in-chief were all-powerful. But a hereditary monarchy is no guarantee of peace-time efficiency; so every year by the vote of the Assembly five executive officials known as "Ephors" were appointed. Their power grew with time, and at last they even took to interfering in the king's direction of campaigns. This curiously mixed constitution—a blend of monarchy, aristocracy and popular representation—continued almost unchanged for hundreds of years.

The political conservatism of Sparta sprang (as we have hinted) from certain historical causes, and to understand these we must first consider the lie of the land. Between the three great southerly spurs in which the Peloponnese terminates, lay two fertile valleys, the Vale of Lacedæmon, in which Sparta itself stood; and westwards of this, beyond a high mountain range, the Vale of Messenia. When first the Dorian invaders, the Spartans' forbears, settled, they had reduced the natives of the eastern valley to serfdom. But, even with these serfs to work it, the territory proved insufficient for their needs; and towards the close of the eighth century they had crossed the mountain barrier and annexed Messenia, making serfs of its natives too. A couple of generations later—about 650 B.C.—the Messenian serfs rebelled; and only after a lengthy struggle during which their warlike poet, Tyrtæus, sustained their flagging spirit, did the Spartans fight them down. For the master-race this revolt had been a terrible warning, a matter of life and death, and to prevent the possibility of its recurrence the Spartans undertook a drastic reform. Hitherto, we are told, they had been a normally pleasure-loving and even luxurious people; but now, by an effort of will-power unparalleled in history (though the rise of National Socialism in Germany bears it a certain resemblance), they transformed their whole manner of life. They appointed a law-giver named Lycurgus,[1] and he instituted a system, the main object of which was to turn every free-born Spartan into a professional soldier. Henceforward the interest of the community was all-in-all; the individual counted for nothing; and from the cradle to the grave the Spartan citizen became, as it were, the chattel of the state.

This totalitarian regime began at birth. If adjudged a weakling, the Spartan boy was exposed on the mountainside to die. If fit for survival, he remained seven years in his home. Spartan women were as tough as their menfolk. They were much valued as nurses in the rest of Greece, and their own children had a rigorous upbringing. "Come back *with* your shield or *on* it," these mothers used to say when their sons went off to the wars; and their scorn was even known to drive the survivors of a lost battle to suicide.

At seven the boy left his mother's side and was drafted into a troop. Here an adult Spartan presided, assisted by attendants called "Floggers."

[1] No details whatever are known of Lycurgus' life. It may be that he was a mythical figure invoked to lend authority and sanctity to the reforms.

Some boys were made "prefects," and permitted to fag their subordinates. They were scantily clad and went barefoot in winter. Physical training was their chief occupation. They learnt to swim, run, jump, wrestle and box, and, above all, to dance. For in Greece rhythmical movement was thought a good training, not for body merely, but for character. Even sports like wrestling were normally accompanied by the pipes. War-songs were chanted by massed bands of boys in a sort of musical drill. Every Spartan was expected to be able to sing; and all learnt by heart the ballads of their patriot-poet Tyrtæus.

Great attention was given to the training of character. Self-control, modesty and strict obedience were the primary virtues. Once a year there was a competition of endurance held at an altar—a survival probably of some early barbaric rite. Youths were flogged till they fainted, sometimes even died. He was winner who stuck it out longest. In behaviour the Spartan boy was a model of propriety. When walking down the street, he held his eyes on the ground and his hands under his cloak. If taken by his father to the men's mess-room, he sat on the floor, seen but not heard, listening to the adults' conversation. He was expected, when asked, to answer such questions as "What makes a good citizen? Who is the best of the grown-ups?"

His mind was not entirely neglected. Great stress was laid on the cultivation of memory. The code of state-laws and the poems of Homer were learnt by heart. But, if one Athenian author spoke truly, few Spartans were literate. "They will never even hear of my works," he complained, "unless they are read out loud to them." Arithmetic was considered superfluous. Citizens were not permitted to trade, and so had no need to count. Rhetoric and the art of argument (so popular elsewhere in Greece) were thought dangerous to discipline and accordingly banned. Yet Spartans had a rough wit of their own and affected a terse manner of speech. "Breakfast here, supper in Hades," one remarked on the morning of a battle. On another occasion, an envoy of a foreign state, seeking military aid, addressed a long speech to the Council. When it was finished, he was told that they could not remember the first half nor follow the second. Next day, accepting the hint, he reappeared with an empty sack. "Sack wants flour," was all he said. "Sack" was one word too many, was the Council's retort.

So a Spartan grew up intellectually starved. Much better he should not use his mind or learn to think for himself; his duty was to obey and keep his body fit. At eighteen he was drafted into the "Secret Corps"— the Spartan "Gestapo." Its business was to keep a watchful eye on the serfs or, as they called them, Helots. Dangerous characters among them had to be "liquidated," and the quicker and more quietly the better. On one occasion, Thucydides tells us, "the authorities announced that, whoever of the Helots could make out a claim to have rendered special service in war, should receive his freedom. Two thousand or so then applied. They were fêted with flowers and marched the round of the temples in triumphal procession. Everyone presumed that their liberty was assured. But before many days passed, every one disappeared, and nobody knew how they came by their end."

From this horrible tale, it is clear that at the back of the Spartans' mind still lay the haunting fear of revolt. They were living, so to speak, on a volcano, a tiny handful of men never more than 8,000 strong in the midst of a population of potential rebels numbering perhaps 200,000 souls. Little wonder that their manhood as well as their youth was spent in the practice of arms. Their daily life was passed in messes. Their food was brought in by Helots from the farms, so they had no need to engage in agriculture. They were forbidden to trade; that was left to a half-privileged class—neither serfs nor citizens—who appear to have been Achæan survivors of the original Dorian Conquest. Even the hoarding of money was rendered almost impossible; for the state-currency was deliberately confined to old-fashioned iron "spits" or ingots. So most of a Spartan man's day was spent in physical exercise or on the drill-ground. They became, in consequence, the finest soldiers in Greece. Other states called up their amateur militia from farm or workshop only when war broke out. In the long run it was impossible for these to stand up to the professional Spartans.

There were protracted wars, stubbornly fought; but before the Lycurgan reform was a century old, Sparta had brought under her hegemony nearly the whole of the Peloponnese—the Arcadians of the central plains, the Corinthians on the Isthmus and many other less important communities. The Argives, though suffering a severe defeat, were alone successful in maintaining complete independence. They were forced to cede some territory, it is true; but Sparta's real object was not annexation. She already had as much land as she wanted. Nor did she seriously curtail the liberty of her subject-allies. They were bound, if required, to join her in war and to contribute a war-tax; but such issues were decided by a Confederate Council, and on this each of the subject-allies had a vote. For the rest they were left to manage their own affairs as they liked.

The truth is that in her foreign policy, as in everything else, Sparta's actions were dictated by her fear of the Helots. What she chiefly desired was that neighbouring states should be sympathetic to her own ways or life. What she chiefly dreaded was the emergence of revolutionary or popular governments, which might put dangerous ideas into the heads of her serfs. So, wherever possible, she encouraged an oligarchic regime in the states of her Confederacy.

The historian Thucydides has left a shrewd analysis of the Spartan character. "They were conservative," he says, "and slow to act even in emergencies. Cautious even when caution was unnecessary, they never dared to put out their full strength. Their stay-at-home habits inclined them to hang back from foreign adventure; and where others thought only of adding to their possessions, the Spartans were haunted by the fear of losing what they had." And then there were other defects on which Thucydides is silent. They produced no art,[1] and, of course, no literature. Only once or twice in their history did they throw up a really great leader. They were bullies at home, and, if it suited them, they could be bullies abroad. Even their boasted discipline had its flaws, and when in foreign lands and so beyond the reach of watchful authority, it was not unknown for them to take to drink.

Yet Sparta was successful, dominating mainland Greece for the best part of two hundred years. Success is always admired; and there was much, too, in the Spartan character and institutions which appealed strongly to Greek instincts. Their courage, their splendid physique, their athletic prowess, their complete subordination of the individual to the State, above all, perhaps, the unique stability of their constitutional regime—these were virtues which held a high place in the moral and political code of even the best Greek thinkers. So a blind eye was turned on the cruelties, the squalor and the many vices or deficiencies of "Black Sparta." It is scarcely too much to say that Greece looked up to her; and even in Athens, where, at least, men should have known better, many conservative-minded gentry made it a fashion to sing her praises. One day—though this was still far distant—they were to be sadly undeceived.

2. IONIA

The cult of the body bulked large in Greek life. Exercise on the sports-ground was a daily habit with those who had the leisure. Many carried it well past middle-age; and one Attic vase-painter has left us a comical picture of a pot-bellied gentleman stripping for the fray. Successful athletes were fêted like national heroes; even philosophers, when enumerating the qualities essential to happiness, gave a high place to good

[1] Before the Lycurgan Reform, however, the art of Sparta—particularly in carving of ivory—showed distinct promise; but this, though not immediately extinguished, gradually decayed.

physique and good looks. The unathletic, correspondingly, were regarded askance. The dramatist got an easy laugh who portrayed some seedy-looking scholar engaged on his studies. Special contempt was felt for soft Eastern peoples, luxuriously lounging on litters or propped among pillows in their dimly-lit houses. Even the Ionians were thought to be somewhat tainted by this enervating oriental culture, and to lack true virility. Nevertheless, the best Greeks were too much interested in things of the mind to ignore the other side of the Ionians' character. They recognized their debt—a debt we ourselves must acknowledge—to the brilliant intellectual initiative of this remarkable people.

Environment played its part in their precocious development. Something was probably due to the native inhabitants of the coast, among whom they had originally settled; for these, as the splendours of Troy showed, were by no means a backward race. More fruitful, however, were the contacts which were very soon made with other and greater civilizations. Phœnicians, hailing from the Syrian coast-towns of Tyre and Sidon, did much early trade in the Aegean; and from them the Ionians learnt a highly important art, lost apparently since the palmy days of Crete, the art of writing. Its reintroduction may well account for the culminating stage in the creation of the Homeric poems; for to compose such lengthy works without writing them down would seem an incredible feat. In any case, the Phœnician alphabet was certainly adopted in Ionia not much later than 1000 B.C. It required some adaptation to suit the Greek language; for as in the Hebrew [1] (which it closely resembled), vowel-symbols were lacking, and to provide these other of its letters were pressed into service. From the Greeks it was ultimately passed on to Rome, and from Rome to the rest of Europe, where it still, of course, remains our own script of to-day.

Another valuable invention, the minting of money, came from Lydia. This kingdom in the hinterland of Ionia was to prove a dangerous neighbour; but at least it was commercially useful, serving as a link with the great civilization of Mesopotamia.

But the main channel of trade was by sea; and for this Ionia was excellently placed. Her principal produce was wool drawn from the upland sheep-farms; and the chief mart of export and exchange was the town of Miletus. This prosperous port, standing on a headland near the mouth of the River Meander, came into prominence during the eighth century B.C. The enormous effort, which sent overseas no less than eighty colonies, was good proof of its people's energy; and much of that energy

[1] The names of the first Greek letters—Alpha, Beta, Gamma—may be recognized as identical with Aleph, Beth and Gimel, which appear in the Bible as the alphabetical headings of the first three sections of the 119th Psalm.

was presently thrown into commerce with Egypt. At Naucratis in the Nile Delta a merchants' settlement was founded, and the intercourse thus established with the oldest of civilizations was to have surprising consequences.

Where traders go, travellers can follow. The Greeks were an inquisitive race; and Herodotus mentions how many went to Egypt, "some on business and some simply for sightseeing." Milesians who went in these earlier days came home much impressed. The "wisdom of Egypt" had set them thinking, and some began to undertake researches of their own. One, Anaximander, made the first map of the world. His geographical ideas were peculiar. The whole earth was divided into two roughly equal continents, Europe and Asia ("Libya" counting as part of the latter), and cutting across either continent ran the two Rivers Danube and Nile. Besides his map, Anaximander constructed a sundial and a globe of the heavens. Astronomy in those days was of great practical use (for navigation at night was impossible without it) and important work had been done by Egyptian astronomers. Inspired by this, another Milesian named Thales took up the study and succeeded in predicting an eclipse of the sun, which duly took place on May 28th, 585 B.C.

But something else of far greater importance resulted from Thales' astronomical interests. His inquisitive Greek mind was not content with mere mathematical calculations; and he began to speculate on the profounder problem—"Of what is the universe made"? It was not the first time that a guess had been hazarded. In the account of Creation, as it appears in the Bible, there is a curious assumption. Jehovah apparently did not create water; it already existed, waiting to be divided into the Sea and the Sky. This idea—no doubt Babylonian in origin—was also current in Egypt; and Thales seems to have taken it as a basis for his own speculation. "Everything that exists," he said, "comes ultimately from water." He had evidently thought it out. Evaporated water makes the sky; deposit at river-mouths shows that water also makes soil; all animals and vegetables depend on the same life-giving source. In some such way Thales must have reasoned—primitive logic perhaps, but an intellectual advance of supreme significance. For in reasoning thus he gave a *rational* basis to what had hitherto been little more than a Babylonian fairy-tale. He assumed, in short, that natural phenomena were no mere conjuring-trick on the part of some god; they were explicable by the reason of man. And from that assumption was born the conception not only of Science, but in embryo form of Philosophy itself.

Once Thales had posed his great question, other Ionians carried on the enquiry. Rival theories were formed; but, ingenious as these were, their authors relied too much on the guesswork of their own brilliant minds and too little on observation of facts. Most interesting of them all was Pythagoras, who broke clean away from current Ionian thought as initiated by Thales and rejected the pure materialism on which its explanation of the Universe was based. Though an Ionian himself, born on the island of Samos not far from Miletus, he migrated to South Italy and settled at Croton. There he gathered round him a body of pupils. Disciples would perhaps be a better word; for the master's doctrine had a strong religious trend. Mathematics was the chief object of his study, and a famous geometrical theorem still bears his name. But what the Egyptians had treated mainly as a technical art with many practical uses, became in Pythagoras' hands an abstract science worthy to be pursued for its own sake alone. Nor was this all; for he went on to build up a philosophy on a mathematical basis. Harmony, he believed, was the root principle of the Universe; and the numbers, which governed such harmony, possessed a mystic significance. Just as he discovered the vibrations of a harp-string to be related to the length of the string, so similar relations, he thought, might be discovered among all created things. Indeed, the mysterious properties of numbers might even extend to a much wider field—moral laws, for example.

All this sounds like nonsense, yet it finds an odd counterpart in some modern theories. Rhythm indubitably plays a part in natural phenomena, the movement of heavenly bodies, the rotation of seasons, the breeding of animals, and the pulsation of blood. Hence harmony, it is argued, may very well react on spiritual as well as on physical health; and by careful measurement of bodily proportions some psychologists have even claimed to discover a relation between these and personal character. Be that as it may, in Pythagoras' own age his ideas found still stranger application to practical life. His formulæ of mystical numbers were used in town-planning. Architects studied them when designing their buildings, and one sculptor even worked out mathematically the ideal proportions of the human figure.

The religious trend of Pythagoras' philosophy was reinforced by a mystical religious cult which about this time swept the Greek world. It was known as Orphism, and in accordance with its tenets Pythagoras himself held the theory that the human soul comes from God; man's duty, therefore, is to keep free the divine element from the contaminations of body, and this could only be done by ritual purifications such as abstention from certain foods and other ascetic practices. It was also part of Pythagoras' creed that the soul migrates from one body to another; and a famous parody represented him as banning the bean from his diet lest he might unwittingly swallow his grandmother's soul. But however others might scoff, the austere mysticism of the master drew many devoted followers round him; and the community over which he presided lived in almost monastic observance of his rigorous discipline.

There had now arisen, as may readily be seen, a serious divergence between the two schools of thought. The Ionians had sought to trace the whole universe to a purely physical source, while the Pythagoreans insisted that the soul, being divine and immortal, was but temporarily entangled with Matter. It remained for Heraclitus, an Ionian of Ephesus, to try and harmonize the conflict. Fire he held to be the fundamental source of existence, and from Fire, he argued, came mist, from mist moisture, and from moisture soil. From these four elements—Fire, Air, Water and Earth—all things are composed. But more than this, Heraclitus saw that all phenomena, as perceived by the senses, are perpetually changing and never remain long the same. Change then, and not Harmony, he declared, was the principle of the Universe. "Everything," he said, "is in flux." "We are and are not; waking is the same as sleeping; youth the same as age." In other words, whether young or old, awake or asleep, a person remains the same person still. But at the centre of all contemplating the eternal mutation of things stands the Reason of Man; and this reason he identifies with the divine element Fire, out of which the whole universe springs. Not that Heraclitus thought of Mind as anything else but material. Such an idea had not as yet dawned. But implicit at least in his thought was the truth that in man's self must lie the key to all problems. "Everyone," he said, "has a private insight of his own."

When we turn from the intellectual work of the Ionians to consider their art, its precocity, if perhaps less striking, was yet full of promise; and here, though again it was the peculiar genius of Greeks to transform what they borrowed, their debt to the great civilizations of the East was equally great. From the Mesopotamian peoples they drew many of their decorative patterns; from Egypt almost certainly many details of their architectural styles. Among the latter we may note their practice of surrounding their temples with an external row of columns. The fluting of the columns themselves was also an Egyptian device—probably an imitation of reeds tied round a pole. Similarly, the so-called "Ionic" capital (resembling a pair of tightly-curled ram's horns) appears to be a conventionalization of the papyrus-lily of the Nile. But the Ionians gave to such details a liveliness of form and delicacy of treatment which were lacking in the more ponderous art of the East. The same was true of their sculpture. Early Greek artists must often have gone to study their craft in Egypt. But the smile they learnt to give to the mouths of their statues, soon gained a new vivacity. Their handling of drapery was more elegant than the severe traditions of Egyptian craftsmanship permitted. They even began to differentiate between textures, treating wool in one way and linen in another; and, generally speaking, new life was infused into the old conventional types. It would be difficult to imagine the statue of some seated Pharaoh rising up from his throne; but even in the early Greek figures, however crude their anatomical detail, there lurks as it were a latent capacity for movement.

In literature it is difficult to believe that the Greeks owed anything to anyone. Whence Homer got his metre—the rapid, colourful, yet immensely dignified hexameter [1]—cannot even be guessed at. In the Iliad and Odyssey, it appears suddenly full-grown and in its perfection; and never again was it handled with such magical skill. In other forms of Greek poetry—to which Ionians gave also an early lead—the metre was dictated by the rhythm of music and usually dance-music at that; for singing and dancing habitually went together to the accompaniment of the lyre. The examples of early lyric poetry we possess came not from the Ionian mainland, but from neighbouring islands. Some were by Anacreon the famous writer of drinking songs; but none can compare with the work of Sappho the poetess of Lesbos. Of her love-lyrics only a few fragments remain; but even from these we can safely say that no more poignant utterance of passion has ever been known.

> The moon hath sunk and the Pleiads,
>   and midnight has gone;
> and the hour is passing, passing
>   and I lie alone. [2]

Or this other, which begins:

> It seems all heaven here to sit
>   beside you listening lover-wise
> To your sweet voice and sweeter yet
>   your laughter's witcheries.
>
> But O why beats my heart so wild?
>   one look at you and swift as thought,
> I am as tongue-tied as a child;
>   words die in my throat.

If we possessed no more of Greek literature than the epics of Homer and the few fragments of Sappho, these alone would be sufficient to prove

---

[1] The Hexameter, with its alternations of the dactylic foot (tum-te-te) and the spondaic foot (tum-tum) suggests a marching rhythm accompanied by a drum. If this was its origin, it is more likely that the Greeks invented it, for they were far better drilled than oriental soldiery. They *marched*, and the others shuffled.

[2] Translated by W. Headlam.

the unique genius of the Greek language for expressing emotion. There is in it "the feeling of morning freshness and elemental power, the delight which is to all other intellectual delights what youth is to all other joys. Beside it Vergil's speech seems elaborate, and Dante's crabbed and Shakespeare's barbarous. For Greek had all the merits of other tongues without their accompanying defects. It had the monumental weight and brevity of Latin without its rigid unmanageability; the copiousness and flexibility of the German without its heavy commonness and guttural superfluity; the pellucidity of the French without its jejuneness; the force and reality of the English without its structureless comminution.[1] And never, the writer adds, can there be such a language again.

But vivid as the life of Ionia was, and full of still richer promise, it was none the less precarious; for her geographical position, to which she owed so much of her culture and prosperity, exposed her also to attack from at least one powerful neighbour. Lydia's growing strength had already begun to menace her, when about the middle of the sixth century the throne of this inland kingdom passed to a man of high ambition, Croesus. Nothing comparable to his power had ever been known in the vicinity of Greece. The splendour of his court and the riches of his treasury made a deep impression even across the Aegean; so that his name became a byword for fabulous wealth. Croesus seems to have admired the Greeks and done his best to conciliate them. He sent gifts to the shrines of their chief religious centres. He welcomed them courteously to his palace. But they feared him, and not without reason. Without provocation he fell on the Ionian city of Ephesus. In a desperate bid for divine protection, the Ephesians (so Herodotus tells us) stretched a rope from the town-wall to the shrine of their goddess Artemis—the "Great Diana" of the Biblical story. But Ephesus fell; and soon the whole coastline passed under Croesus' sway. Miletus alone preferred to compromise with the enemy and retained some measure of her independence. Nevertheless, the days of Ionia's greatness were numbered; and the leadership of Greek civilization was presently to pass across the Aegean to their supposed blood-cousins and their spiritual heirs—the Athenian people.

[1] Frederick Myers. Comminution signifies a "splitting-up" into isolated sentences.

CHAPTER IV

FROM OLIGARCHY TO DEMOCRACY

I

During the sixth century B.C., while Sparta was engaged in extending her hegemony over the Peloponnese and Ionian philosophers were showing the world how to think, Athens, for her part, was entirely absorbed in her own domestic problems. When the century dawned, she was only just emerging from comparative obscurity. Her people were still farmers in the main. She had as yet produced no great poet, no scientists, not even any art of importance. Nevertheless, the spell of Ionia had fallen over Attica. Luxurious Ionian habits were spreading among the gentry. They had caught the fashion for curls, perfumed robes and "grasshopper" brooches. Music and song enlivened their banquets.[1] They patronized craftsmen; and in their employment worked sculptors who within a generation or two were to develop an art of rarely sensitive beauty.[2] Among the Attic nobility, in short, there was already evidence of a refined aristocratic taste; and even the ferment of Ionian ideas was beginning to work in the minds of the more thoughtful. Athens, sure enough, was on the move; and the next hundred years were to see in her a rapid political and intellectual development which would end in placing her head and shoulders above the rest of the Greek world.

In an agricultural community possession of the soil is always the one sure passport to authority and esteem. Not so long ago, on however modest a scale, this could be seen in our own English villages. There it was the squire and leading farmers who counted for everything in the community's life. From them would be drawn the members of the Parish Council, who alone perhaps understood the "ins" and "outs" of local affairs—how many "legs" each villager might graze on the common, where turf might be cut and firewood gathered, and so forth. They, too, would supply the wardens of the Parish Church; and, if there had been a village tribunal, they would certainly have filled its bench. So it was also in Ancient Greece, and not least in sixth century Attica. There the hereditary aristocracy of landowners, having ousted the king nearly a hundred years before, now ruled the roost completely. Their Council exercised control over all public affairs, holding its sessions on the slopes of the Areopagus—the Mars Hill of St. Paul's famous sermon. From

---

[1] See Plate II, page 51.   [2] See Frontispiece.

among them, too, were drawn the officials or "archons," chosen annually by the Council to perform the executive duties previously discharged by the king.

Needless to say, this close oligarchical clique stood for the vested interest of their own selfish class. Nevertheless, as always in an agricultural community, respect for ancestral custom was still immensely strong; and the aristocrats' right ro rule was scarcely as yet questioned. That right rested, at bottom, on a twin foundation. Firstly, in war (though to a lesser degree than in Homer's day) they still bore the brunt of the battle; for no one but a man of substance could then afford the expense of a fully-armed warrior's equipment, let alone the leisure to practise its use. Secondly, the traditions of public administration were in their keeping. They alone understood the proper procedure of religious ritual, and theirs, too, was the accumulated experience of legal custom, inherited from many generations of aristocratic judges.

But aristocracy was not now what it had been in the Heroic Period. There had been a sad change for the worse; and the poet Hesiod who wrote a century earlier in a neighbouring country, had already recorded the change. The Golden Age is gone, he lamented. An Age of Iron has set in. The nobles are no longer what Homer had called them the "Shepherds of the people." Even as judges their honesty is not to be trusted; they "swallow bribes." Old neighbourly habits, in fact, had given place to avarice and oppression.

Since Hesiod's day there had been a further deterioration. The introduction of money had helped the rich man and hit the poor man hard. For money will keep where corn or oil will not; and so the big landowner, having accumulated his hoard, could now lend to the small peasant when crops failed and rents could not be met. But for the debtor there was danger in this. Repayment must now be in coin; and if bad times lasted, he had no alternative but to pledge his land in security, or if he did not own the land, his person. If still insolvent, the bankrupt was liable to be sold into bondage. Slave-labour was increasing, imported mostly from abroad; and this told equally against the peasant. The large landowner, getting his work done for nothing, could undersell him and crush him.

Such a condition of things was a scandal; and already there was dangerous unrest. In 621 a concession was made. The unwritten custom of the courts was set down in "black and white." To the common folk this was real gain; for now at least they knew where they stood; and sentences were no longer dependent on the arbitrary interpretations of an aristocratic judge. But the code, like the custom, was terribly severe—"written in blood, not ink," as a later writer remarked. The penalty for stealing even a cabbage was death. This alone goes to show how bitter was the struggle for existence. Feelings seldom run high, unless men are hungry, and they were running high now. The increase of landless citizens was becoming a danger to the community. Factions were forming; and wild demands were put about that "debts should be cancelled," or that "all land should be redistributed." Even in high places the voice of protest was raised. "Avarice has laid hold on the leaders," wrote one would-be reformer, "they enrich themselves unrighteously and heed not the holy foundations of Justice."

Solon, the man who wrote these words, was himself an aristocrat, and therein lay the hope of the future. Among Athenians, if anywhere, there was a genius for political compromise; they were willing to listen to reason and to pursue the ideal of moderation which the "prophets" so sedulously preached. Solon was one of these "prophets," and happily he did not preach in vain.

By the year 594 the danger of faction had become so threatening that a "Peacemaker" was appointed with dictatorial powers and the choice fell upon Solon. This remarkable man was a poet and philosopher as well as a practical statesman. Though representing the high moral tradition of the good old days, he was also a student of the new intellectualism that was spreading across from Ionia, a friend of Thales, and much interested in the "wisdom of Egypt." By the later Athenians he was regarded as a founder of their political institutions. Posterity counted him among the Seven Sages of Greece; and a modern historian has called him the greatest economist whom the Mediterranean world produced before the foundation of the Roman Principate.

With wild schemes of reform Solon would have nothing to do. Beyond limiting the size of estates, he did not alter the system of land-tenure; nor did he cancel all debts, though he put an end once and for all to the enslavement of debtors. His measures, in fact, were not so much remedial as constructive. Solon's father, though an aristocrat, was engaged in trade; so he himself knew something about his country's economy, and he saw that the solution of Athens' troubles lay in making her prosperous. The problem of food came first. Attica was poor soil for grain, and there was nothing to spare for export. This, therefore, Solon forbade. The olive-tree, on the other hand, throve; indeed, it was the national boast that Athena, the country's patron goddess, had planted it there. So the export of oil he encouraged. But something more was needed to ensure prosperity; and with astonishing prevision Solon undertook a deliberate policy of industrial expansion. First he ordained that any father failing to have his son taught a trade, should forego all claim to his support in old age. Secondly, he sought to entice artisans from abroad by guaranteeing them full rights of citizenship. These measures soon bore fruit. Amongst other things there was a boom in the manufacture of pottery. Near the city were good beds of a reddish-brown clay, and Attic potters and vase-painters developed great skill, outstripping in time their rivals of Corinth, Rhodes and elsewhere. Their technique underwent an interesting development. At first they washed in the patterns and figures with black; but later they learnt to leave the terracotta surface to represent flesh-tint and washed in the background with black.[1] Jars of this ware were designed to contain oil or wine for exportation, and great quantities of them were sent overseas. But, though serving a practical purpose, they were masterpieces of draughtsmanship, and many of them now rank among the chief treasures of European museums.

Solon's policy had one result which he himself can hardly have failed to foresee. The population of the city rapidly increased—and more particularly those sections of it which were engaged in commerce or crafts. It was this urban and industrial development which more than anything else was to determine Athens' political future.

Solon's own political reforms were cautious almost to the point of conservatism. He was too wise to imagine that the people were then and there ripe for self-government. He may have foreseen—who can tell?—that the new industrial and commercial classes would prove politically conscious and politically ambitious; and in that sense at least he was indeed the founder of Athenian Democracy. He is said to have instituted a popular tribunal of appeal by which even the decisions of officials might be overridden; but to what extent it really functioned is hard to say. The Citizen Assembly he clearly meant to encourage; for he admitted to its membership men of all classes, even the poorest; and he set up an elective body of four hundred members to supervise and prepare its business. But he left the supreme power, as before, in the hands of the Aristocratic Council. The chief administrative offices, too, he confined to the large proprietors. The net result therefore was that Athens remained an oligarchy.

So long as the land-owning class controlled the policy of state and filled all high executive posts, it could make little real difference what views the popular Assembly might hold or which aristocratic candidate they elected to office. Vested interests were in the long run bound to prevail. There was, however, one change which Solon introduced and

[1] See Plate II, page 51.

48

which was perhaps the most significant feature of his whole legislation. He made property and not birth, as heretofore, the qualification for high office. By this he must clearly have meant to broaden the basis of the administration. For merchants could now save money and buy land; and so they too might qualify for election. Thus through Solon's foresight began the process—familiar enough in English history—whereby the hereditary governing class was compelled to admit recruits from the bourgeoisie.

His legislative task accomplished, Solon went off on his travels, and deliberately left his countrymen to work out their own salvation without his embarrassing presence. But legislation is one thing, and its application in practice is quite another. Athens was still gravely disturbed. Discontent would take time to allay. The factional spirit had by no means vanished; and there was even danger of revolution. No one knew this better than Solon himself. He was accustomed, as we have said, to express his views in poetry (indeed, men had not yet learnt to write prose), and among the few fragments which survive from his writings there is one that voiced his fears. "From the clouds," he said, "come snow and hail; and lightning is followed by thunder ; so too by powerful men the city is brought low and the people in its folly comes under the rule of a Despot." Solon's fears were but too well justified.

2

Once a King of Persia, Herodotus relates, was caught in a storm at sea; and on the skipper's advising him to lighten the ship, he called his courtiers on deck and ordered them to jump overboard. On reaching land, however, he first decorated the skipper for saving his life, then chopped off his head for causing the death of his courtiers. Such an act was inexpressibly shocking to the Greek mind, not so much because it was morally wrong, but because it was politically irresponsible. Whoever was armed with executive power, should always, it was felt, be answerable for its use, and a Persian King was answerable to no one. Nevertheless, from time to time in Greek history—more especially in their turbulent early period—adventurers were found ready to seize control of the state and govern as despots. Their rule, of course, could never have succeeded without some popular backing; and usually, in point of fact, the masses approved of it. In particular, the rising class of artisans and merchants seem to have preferred it to the nobles' misgovernment. Autocracy, as it proved, was no more than a passing phase; but it did much to stimulate the growth and ambitions of the bourgeoisie, and thus, like the rule of the Tudors in England, to pave the way for democratic advance.

To the nobility, however, whom the autocrats displaced and whom they usually sought to destroy, the breach of constitutional practice seemed unforgivable; and in later days, whatever may have been the general view of them in their lifetime, there was a deliberate campaign to blacken the memory of these political upstarts. The name applied to them was "tyrants"—a title which significantly enough was borrowed from monarchical Lydia; but tyrannical in our sense the autocrat seldom was, except towards the nobles. Indeed, if only for popularity's sake, he often did a great deal for the lower orders. Yet his rule was an offence not to establish custom merely, but to the deep-rooted belief of the Greeks that reason should govern human affairs. On that score alone the adverse verdict of posterity was justified.

Elsewhere tyranny was no new phenomenon. It has already existed at Corinth and Megara and, across the Aegean, at Miletus; and even in Athens there had been an attempt at it which was narrowly foiled. Solon must have witnessed this attempt in his youth; and his warning against its repetition was timely. For soon after he had laid down his office and gone abroad, faction broke out once more, and the opportunity for a *coup d'etat* suggested itself to a certain Pisistratus. He was by birth an aristocrat, and had distinguished himself in a recent war against Megara. The neighbouring island of Salamis had been captured; and Pisistratus was popular. The story of his coup is told by Herodotus: Collecting partisans from the rough mountaineers "he planned an ingenious stratagem. First he wounded himself and his mule-team, and then, driving into the market-place, pretended that his enemies had made an attempt on his life, as he was on his way to the country. This took the Athenians in, and a body-guard of citizens was granted him, armed not with spears but with wooden clubs; and, aided by this following, he seized the Acropolis."

It was much in this way that the Reichstag fire was used by the Nazi revolutionaries; indeed, though their ideals were very different, it is tempting to see a resemblance between the methods of the Fuehrer and the tyrant. Pisistratus also understood how easily the masses may be gulled; and, when presently driven out by the two other factions, he resorted to a much stranger ruse. "There was an Athenian lady," Herodotus continues," of remarkable beauty, and only three inches short of six foot. This woman Pisistratus dressed up in full armour, then, mounting her in a chariot and arranging her in a suitable pose, he drove her into the

PLATE I

The Acropolis at Athens from the west. The view is taken from the Pnyx Hill where the Assembly was held. To the left lies modern Athens on the site of the ancient city. Beyond rises the conical hill of Lycabettus, and in the further distance Mt. Hymettus.

50

PLATE I

PLATE II

town. Meanwhile he sent runners ahead to make proclamation that the goddess Athena was doing honour to Pisistratus and conducting him back to her own citadel; everyone should make ready to give him a welcome." This rudimentary propaganda succeeded; and though again ejected by his rivals, Pisistratus was not to be put off and after ten years absence he again returned, this time for good.

The nobility, of course, suffered, and he drove many of them into exile. But otherwise he showed himself a beneficent "tyrant." "He did not," so Herodotus says, "abolish the existing magistracies or change traditional usages, but ruled the city in accordance with the established order of things and gave it good government." This showed a shrewd judgment of the Athenian temper, and no doubt it made the regime more palatable even to more prominent citizens—Hitler himself did much the same. But it was the common folk especially that Pisistratus sought to please. Water was short in Athens; for though the population had grown, no provision had been made for its increase. So he constructed conduits, and near the foot of the Acropolis he built a handsome fountain, known as The Nine Springs. Similarly, he conciliated the peasantry by providing seeds and stock animals for their farms; and he distributed among the landless the property he had confiscated from the exiled nobility.

Such schemes of social and economic betterment, though modest in themselves, serve at least as some indication of Pisistratus' policy. But his real contribution to the communal life went far deeper. So far as may be judged from the evidence, he set out to make Athens—what she eventually was to become—the cultural centre of Greece. Details are unhappily scanty. But we know he attracted foreign poets to his court, among them Simonides the well-known author of epitaphs. Later, under his son and successor, Anacreon the writer of drinking songs also came over. Besides this Pisistratus patronized artists in sculpture and painting. He improved and adorned Athena's shrine on the Acropolis; and he planned, though he did not complete, a magnificent temple to Olympian Zeus.

All this was something more than the mere gratification of the tyrant's own æsthetic instincts. It was part of a policy which only a man of real vision could have conceived.[1] Hitherto the appreciation of art and literature had been limited to a very narrow circle. The Athenian gentry were, in fact, the cultural heirs of the long-past Heroic age when the

[1] For further consideration of its motive, see page 82.

PLATE II

Above: a scene from a Red-figure Vase, representing an Athenian noble of Cleisthenes' day, reclining on his dinner-couch; a drinking-vessel beside him on a stool; a girl plays to him on the pipe.

Below: scene of a chariot being got ready. (From a Black-figure vase.)

"sweet-voiced minstrels" of Homer's poems were attached to the palaces and sang at the feasts of the great. Pisistratus' aim was to make available to the many what had till now been the privilege of the few. In other words, he sought to democratize culture.

Here again our information is scanty, and two instances must suffice. Drama in Greece was no sudden growth. Dances in which dialogue played a part were already popular; but the performances took place in the countryside. Pisistratus transferred them to the capital and made them a central feature of one of the national festivals. There drama rapidly developed, and within a generation or two the great tragedies of the Attic stage were to be numbered among Athens' chief glories.

Another of the public festivals—the Panathenæa, held in honour of the city's patron goddess—was also reorganized and elaborated. And here, too, Pisistratus introduced a new feature. He arranged for professional minstrels to give recitations of the Homeric poems. This popularization of the great Ionian masterpieces was to have a profound influence on the cultural life of the city; and her dramatists in particular came more and more to rely on Homer for moral as well as artistic inspiration. Even outside the Attica the effects of so enlightened a policy made themselves felt; and other states tended to look increasingly to Athens for the spiritual leadership of Greece.

To suppose that Pisistratus had any clear vision of unity in the Greek world would be going too far; but some such instinct, however dim, may have lain at the back of his mind. Culturally, at least, his popularization of the Homeric poems pointed in that direction. The Iliad and Odyssey are no product of a narrow provincialism, they are significantly catholic in outlook. The gods, as therein depicted, are something more than mere local deities. They rule from Olympus over the entire Achæan race. And one thing is certain, Pisistratus deliberately cultivated a friendly relation with the Ionians themselves. He is known to have been a bene-factor of their shrine at Delos—an island which was the traditional religious centre of the Ionian race; and it is evident that in so doing he had in mind the claim that Attica was the motherland from which they sprang.

That Pisistratus also kept in close touch with fellow-tyrants in other Greek cities, may have been no more than a precaution. Mutual support between such men was common prudence. For tyranny was never too firmly seated in the saddle, and it seldom lasted long. The regime founded by a capable father was usually mishandled by an incompetent son, and came to a swift end. On Pisistratus' death in 527, his two sons, Hipparchus and Hippias succeeded to his power. Hipparchus was presently assassinated by Harmodius and Aristogeiton two creatures of the court. In later days they were honoured as national heroes; but such a claim was baseless. Their action arose from a sordid personal grievance.

Meanwhile Hippias, unnerved by his own narrow escape, grew suspicious and oppressive. His real danger, however, was from outside. Exiled aristocrats were plotting to overthrow him; and they worked on Sparta's habitual distrust of revolutionary regimes till she finally intervened. Hippias was driven out, and the exiled nobles returned; but their return had an unexpected sequel. One influential section of them espoused the popular cause. Sparta again took alarm; but this time her interference was unavailing; and under the direction of Cleisthenes, the new party's leader, a thorough-going democratic constitution was established at Athens.

3

Cleisthenes, like Solon, was a statesman of the first order; and he could afford to be more adventurous. Pisistratus' regime had been an educative experience, and in the nobles' absence the masses had become more politically-minded. They now seemed ripe for self-government, and Cleisthenes had the courage to give it them. But he had learnt the lesson of the past hundred years. So long as partisan rivalry lasted, there could be no political stability.

Now such partisanship had its roots in the old electoral system. Hitherto the leading state officials had been chosen by the people voting in clans or family groups (all MacDonalds, as one might say, would vote in one group). So inevitably at the polls each group tended to rally to its own traditional leader—the "head of the clan"; and here, then, automatically was faction in the making. Cleisthenes determined to end this system. So he reorganized the electoral constituencies. Instead of kinship he gave them a *territorial* basis; and each constituency was so distributed as to include a representative cross-section of the whole community—city-dwellers, country-peasants and mercantile folk at the port. By this ingenious rearrangement the old clan grouping lost all political significance (MacDonalds could no longer vote together), and thus no elected official could count on an automatic partisan backing.

But Cleisthenes was taking no chances, and he introduced another device to check dangerous political rivalries. Once a year a referendum was to be taken whether any individual's presence in Athens was against public interest. Whoever desired to see some individual banished, recorded the name on a potsherd or "ostracon" (whence the referendum was known as "Ostracism"); and if more than six thousand votes were cast against any one man, he had to leave Athens for ten years.

To establish a pure democracy must at any period be a great act of faith; but under the safeguards already described Cleisthenes was ready to make the experiment. The old Aristocratic Council of the Areopagus was, so to say, by-passed. Though not actually abolished, it fell gradually into the background—a survival of the past which, like our own House of Lords, commanded respect but less and less real power. Ultimately even its prestige vanished, and it ended as a High Court of Appeal in cases of homicide.

The Assembly of citizens now became the sovereign voice in the State. All public policy was determined by its vote. All officials were responsible to it alone. No one could challenge or alter its decision. The People's decree was final. The Council specially created by Solon to prepare the Assembly's business and preside at its sessions, was retained by Cleisthenes. But he raised its members from four hundred to five hundred and threw open its membership to all classes. The method of its election, too, was revised. A panel of candidates was chosen in the constituencies, and from these the final Five Hundred were selected by lot. Bribery was thus made impossible.

It would be hard to imagine a machinery of government more genuinely democratic. Under our modern representative system, the individual can only express his will directly at widely-spaced intervals, and then only on the most general issues of policy. In day-to-day decisions the Parliamentary member must be left to interpret the view of his constituents. At Athens such decisions were made by the citizen himself. In the Assembly's debates he could influence speakers by his applause or dissent; he could, under certain circumstances, move his own motion[1]; he could make his own speech and, above all, he could cast his own vote. But political education is bound to be a slow process; and the art of public address is not learnt in a day. At first, therefore, it was inevitable that the aristocratic spokesman, a practised hand in debate and with long experience behind him, should retain his traditional leadership. To all intents and purposes he retained it for the best part of a century.

It is likely enough that Cleisthenes and his aristocratic supporters even foresaw something of the sort. What they cannot have foreseen was the peculiar circumstances under which their great experiment would have to work. In the not far distant future, democratic Athens would be faced with problems and responsibilities of a wholly new order. First through her leadership and example she was to save Greece from national extinction by Persia. Then in the consolidation of this victory she endeavoured

[1] Some safeguards undoubtedly existed against irresponsible motions. In Aristophanes' parody of an Ecclesia (quoted on page 88) a private citizen is restrained from initiating a discussion on peace. Decrees were normally proposed by some official.

to unite a part at least of the Greek-speaking world. Voluntary union—
through no very great fault of her own—proved a failure; and she thus
found herself committed to imposing unity by force. A democracy is
not ideally adapted to the exercise of imperial rule: certainly not a
young democracy like Athens; and the wonder is not that she
ultimately failed to solve its problems, but rather that she succeeded as
well as she did.

CHAPTER V

UNITY OR ANNIHILATION

I

There was so much that was admirable in the life of the Greek City States—the healthy diversity of their institutions, the vitality of their artistic and intellectual growth, the strong individuality of their leaders, and above all the many-sided activities and burning enthusiasms of their citizens—that it is tragic to contemplate the price they had to pay for the political independence from which in the last resort these many virtues sprang. For, unless they were prepared to sacrifice their separatist instincts and merge in some sort of political union, nothing could be more certain than that sooner or later they would be overwhelmed piece-meal by some foreign power. Already, as we have seen, Ionia had fallen to Lydia; and now at the very moment when Cleisthenes was launching his great experiment, a far more serious threat was looming up in the East. The power of Persia would have carried all before it, had not the Greeks at the moment of crisis sunk their differences and formed a common front. But the crisis over, they fell apart once more into the two traditional groups, Sparta dominating the Peloponnese, and Athens dominating the Ionian and other Aegean states. The antagonism between them deepened; and eventually the two groups were to clash in a war so devastating that Greece never properly recovered her strength: till her weakness and continued disunity made her an easy prey to the ambitions of a Macedonian King.

Yet, incurable separatists as they were, the Greeks did not by any means lack a sense of racial brotherhood. Hellas—the name by which they themselves always called their country—meant something much more to them than a mere geographical expression. They were all Hellenes at heart; and go where they might to settle—north to the Black Sea or south to Libya, to Cyprus at one end of the Mediterranean or Marseilles at the other—Hellenes they obstinately remained; and though in early times there may have been some intermarriage with the surrounding natives, these settlers never allowed themselves to be absorbed. In the Roman epoch, after seven hundred years of history, the Greek character of Marseilles was still the boast of its inhabitants.

What was the real foundation of this racial pride is not so easy to say.

Religion certainly played some part in it. Homer, as we saw, had encouraged the belief that the gods of Olympus were gods of the whole race. Local shrines, of course, they had; but the more important of these were held in universal reverence and pilgrims visited them from all over Greece.

Two such religious centres enjoyed a special pre-eminence; and each in its way helped much to foster the sense of Hellenic unity. One was Delphi, a beautiful spot in a high mountain valley looking southward over the waters of the Corinthian Gulf. Here was situated the famous shrine and sacred precinct of the god Phœbus Apollo and, in close connection with the shrine, his still more famous oracle. Most early peoples have claimed by some means or other to receive direct communication from the deity; did not Saul, King of Israel, pay a visit of enquiry to the witch at Endor? And the Greeks believed in all seriousness that Phœbus Apollo spoke through the mouth of a prophetess. This woman was known as "the Pythia"; and when one holder of the title died another succeeded her. In a fit of convulsions—induced no one knows how—she gave vent to the oracular response; and no matter what question was asked there was always an answer. Some came with their personal problems: Why was a wife childless? What career should a son pursue? States, too, sent to seek advice on questions of policy. There was endless variety. More often than not the response was couched in a distinctly cryptic style, sometimes susceptible of a double interpretation. One monarch, for instance, was told that, if he crossed a certain river, he would destroy a great empire, and optimistically crossing it, he destroyed his own. There was another suspicious feature about the working of the oracle. It always reached the enquirer neatly composed in hexameter verse. This suggests that the priests had some latitude in the interpretation of the Pythia's ravings. They seem, too, to have been well informed about the affairs of the outside world, and possibly they even relied on some kind of secret service. During the epoch of colonization they were able to direct enquiries to suitable fields for settlement. One man, who had come to ask about his stammer, was irrelevantly told to go and colonize Lybia—advice which he eventually took, and with surprising success.

In any case, whether by luck or intelligence, the Delphic oracle gained a great reputation. Foreigners came to consult it, Crœsus of Lydia among them. Presents of gold and silver plate flowed in from the grateful; and an enormous treasure was accumulated in the precinct. Nor was the influence of the oracle confined to purely secular affairs. The voice of Apollo joined with that of the "prophets" in urging the ideals of Reasonableness and Moderation. On the outside of his temple were exhibited two mottos, one the "Mêden agân" or "Nothing in excess" which we quoted above; the other "Gnôthi seauton" or "know thyself" as who should say "Do not overreach yourself: recognize your limitations." Whatever hocus-pocus went on behind the scenes at the Pythia's séance, the oracle undeniably preached good sense and did what it could to promote order and harmony in the Greek world.

The other religious centre, rivalling Delphi in popularity, was Olympia. It lay up a river valley [1] near the west coast of the Peloponnese. Here stood the temple and precinct of Olympian Zeus, where at four yearly intervals were held the famous Games. These, too, were religious in origin—a survival from some early ritual of human sacrifice which a kindlier age had commuted to ordeal by trial of strength. The opening day was devoted to ceremonial in front of the Temple; and during the period of the festival a Sacred Truce was proclaimed; and throughout Greece all wars were interrupted. To the games came not athletes merely, but every sort of person who had goods to barter or skill to exhibit; hucksters, conjurers, acrobats, professional lecturers, and even authors of note; Herodotus himself is said to have given a public reading of his history there. It was a regular World's Fair, and from all over the Hellenic World—especially from Sicily and Southern Italy—pilgrims and sight-seers poured in. The contests were very varied, and included chariot-races and a competition for heralds. But to describe the events in detail would be superfluous in an age which has seen their revival. A few points, however, deserve mention.

First the competitors stripped naked, as was usual in all physical exercise; and, though women were excluded, the ban was simply a survival of an ancient taboo and not due to any sense of propriety. The Greeks were perfectly frank and unashamed about the human body. Many of the events were intended to be a test of endurance even more than of actual skill. Races were run in thick sand; and in one the competitors ran in soldier's equipment. Special feats might be remembered; but, where there were no stop-watches, records could be no object. Extraordinary toughness was shown; and in the "all-in wrestling" men were known to suffer death from strangulation rather than admit defeat.

Secondly, in the palmy days of the Games competitors were all amateurs. For a long period the Spartans not unnaturally swept the

[1] See Plate V, page 62.

PLATE III

PLATE IV

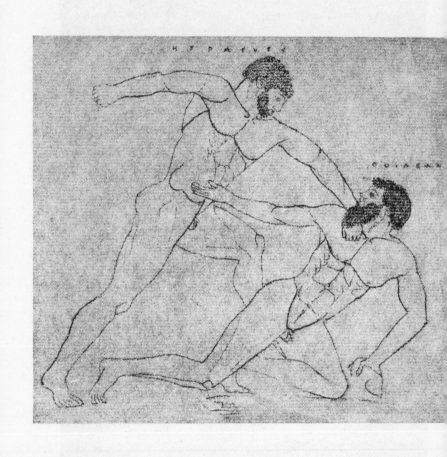

board; and it was not till a fashion for specialized training set in that their supremacy was challenged. Even then they refused to follow the fashion, preferring an all-round physical development. The professional athlete did not make himself beloved. His braggart talk and greedy appetite were thought out of taste—"one of the worlds' abominations" an Athenian playwright called him. Nevertheless, a victor in the Games was always a hero in his home-town. On his return he was fêted by the whole population, and rewarded with free meals for life at the public expense.

Lastly, it should be said that before the Games a careful scrutiny was held into the entrants' parentage and antecedents. It was useless for a half-caste to apply. The competitions were for Greeks and Greeks alone. So it was an exclusive gathering, yet none the worse for that. Here for once in a way at least, all Greeks could meet together as a harmonious family and in conscious pride of their common brotherhood.

Such exclusiveness was a gradual growth. There is no hint of it among the Homeric warriors; there was nothing to choose between Achæan or Trojan. But the later Greeks, though great travellers and good mixers, developed a strong sense of racial superiority. The word "barbarian," by which all non-Hellenes were known, had more than a tinge of contempt in it. Most of all was this felt for the soft luxurious Oriental; and dramatists could always make a good hit by holding him up to ridicule. After the defeat of the Persian invasion the feeling seems to have grown; and the Greeks painted an exaggerated and not wholly justified picture of the cowardice and feeble spirit of their enemy. Some elements of the invading host were no doubt unreliable, and its training and equipment no match for the heavy-armed Greek warrior. But the Persian regiments at least were tough fighters, and racially they belonged to the same Aryan stock as the Greeks. It was to be a stern bitter struggle, and for a while the future of European civilization hung in the balance.

2

During the twelfth and the five succeeding centuries the cruel military domination of Assyria had lain heavily over Mesopotamia. About 600 B.C., however, the empire of the Ninevite kings went to pieces, and its territory was divided between Babylon and Media. Among the dependencies of the latter was the mountainous district of Persia, and fifty years later some change of dynasty set a Persian prince on the Median throne. His name was Cyrus. He was a strong ambitious character; and from Susa, the new capital, he began a career of conquest which was to carry his realm to the shores of the Aegean. First he attacked and annexed Babylon. Next he entered Asia Minor, overwhelmed the Lydian army, captured Sardis and made Crœsus a prisoner. The fate of the Ionian Greeks followed swiftly. They were placed under the rule of "quisling" tyrants supervised by a Persian Satrap who was quartered at Sardis.

Cambyses, Cyrus' son and successor, followed in his father's footsteps and added Egypt to the Empire. On his death the crown passed to Darius, a man of great energy and a master of organization. The empire was now divided among some twenty satraps. Great trunk roads were built, one from Susa to Sardis, a distance which by the aid of a courier system could be covered in a week. It is a commonplace of history that improved communications upset the balance of world affairs; and Europe was now brought within the orbit of Persian ambitions. In 514 Darius crossed the Bosphorus, intending apparently to conquer the Danube basin. The expedition proved a fiasco and he narrowly escaped destruction by the wild Scythian tribesmen.

Persian prestige was badly shaken; and in 499 the Ionians, restive under alien rule, rebelled. They put up a plucky fight and even marched inland and burnt Sardis. But the odds were too great, and in 494 they were crushed. Miletus was sacked and its inhabitants slaughtered.

But the most significant part of the story has still to be told. The organizers of the Ionian Revolt had appealed for help to European Greece. There, odd as it may seem, opinions were divided. Men's vision was short; only a few years before Lydia had been the closest and seemed the most dangerous enemy, so that her overthrow by Persia had been hailed with relief. As yet little was known of the new power which had appeared out of the East; and few felt inclined to take up the cudgels against it. Cleisthenes himself had favoured a policy of appeasement, even hoping that Persia might prove a useful ally against Sparta. One Greek island lying close off the Peloponnese was actually ready to place herself under Persian protection.

So when the Ionian envoy, seeking military aid for the revolt, had arrived in Greece, his prospects were not promising. At Sparta he met with a cool reception. "He had brought with him," says Herodotus, "a bronze tablet on which the whole circuit of the earth was inscribed with all its seas and rivers," and, pointing with his finger, he explained the geographical position of Lydia and the rest. "How many days' march is it from the sea to Susa," the Spartan King presently asked. "Three months" was the unguarded reply. "Milesian stranger," said the king, "quit Sparta by sunset."

Athens, however, was by now awake to the peril from Persia. She had strong ties of sentiment with Ionia and agreed to send twenty ships to aid the revolt. Then came the news of Miletus' destruction. The dismay at Athens was terrible. When next year a dramatist made the catastrophe the subject of a play, the whole audience burst into tears, and the poet was heavily fined for his tactless reminder.

3

"The sending of those twenty ships," says Herodotus, "was the beginning of trouble to both barbarians and Greeks." For Darius was set on revenge. In 490 he sent an expedition across the Aegean, and Athens found herself compelled to face invasion alone. The Spartans, still blind to the reality of the danger, deliberately dallied; and when at last their troops came, they arrived too late. Athens had in the meanwhile fought and won single-handed.

The Persians' strategy was ingenious. They had brought with them Pisistratus' son Hippias, now twenty years an exile. This man still had his friends in Athens; and a section of the populace, remembering his past benefactions, was in favour of receiving him back. So when the Persians disembarked in north-east Attica, the government were caught in a dilemma. To send out their fighting men and leave the capital at the mercy of the traitors seemed a big risk; but their leader, Miltiades, an aristocrat of the old school, insisted on taking it. He led the army across and stationed it on the mountain-slope overlooking the Plain of Marathon where the enemy were encamped by the seashore below. So things remained for some days. The next move was for the Persians.

Herodotus' account of what followed is far from explicit; and some gaps must be filled in by conjecture. But what happened seems to have been this. One morning the Persian cavalry was seen to re-embark and sail away southward. They had only to round the tip of the Attic peninsula to reach the coast near Athens; and if their main forces meanwhile took the overland route to the city, it would be caught upon two sides. That the traitors within were in readiness to open the gates, seemed only too probable—indeed, the story was that a shield flashed on the hills that same afternoon had been their prearranged signal. So for the Athenian army on the mountain-slope it was now or never. They moved down and "charged," so Herodotus says, "at the double, the first Greeks to my knowledge who introduced such tactics." There was hard-fought struggle, and then they drove the Persians back into the sea. But there was still no time to be lost. Weary as they were with the day's fighting, they marched back to Athens. They arrived in the nick of time; and at the sight of them the Persian fleet, already in the offing, turned on its tracks and sailed for home.

The victory of Marathon was a signal triumph for the Athenian aristocrats and their great leader Miltiades. For it had been the popular party—or a section of it at least—who had been prepared to turn traitor and receive Hippias back. Happily their miscalculation provoked no change in the regime, and this, as it proved, was to save not only Athens, but Greece. For they had not done with Persia yet; and aptly to the moment a democrat leader was now to the fore who appears to have known it. This leader was Themistocles, a type of statesman not hitherto known, and the first fruit, as it were, of the new democratic regime. He was the son of a bourgeois merchant, and his father had not given him the old-fashioned aristocratic schooling. His music—normally the accomplishment of a gentleman—had been entirely neglected; he could not even play the harp. Instead, he had studied under teachers of the new-fangled art of Rhetoric. This had sharpened his wits. He was adaptable, imaginative, and possessed of an extraordinary faculty for quick decision. Many stories were told of his brilliant retorts and ingenious strategems; and, if there was any truth in such tales, he does not seem to have been much troubled by scruples.

Themistocles' upbringing had made him sea-minded in a way that his aristocratic contemporaries were not; and if (as seems certain) he foresaw another Persian attack, he must have known that Athens' only hope of salvation lay in sea-power. To convince his countrymen of this was another matter. But an excuse for increasing the size of the fleet was opportunely provided. A war was in progress against the neighbouring island Aegina, and it was going none too well. As luck, too, would have it, a rich vein of ore had recently been struck in the Attic silver mines at Laureum. Themistocles had his way and the windfall was devoted to the construction of two hundred new galleys. Previous to this he had initiated a scheme for making a new harbour. The sandy bay of Phalerum, hitherto used, was no protection against storms; but at Piræus, some six miles from the city, was a rock-bound inlet which offered far better accommodation. This Themistocles planned to convert into a serviceable road-stead. But he had not the opportunity of completing it; for even his other precautions were taken barely in time (483).

Darius in the meantime had died; but Xerxes, his successor on the Persian throne, had decided to carry out his father's intention and renew

PLATE V

PLATE VI

the attack on Greece. Preparations were made on a gigantic scale. This was to be no mere raid across the Aegean, but a highly-organized expedition of the combined fleets and armies of the Empire. The strategic plan was to follow the coast-line round the Northern Aegean and so descend upon Greece, fleet and army moving side by side. The Dardanelles was bridged in advance with pontoons, and a ship-canal was even dug through the peninsula of Mt. Athos—one of the three finger-like promontories in the north-west corner of the Aegean—off which an earlier expedition had foundered through storms. A convoy of ships was to help in provisioning the huge land army—put down by Herodotus at 1,700,000 men, but unlikely to have numbered more than a quarter of a million. The fleets of Phœnicia were accompanied by Ionian vessels pressed into service, and the whole constituted a formidable armada.

When in 480 this vast assemblage of men and ships began to move, panic seized Greece. The northern states of Bœotia and Thessaly determined on a policy of appeasement. Even the Delphic Oracle doubted and warned the Athenians of impending doom:

> Wretches why sit ye here? Fly, fly to the ends of creation!
> Nay, not alone shall ye suffer; full many a town shall be levelled;
> Many a shrine of the gods will he give to fiery destruction
> Get ye away from the Temple and brood on the doom that awaits you.[1]

The prestige of Apollo never recovered after this disastrous failure of nerve. Happily, however, the Spartans were staunch, and, if only to secure the invaluable services of the Athenian fleet, decided on an attempt to hold Northern Greece.

Parallel with the upper tip of the island of Eubœa the mountains of the mainland come down close to the sea. The narrow passage left between cliffs and water was known as the pass of Thermopylæ; and here the Spartan King Leonidas elected to make his stand. He had brought with him three hundred Spartan warriors, a contingent of loyal Helots, and some forces drawn from the more reliable northern states. His position could not be by-passed except by an inland track through the hills, which he took steps to secure. The holding of the pass was therefore by no means a forlorn venture. The Greek warrior was well equipped for defence. With head covered by vizored helmet, body and thighs by shield and

---

[1] Quoted from Rawlinson's "Herodotus."

cuirass, and lower legs by greaves, he was almost invulnerable from in front. In the narrow pass the Persians were at a disadvantage. Their numbers could not tell and of their two most dreaded arms the cavalry and the archers, one could not operate and the others' volley could make little impression on their well-armed opponent. The story of the battle shall be drawn (in an abbreviated form) from Herodotus' account written a generation later.

'First Xerxes sent forward a mounted scout to find out what the Greeks were doing and how many they were. The man found the Spartans posted in front of their encampment, some engaged in athletic exercises, others in combing their long hair; and his report sorely puzzled the King; for the simple truth never struck him that they were preparing to do or die like heroes. So he let four days go by, in the hope that they would decamp. But on the fifth he decided they were a set of obstinate fools and sent forward the Medes with orders to capture them and bring them to his presence alive. The attack was pressed home, but with terrible losses; and what was clear to everyone else, at length dawned on the King; his fighting-men were numerous, but the warriors among them rare. Finally the Persian Corps, known as the Immortals, were ordered up in the Medes' place. These, it was thought, would soon end the business. But they in their turn proved no more successful. Their lances were shorter than the Greeks, and fighting on a narrow front they could not deploy their numbers. The Spartans' remarkable handling of the battle, too, showed the superiority of their tactics. Often they would feign flight, and then, when the noisy, yelling rabble pursued, they would swing round and slaughter them in heaps. Three times, it is said, Xerxes leapt from his throne in terror for his army.

'Next day the assault was resumed; but, faring no better, the Persians again retired. In this predicament the King was approached by a certain Ephialtes, a native of the locality, but now in exile. He revealed the existence of the track through the mountains leading to the rear of the Greek position. The Persian Corps under Hydarnes was entrusted with the mission. They set out about the time of the lighting of lamps, and, marching all night, found themselves at dawn near the top of their climb. Here Leonidas had posted a thousand Phocians; but they were at first unaware that anyone was approaching. The air, however, was very still; and the Persians' feet, tramping through the leaves, made a rustling. This awoke the Phocians to their peril, and they rushed to arms; but under the hail of arrows fell back to the crest of the mountain, meaning to sell their lives dearly. But the Persians passed on and dropped swiftly down towards the coast.

'When scouts ran in with the news, the Greeks held a council of war. Many elected to march off home; but the rest made up their mind to stand by Leonidas to the end. Hitherto all the fighting had been done in the narrowest part of the gap; but now, seeing death near, the Greeks advanced to the point where the pass opens out. Here terrible havoc was wrought on the barbarian host. Their captains kept urging them forward with blows of the lash. But many fell in the sea and were drowned. Still more were trampled underfoot; and no account was taken of the dying. When their spears were shivered, the Greeks went to work with their swords. And here Leonidas fell fighting bravely.

'Presently came tidings that Ephialtes' party was approaching. Then the Greeks fell back again to the narrow part of the pass, and formed a compact body on a hillock. Here they fought on with swords, if swords were left them; if not, with hands and teeth; till finally they were overwhelmed by the shower of missiles.

'So died the Spartans and their remaining allies, and over the Spartan grave was set this inscription:[1]

> Go, way-farer, bear news to Sparta's town
> that here, their bidding done, we laid us down.'

Northern Greece was now lost. Athens was speedily evacuated; and all the women and children were ferried over to neighbouring islands. Only a few fanatics stayed behind to make a brave but futile stand on the Acropolis. To save the Peloponnese seemed the one remaining hope. The fortification of the Corinthian isthmus had already begun, and hurried efforts were made to complete it.

Meanwhile the Greek fleet, though successful in holding the Euboean narrows, had no choice but to retire in conformity with the strategic situation. It took up its station at the island of Salamis; but scarcely had it done so, when the Persian fleet arrived and anchored near the Piræus opposite.

Among the Greek captains, two views now prevailed. The Peloponnesians were for retiring to the Isthmus and there linking up with the land forces. This course, however, would have committed them to an engagement in open water, where with their inferior numbers they were bound to be outflanked. Themistocles took the opposite view. The best hope, as he saw it, was to lure the Persians into the narrows between Salamis and the mainland, where numbers could not tell. There was a heated debate, in which he actually threatened to withdraw the Athenian fleet altogether and sail off to Italy. By this threat he carried the day, and the Greeks remained at Salamis.

[1] By Simonides.

The Persians behaved as Themistocles had foreseen. They entered the narrows. Cramped for space, their vanguard alone was able to deploy; and the remaining ships, crowding in on its rear, created indescribable confusion. The nimbler Greek vessels made rings round their disordered opponents, and by the end of the day there was little left of the great Persian armada. Xerxes himself had been watching, seated in his throne on "the rocky brow which looks o'er seaborn Salamis." What he had seen decided him. He was terrified of a fresh revolt in his rear and departed at once for Asia Minor. But he left the Persian land army behind him with orders to withdraw into winter quarters in Thessaly.

This was clear evidence that the permanent occupation of the northern half of the country was still in contemplation; and the Greeks were now well alive to their danger. With spring they decided to take the offensive. All, for once, pooled their military resources; and under Spartan leadership a formidable army marched north from the Isthmus. The enemy, too, had moved down to meet them; and at Platæa, on the frontier between Attica and Bœotia, a decisive battle was fought. Here, at least, the Persians gave proof of their soldierly qualities. During the opening stages of the campaign, in which for many days both sides manœuvred for position, their redoubtable cavalry severely harassed the Greeks; and in the pitched battle that followed, their archers, posted behind a barricade of wicker shields, put up a stiff fight. But the Greeks won, and never again was a Persian army to set foot in Europe.

Much, however, remained to be done. There were Persian garrisons to be cleared out of Thrace; and there was Ionia to liberate. This last was achieved by a crowning success won at sea off Cape Mycale near Samos. In the course of the battle the Ionian naval contingents, hitherto timorously loyal to their Persian masters, deserted to the Greek side.

Victory was now complete; but in the aftermath of victory unity was lost. Sparta, who with her eye on the Helots shrank from risking her forces far from home, gradually withdrew from the alliance; and her Peloponnesian confederates did the same. Such over-confidence was premature. There could be no lasting guarantee against renewed Persian aggression, unless an adequate fleet were kept in being. For this Athens alone would scarcely have the resources. Shipbuilding was expensive, and Attica was not a rich country. What was needed was a co-operative effort of all maritime states—the Eubœan cities, the colonies of the Northern Aegean, the islanders, and the Ionians and other Greeks of Asia Minor. So a League was formed. All members of it were to contribute according to their means. Athens, of course, contributed the bulk of the fleet. Others, notably the three large islands, Lesbos, Chios and Samos, contributed ships too. The rest paid an annual quota of money. The collection of the latter was entrusted to the Stewards of the League; and the League Treasury was kept on the island of Delos, the old religious centre of the Ionian Greeks. Here, too, met the delegates sent by League members to discuss common policy. Thus the constitutional arrangements were democratic enough; but from the first, as was inevitable, Athens took the lead; and it was primarily to her efforts—and in particular to the forceful commandership of Cimon the son of Miltiades—that the League's military successes were due.

For Persia was not yet done with. The loss of Ionia still rankled and she had by no means abandoned hope of its recovery. In 466, it became known that the Phœnician fleet accompanied by a land army was moving towards the Aegean. It had got more than half-way along the southern coast of Asia Minor before the Greeks under Cimon encountered it. The battle was fought near the mouth of the River Eurymedon. The Persians' fleet was first overwhelmed and driven into the estuary; Cimon then disembarked his army and destroyed their forces on land.

Though formal peace was not declared for a dozen years or more, two generations were to pass before Persia sought to meddle again in the affairs of the Greeks. To whom in the last resort their salvation was due was controversial even in antiquity. Some gave the credit to Sparta, whose eadership had clinched the decisive victory of Platæa; others, perhaps with more justification, to Athens whose resolute policy at Salamis had first turned the tide. But the final explanation of the miracle lay in the fact that the Greeks had for once sunk their differences and united in defence of their common freedom. The tragedy was that the lessons of the war were so quickly forgotten in the peace.

CHAPTER VI

THE AGE OF PERICLES

1. A NEW CHAPTER

The magnitude of their double triumph over the greatest known military power was not lost on the Athenians. Long after, their elders prated about the "Marathon-heroes," and Salamis became a part of every orator's stock-in-trade. As a people they felt themselves suddenly to be "on the top of the world," and from this in a large measure sprang the reckless confidence and boundless energy which now carried them forward to the greatest phase of their history. Athens' heyday lasted less than eighty years, and the number of her adult male citizens scarcely exceeded fifty thousand. Yet this handful of men attempted more and achieved more in a wider variety of fields than any nation great or small has ever attempted or achieved in a similar space of time.

After Salamis, clearly, things could never be quite the same again; first the mass-evacuation, in itself a great leveller, a breaker-up of traditions as well as of homes, and then the victory in which every man equally had played a part, the rower at his bench and the man-at-arms on deck, no less than ship's captain or the admiral himself. The twofold experience was bound to breed a sense of social and political equality. The tide of Athenian democracy now set in at full flood; and more and more through the coming years the People's will determined the city's policy.

The social advance was scarcely less striking. The whole temper of Athens was changed. Among a society of merchants and craftsmen and shopkeepers there was little room for the beautiful but exotic culture of the pre-war gentry with their Ionian robes and oriental perfumes and "grasshopper" brooches. Its gay insouciance was replaced by a very different spirit, the spirit of men who had been—and still were—at close grips with life, purposeful, serious-minded, at times almost morose. The transformation is well reflected by the art of the two periods. In the reconstructed foundations of the Acropolis wall, where after the Persian sack they had been thrown like so much rubble, many pre-war statues have been unearthed—lovely female figures, with dresses falling in dainty folds and picked out with brightly-coloured patterns, and with a charming, if highly conventionalized, smile on their delicate faces. To pass from these to the austere sublimity of the Parthenon statuary is like passing from the gay fantasies of Watteau to Millet's serious canvasses, or from the poignant sweetness of Mozart to the solemnities of Beethoven.

And the Athenians had need to be purposeful. On their home-coming after Salamis there was much to be done. They had their ruined houses to restore. At Piræus there was the rock-harbour planned by Themistocles to complete; and, as a permanent safeguard of their communications with the port, they proceeded a little later to build a pair of Long Walls linking it with the city. Yet these tasks absorbed but a part of the people's energy. The war had shaken Athens out of herself; it had brought her more into contact with the rest of the world. During the campaigns for the liberation of the Aegean large numbers of her citizens had seen service in Thrace, Ionia, and even further East. Familiarity with other people's habits and with more luxurious standards of life could not fail to leave its impression; and many must have come home with their heads full of new commercial ambitions. The main fields of their enterprise lay, of course, in the directions above mentioned; but even these did not satisfy them. They began to push their voyages round the Peloponnese and across the Adriatic where in Sicily and South Italy—hitherto Corinth's special preserve—great openings were awaiting them. Friendly relations were established with Corcyra on this westerly trade-route, to be followed by alliances with several Sicilian towns; and meanwhile traffic in oil and wine—previously carried on others states' vessels—could now be carried more advantageously on their own.

Thus a new chapter was begun in Athens' economic development, a continuation no doubt of earlier tendencies, but on a much vaster scale. Both city and port became hives of industry. Foreigners and slaves were increasingly employed on production, and citizens thus left free for the business of export. But, as the number of the inhabitants grew, so too did their needs; and commercial expansion became a necessity of the city's very existence. Geography favoured her. Economically the Mediterranean world had become since the war a more closely-knit unit; and Athens stood more or less at its centre. So into the Piræus, as a comic-poet could boast, goods flowed from every quarter—"hides from Cyrene, ivory from Libya, meat from Italy, pork and cheese from Syracuse, rugs and cushions from Carthage, scents from the East," and to these we may add corn from the Black Sea and Egypt, and metalwork from Tuscany.

Even so, there was never more than enough to keep pace with the mounting population. The strain on Athens was constant, and competition severe. And this, too, had its effect on the people's character. They grew more grasping and aggressive. As their fleet came to assume the control of the Aegean, they began to be more conscious of their strength and less scrupulous in their use of it. We are approaching an era of what we may term Power Politics, an era in which selfish calculations were nakedly advertised and armed might acknowledged to be the mainspring of policy. Athenian democracy, in short, was on the make and ready for every enterprise; and more than anything else its future depended on the type of leadership it found.

Fortunately, perhaps, the masses did not turn for guidance to members of their own class. Few among them can as yet have been ripe for political responsibility. Themistocles himself disappeared from the scene—ostracized through the intrigues of aristocratic opponents; and half a century was to pass before another bourgeois came to the fore. The days of demagogy were not yet. So the Democracy accepted the leadership of the aristocrat—not now from sheer force of habit, but for his practical experience, his superior education, and, perhaps we may add, for his virtues too. For the "gentleman's" code was still upheld in the best Athenian families. The old ideals of Moderation and Justice were still preserved, and they were the constant theme of the writers of the period. Herodotus never fails to point out the dangers of Pride, and Xerxes' fate was to him the classic example of Pride's fall. The same is true of drama. The plots of Æschylus' and Sophocles' plays normally hinge on the Nemesis awaiting the frantic word or foolish boast, and the self-will that will not listen to reason. Even in the calm repose of Phidias' sculptured figures we can discern the same moral idealism.

The urgency of such preaching is evidence enough of how much it was needed; and in the Athenian democracy, as we have seen, dangerous forces were at work which only the firm hand of a clear-sighted statesman could curb and direct; and now, as at previous crises in the city's history, a man was to be found capable of the task—the greatest of all her leaders, Pericles.

Pericles belonged to the same distinguished family as Cleisthenes. He was a man of high culture, the friend of poets and philosophers. But he was also the most adroit of leaders. Shrewdly he kept himself secluded from public view, never wishing to make himself cheap, yet never afraid, if need be, to speak out against public opinion. They nicknamed him the "Olympian," and on the rare occasions when he appeared on the platform, he spoke with grave but dynamic dignity. "The Olympian, lightened and thundered," said one of the poets. From Thucydides we have versions of some of his speeches. How much of them is Pericles and how much the historian, is not easy to say; but their tone is deeply impressive, and something at least of the speaker's idealism must have found an echo there.

Both by his oratory and still more by his personality Pericles wielded an immense influence over the Assembly. At one period, indeed, his authority seems to have gone almost unchallenged. Nevertheless, we must beware of assuming that he had a completely free hand in his direction of policy. He was the leader but only the leader of an extremely high-spirited people, on whose vote year by year he was dependent for his continuance in office. He had to take his countrymen as he found them. He was bound in some degree to interpret their wishes. Still more was he bound to diagnose the deeper and unexpressed needs of their spirit, and to direct, so far as possible, the economic and other forces which were driving them along perilous and difficult paths. In this task he largely succeeded. His only real failure was that, once he himself was removed, the lessons he had striven to teach them were so soon forgotten. But few even of the greatest statesmen can educate their posterity.

2. FOREIGN POLICY

In the aftermath of Salamis, Pericles was not yet old enough to take the political stage. After Themistocles' fall, therefore, the leadership passed to Cimon, already the most energetic spirit in pushing the counter-attack against Persia. Like his father, Miltiades, he was an aristocrat of the old school, frank, chivalrous and athletic, a thorough "good fellow." His pet project was to maintain good relations with Sparta whose institutions he greatly admired; and in 464 an unexpected chance came. In that year a terrible earthquake shook the Peloponnese. Sparta was laid in ruins. The Helots, seizing their opportunity, rebelled and gathered their forces to the impregnable hill of Ithome in Messenia. All attempts to dislodge them failed. Cimon conceived the idea of going to the Spartans' assistance. Leave was granted him, but he was no more successful, and on his return home he was not re-elected. Pericles had been foremost in ridiculing the notion that Sparta and Athens could work together; and in the following year (461) he found himself in power in Cimon's place.

The thirty-two years of Pericles' rule—and it was almost uninter-rupted—fell roughly into two halves, a period of continuous warfare followed by a period of nominal peace. The first half was crowded with events. Campaigns were fought in half a dozen different countries. On a war memorial, which has survived, were recorded the names of the fallen in one Attic clan alone: "Of the Erechtheid tribe, these died in one year fighting in Cyprus, Egypt, Phœnice, Halieis, Aegina and Megara." A remarkable record; but at the same time for the historian a complex situation not easy to disentangle. Three spheres of action, however, may be distinguished: first, against Persia; second, against members of the

Delian League; third, within Greece itself. We will deal with them in that order.

About the time that Pericles came into power, the Egyptians under a prince named Inaros had revolted against Persia. Athens depended somewhat already on corn supplies from the Nile, and the chance of assisting Egypt's liberation seemed too good to miss. A fleet of two hundred galleys was sent, but after a promising start the expedition failed disastrously. Not a ship returned; and a second squadron sent in reinforcement fared little better (454). Pericles had the wisdom to close at last the long chapter of hostilities begun at Marathon and in 448 he made peace with the Great King.

Meanwhile the prolongation of the struggle with Persia had had important repercussions in the Aegean. As the peril from the East appeared to recede, the members of the Delian Confederacy had grown increasingly restive. The annual contribution to the Central Fund irked them. They were discomposed, too, by Athens' high-handed methods. As early as 467, the year before the Eurymedon battle, the island-state of Naxos tried to secede and had been crushed. After the Eurymedon further precautions against Persia seemed needless, and a more general rot set in. There was no concerted movement. One by one the members of the League sought to evade their obligation; and one by one Athens held them to it by force. By the middle of the century the three large island states, Lesbos, Chios and Samos, alone remained with a nominal autonomy and fleets of their own.

The ethics of secession are never easy to determine (as the United States found to their cost); and Athens strong policy was not without its justification. Though at the moment the Persian Empire was enfeebled, another Xerxes or Darius might any day succeed to the throne, and the bulwark of the Delian League was not a thing lightly to be thrown away.[1]

Athens, however, was not content simply to hold the League together. She was assuming the role of mistress rather than leader. The meetings of the Confederate Council were discontinued, and in 454 she took a still more significant step. It was a critical year. The best part of her fleet had been lost in Egypt; and if the Persians cared to enter it, the Aegean was at their mercy. Pericles took his precautions. He removed the League treasure from Delos for safer keeping on the Acropolis. But it was never sent back. Thus the seal was set on a policy to which perhaps Athens was already committed in her suppression of the secessionist movement. The League was a league no longer: it had become her Empire.

[1] At the end of the century when Athens fell, Persia very soon resumed the control of Ionia.

The ethics of Imperialism, as of secession, are subject of controversy; and it is not for ourselves to cast a stone at Athens. But in the last resort the issue must turn on the use to which Empire is put; and Athens' use of it was certainly open to criticism—not least her sequestration of the tribute-funds wrung from unwilling subjects. Yet there is also much to be said on her side. Normally even the tribute itself cannot have been exorbitant, else it would scarcely have been possible later on, under the exigencies of war, to treble its rate.[1] If part of the fund was spent on the beautification of Athens, the bulk of it went to the upkeep of the fleet, which kept Persia at bay and policed the Aegean. In this and other ways the subject-states gained as much as they lost. Piracy was suppressed. They enjoyed the use of the Athenian currency, a great stimulus to their trade. The importation of Black Sea corn was regularized. Most of it went first to the Piræus for subsequent distribution; but direct traffic was sometimes licensed. Nor politically were the subject-states too badly off. With each state, as it sought to secede and was brought to heel, Athens had made a separate treaty; and the terms were not onerous. An Athenian garrison was rarely imposed. A democratic constitution was *de rigeur* (since compliance could more safely be counted on from the popular party); but otherwise they were left to manage their local affairs. Law-suits between Athenian merchants and theirs might be taken to the Athenian courts; but since these were notable for their equity, this was less a hardship than a privilege. Evidence, indeed, is not lacking that the benefits of the Empire were even appreciated. Troops from the subject-states served loyally with Athenian contingents, and on one occasion stood by them to the death rather than desert to the enemy.[2] Some cities of the North-West Aegean, though not original members of the League, actually came unasked under Athens' protection, and paid her a voluntary tribute.

Yet it would be idle to pretend that Athens' rule was popular. When a chance came to rebel, it was usually taken. The passion for independence was ineradicable among Greeks, and it was characteristic of them to be always "agin the Government." Yet, taken all in all, it is doubtful whether, in antiquity at least, any imperial rule could boast a more solid justification; and it would be tempting to add, in modern times, too.

The reduction of the secessionists cannot have entailed much serious fighting. Among the Erechtheid tribe, it seems, no lives were lost across the Aegean, and in most cases a mere threat of blockade must have been sufficient. Otherwise, Athens could scarcely have undertaken during this

[1] See p. 112.
[2] During the Sicilian expedition.

73

period a whole series of wars nearer home. The motive of these was pretty clearly commercial expansion. Her chief trade rivals were Corinth, Megara and the island of Aegina. First in 461 Megara, nervous of Corinth, had come under Athens' protection. Then Aegina, though assisted by Corinth, was conquered. Finally, Sparta intervened and drew Bœotia into the war. But this merely gave Athens a pretext for further aggression. In 457 she attacked Thebes, the leading Bœotian city, and by one sweeping victory took under her sway not Bœotia only, but much of the adjoining country westwards. Nearly the whole upper coast of the Corinthian Gulf passed into her hands, and at the narrow exit of the gulf she planted a settlement at Naupactus. Thus she threatened Corinth's vital outlet to the trade of Sicily and Italy.

For a while, indeed, it looked as though Athens would establish over Northern Greece a hegemony similar to Sparta's hegemony over the Peloponnese. But she had over-reached herself. Her reserves of manpower were limited, and her grip on the conquered territory was precarious. In 447 the Bœotian cities rose and defeated her in battle. This was a signal for Megara and Eubœa to rise too; and, to top all, Attica was simultaneously invaded by a Spartan army. Athens surmounted the crisis. The Spartans were bought off by a bribe to their King, and she was left free to reduce Eubœa at leisure. But her Land Empire was irretrievably lost. Aegina and Naupactus were all that remained of her conquests. In 445 she concluded a thirty years' truce with Sparta. It was not to run half of its time.

During the dozen years or so of uneasy peace which followed, Pericles was not idle. He must clearly have envisaged a renewal of the struggle with Sparta and out of the imperial tribute he set aside a war-reserve which, by the time it was needed, amounted in value to seven million pounds of our money. But he found other and more commendable uses for the accumulating funds. He had already embarked on an architectural programme calculated to make Athens the finest city in Greece, and he

---

PLATE VII

A reconstruction of the Parthenon, as seen from inside the Propylæa. It shows (1) in the gable or "pediment" a group of figures representing the scene of Athena's contest with Poseidon for the soil of Attica; (2) under the gable the row of two-figured groups of combatants (known as "metopes"); (3) dimly discernible between the pillars [1] the famous "Frieze," most of which, together with some of the pedimental figures, are now in the British Museum.

All three sets of sculpture were designed, and in part perhaps worked upon, by Phidias.

[1] Along the sides of the temple the Frieze is placed high on the outer wall of the shrine itself. At the ends, however, it runs above the row of secondary columns. In this position it would be invisible from the view-point of this picture; so, to give some impression of its part in the decorative scheme, I have here placed it in the same position that it occupies along the sides of the building.

PLATE VII

PLATE VIII

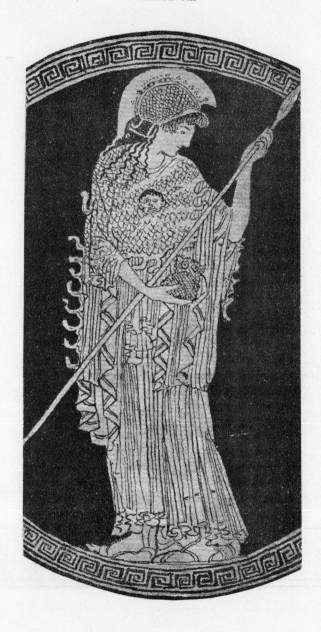

was now at liberty to proceed with it. First on the Acropolis came the building of the Parthenon, a new temple dedicated to Athena. It was completed in 438 and presently adorned with the sculptures of Phidias (now one of the chief treasures of the British Museum). Next followed the construction of an Entrance gate or Propylæa at the western approach of the Acropolis; and nearby the completion of a little temple, already begun, to the goddess of Victory, Nike. The genius of Phidias was further employed on two colossal statues of Athena. One cast in bronze stood just inside the new Propylæa; the other, made of ivory and gold, was placed in the Parthenon itself. Athena's old shrine, the Erechtheum,[1] was rebuilt somewhat later. Phidias' giant statues have long since disappeared, but the buildings above mentioned still stand, albeit in sad disrepair.

Meanwhile down at Piræus a vast scheme of reconstruction had gone forward. Here town-planning—that strange by-product of Pythagorean theories—had free play; and the quayside city was laid out on a rectangular pattern with broad streets leading to stately arsenals and warehouses. Thus the new and populous suburb presented a strong contrast to the older city. There, though the market-place was surrounded by fine buildings and porticos and adorned with masterpieces of statuary and painting, the rest of the town, having grown up at haphazard, was still a medley of narrow winding alleys.

In this contrast, too, was reflected a marked social difference. Compared with the adventurous go-ahead commercialists of the port, the City, as the seat of government and the home of the aristocracy, stood for a more level-headed and cautious conservatism. As time went on, it was the former class rather than the latter that was to weigh the scales and decide the fate of Athenian Democracy.

3. PERICLES' POLITICAL IDEAL

Pericles was a political realist. He had no illusions about the character of the imperial rule. He knew that Athens was hated. "Your Empire," he once said, "has become a tyranny, wrongfully won, some say, but a tyranny you cannot safely surrender." In other words, if Athens was to govern, she must govern strongly, and she did. These were stormy days, with a prospect of worse to come. It was no time for concessions to sentiment; and even at home, for reasons which we cannot fully under-

[1] See Plate IX.

stand, Pericles curtailed the facilities for naturalization and so limited the enjoyment of citizen rights to pure-blooded Athenians only.

Yet we know that Pericles was an idealist too. He had a clear vision of what he wanted his own country to be. What we do not know is whether he had an equally clear vision for Greece. That he consciously aimed at its unification, Thucydides never so much as suggests. Yet what was the alternative? There could be no permanent *modus vivendi* between democratic Athens and oligarchical Sparta. Sooner or later a clash was sure to come; and from it the one or the other was bound to emerge as master of Greece. Pericles was too far-sighted a statesman not to have considered what use should be made of such an opportunity, but no doubt he was also too wise to say so in public.

One move of his was, however, significant. After concluding peace with Persia he had invited all Greek states to meet together in conference and discuss the restoration of temples destroyed in the war. This belated and, as it proved, unsuccessful proposal discloses something at least of what was in Pericles' mind. There is a phrase in one of his speeches which throws a clearer light on it (and of the many sayings attributed to him by Thucydides, none has a more authentic ring). "Athens," he said, "is the educator of Hellas." So it was a cultural unity at the very least that Pericles envisaged—a cultural unity which his own country might give, and, if his claim were true, was already giving to Greece.

All the highest spiritual traditions of Athens were blended, so to say, in Pericles' own personality. Like Solon, he was a student of philosophy; like Pisistratus, a lover of arts; like Cleisthenes, a believer in freedom of thought and speech. He had gathered round him a brilliant circle of intellectuals, among them the poet Sophocles and the sculptor Phidias. Others, if only for a time, he attracted from abroad, Herodotus the historian, Protagoras the educational expert, and Anaxagoras the philosopher. At his invitation many men of distinction came to settle in Athens. One was a Syracusan manufacturer named Cephalos, a friend of Socrates and father to Lysias the eminent legalist. Such aliens, though excluded from the franchise, played a valuable part in the cultural life of the city.

Thus Athens was rapidly becoming what Ionia had once been, the hub and focus of intellectual and literary activity. Architecturally she was the most beautiful city in Greece. Her dramatic performances were witnessed by visitors from all over her Empire. She was setting a new standard of civilization which little more than a century hence Alexander was to

PLATE IX
North Porch of Erechtheum. This temple, which stands on the Acropolis to the north of the Parthenon, was built in the Ionic style.

PLATE IX

PLATE X

spread through the whole Eastern world. And even now, though her subjects might justly complain that they paid a high price for them, these amenities were something which they might themselves imitate and even come to share with pride.

But the "education of Hellas" cannot in Pericles' mind have been entirely confined to the æsthetic or intellectual field. His speech from which that phrase is quoted and which we will reproduce in part below, was one long panegyric of the Athenian way of life. This he passionately believed to be the best in the world. His countrymen, he claimed, were liberal in outlook, tolerant towards their neighbours, law-abiding citizens of the state, versatile and adaptable, ready to face every problem and danger with the enterprising spirit of free men. No doubt he would have wished to see other Greeks follow their example. But the fatal dilemma remained. It was because they were free men that the Athenians had developed these qualities; and yet the very method by which Pericles sought to impose Athenian culture on others, began and ended in depriving them of their freedom. That fatal dilemma had its roots deep in the whole political system of Greece.

This much, however, may be said. Pericles' belief in freedom sprang from a profound faith in human nature. His long experience of Athenian democracy cannot have failed to teach him what the dangers of freedom were; yet despite all the hard tussles he must have had with his countrymen, he was prepared to trust them still. That was the real secret of the success of his leadership: and who can say whether, had he lived longer, his faith might not have carried him on to yet bolder experiments? [1]

4. THE FUNERAL SPEECH

The occasion of the speech, to which reference has been made, was an annual ceremony in commemoration of citizens who had died during the year in the country's service. The main part of it shall be given in full. After a preamble dealing with the circumstances under which he was speaking, Pericles proceeded thus:

"I need not dwell on our military history. You are all familiar with the

[1] When their great war with Sparta was drawing to a close and they were on the verge of collapse, the Athenians extended a grant of citizenship to the inhabitants of the loyal island of Samos—a policy which, if it had been adopted earlier and spontaneously, might have changed the whole course of history.

---

deeds that have won us the Empire and the stout resistance we have always offered to Greek or barbarian invaders of our soil. So I will pass on; but before coming to my main theme, I have something to say about the social background of our success and about the moral and political ideals which have made us what we are. The topic, I feel, is apposite to the occasion, and the gathering of citizens and visitors I see before me will surely benefit.

"Ours is an unrivalled constitution. So far from owing anything to our neighbours, it sets the standard for them. On account of its popular bias, it has come to be called Democracy or the Rule of the Masses. But, in fact, we enjoy, as between man and man, complete equality of legal status. In our public life individual talent is the one thing valued. Preferment depends on merit, not on class; nor does obscurity of rank prevent any from making his contribution to the common weal.

"An equally liberal spirit is carried into our private relationships. Everyday life is not soured by petty suspicions. A man may go his own way and yet incur no resentment, not even the harmless but aggravating sneer. The same absence of friction extends to our public life. There is a wholesome dread of law-breaking. We defer to the government of the day. We defer no less to the legal code, especially when it casts its shield over the victims of injustice. Least of all do we ignore those rules which derive their unwritten sanction from the individual's sense of honour.

"Nowhere else is manual drudgery relieved by so many cultural diversions. The state provides for an annual cycle of religious pageants and competitive performances. The beauty of our homes helps to make life less drab; and the very magnitude of Athens attracts imports from all the world over, so that foreign goods give us as much pleasure as though they came from home.

"Next observe the contrast between the military methods of our opponents and our own. Our gates are kept wide. We never adopt their habit of periodically deporting our aliens. This might check espionage and the disclosure of important secrets. But we are averse to building up armaments on the sly. We prefer to trust in our own stout hearts, when the call for action comes.

"In education, too, there is a similar contrast. The Spartans manufacture men by a rigorous lifelong training. We prefer a free and easy existence; yet man for man we face danger as readily as they. And here is the proof. If they invade Attica, they do not come alone; they bring their allies with them. When we march, we march unaccompanied; yet nine times out of ten we come off best, though our enemies are fighting on their own soil and for all that they hold dear. So far, indeed, our full strength has never been put into the field. What with our naval commitments and the wide dispersal of our forces that is impossible. So from time to time the enemy may encounter a fraction of our army; and then they brag of victory or explain away defeat on the pretence that our whole force was engaged. And, if we like to go as we please, letting courage grow by habit rather than through the organized drudgery of the drill-yard, we are on balance the gainers. We avoid the initial strain of preparation; and yet, when the crisis comes, we meet it just as pluckily as our plodding enemy.

"And we are remarkable for other qualities. We are lovers of beauty, and with us it is within the reach of all.[1] We care deeply for things of the mind, but this does not make us soft. Wealth is with us a means to creative activity. Poverty itself we are never ashamed to admit. The disgrace lies in failure to struggle against it. The claims of public and private life do not clash; and concentration on personal business does not detract from our political flair. As a people we stand out in our condemnation of those who 'wash their hands of politics.' This, we hold, is to shirk responsibility. In debate we are at once critical and constructive; and, while we like to look before we leap, discussion is with us no impediment to action. Nowhere else is coolness in council combined with such daring initiative. Other folk's courage springs from lack of imagination. It soon leaves them, once they stop to think. But the palm must assuredly go to the man who has taken the just measure of life's joys and war's dangers, and so can be deflected by neither from the path of duty.

"My conclusion then is this. As a country, we are an education to Hellas; and individually such is our versatility that each of us is able to fill any or every role and to carry it off gracefully too. Nor is this an idle boast. It is the sober truth; and the proof lies in the proud position we owe to our national character. Athens alone, when put to the test, rises above her reputation. She alone can inflict defeat without her foes resenting their chastisement. Her subjects and hers alone feel no humiliation in serving such a mistress. We have given many tokens of our strength, and our claim to the admiration of this and future ages is well attested. We need no second Homer to chant our praise nor the pleasing tribute of poetic fancy which the facts may later belie. Our evidence is more solid. There is not a sea or a land into which our adventurers have not forced a passage, and which does not bear indelibly the marks we have left there for better or for worse.

[1] Pericles' actual words were, "We love beauty with cheapness." They had a dual significance. First they implied that at little or no cost to himself the citizen might share in the artistic and literary amenities which the State provided. Secondly, that Athenians avoided the luxurious extravagance in which the plutocrats of their rival Corinth indulged.

"It is for such a city that these men have died, her loyal comrades to the end. And it is to such a city that we, their survivors, must dedicate all we have. That is my reason for dwelling at length on our Athenian ways. It is an instructive picture. It tells us that we have a stake in what others have not got; and it lends colour and substance to the panegyric which I am here to pronounce on the fallen. Little indeed remains to add. The heroism of these men and their like has but pointed the moral of my earlier theme—and few Greeks can hope to find their words tally so closely with the facts. For what to my mind stamps a man as a hero—first evidence it may be or it may be final proof—is a soldier's death like theirs. Some perhaps had their failings; but against these must be set their gallantry in the field. Whatever damage they did their country in civilian life, is nothing to the public service they now have rendered her. The self-indulgent may cling to life's comforts and the poor man to his dream that luck will turn; but not men such as these. Their overmastering desire was to be even with the enemy and they proudly resolved to sacrifice all to that. Hoping the best of the unknown issue, they confidently faced the visible task before them and made ready to stand firm at the cost of their own blood. Life was dear, but they held their honour dearer, and so, when the hour came it brought not terror but glory, from which at that high moment of hazard they were suddenly rapt away.

"These men then deserved well of their country; and it is for us to show a courage as dauntless, though leading (let us pray) to a happier close. No words can measure its import. What the security of our frontier means, is known to you all, and why should I labour it. Use the evidence of your eyes. As you go your daily ways, look round you on the visible might of Athens. Fall in love with this fair mistress; and as you come to learn her greatness, call to mind the brave stand of these her chivalrous champions, their proud refusal to forsake her in the evil hour and their last noble contribution to her cause. Their sacrifice has won for them imperishable renown and the most illustrious of sepulchres, not in their present resting-place; but wherever man's word or deed honours their memory, there their glory will for ever endure. The whole world is the sepulchre of the great. The carven stone in some graveyard at home has little significance, but elsewhere their unwritten memory will outlast material symbols, alive in the minds of men. Take them as your model, and remembering that no happiness can be had without freedom and no freedom without courage, make light of the perils of war. To the un-happy creature, for whom it holds out no prospect, life may mean little enough, but he knows no such reason to risk it as those who, having the greatest hostages to offer to fortune, have most to lose by defeat. What daunts a man of spirit is the degradation of a cowardly surrender, not sudden death encountered in the heat of battle and under the inspiration of a common cause.

"I have said my say, as the law ordains and as I could best match the occasion. The funeral rites are over and in part, at least, the dead have received their due. One thing remains for the future. The State will bring up their children at the public charge until they are of age. That is the material prize she holds out to these and all such for a race thus worthily run. Men make the best citizens when character can count on the highest awards.

"Now shed each a last tear for your personal loss and then go your several ways."

5. DEMOCRATIC CULTURE

How much of his own ideas Thucydides has here placed in Pericles' mouth is impossible to determine, but we may at least say that the historian was himself a shrewd and critical observer, and that in the main this description of the Athenian character is borne out by the known facts. At the same time there is no doubt an element of idealization in Pericles' words. He is preaching, as it were, to his countrymen, painting a picture of what he wished them to be rather than of what they already were.

There is, too, an undercurrent of polemics in much of the speech. Pericles is defending his ideal against the criticism of political opponents. There was a party in Athens, aristocrats of the old school and led by another Thucydides, who disapproved of the democratic regime and would probably have liked a return to some modified form of oligarchy. After 447, when the collapse of his Land Empire had brought Pericles into disfavour, these men had enjoyed a brief spell of power; and though by the time the Funeral Speech was delivered their influence had dwindled, it was still worth Pericles' while to discredit their views. Like Cimon, Thucydides and his followers had a great admiration for Sparta; and to this the comparison drawn in the Funeral Speech was a fitting retort. More serious perhaps were their criticism of Pericles' Imperialism. They disliked the expenditure of the tribute-money on the beautification of Athens, "like a vain woman," one of them said, "decking herself out with trinkets." Hence Pericles' contention that Athenian culture was neither luxurious nor "soft"—like that of Ionia or possibly the rich merchants of Corinth. The critics even took up the cudgels on behalf of the tributary-states. And here Pericles answered by a reminder of the commercial advantages of the Empire. A firm grip on the Aegean was vital to the survival of Athenian democracy. Without it half the merchant class would be ruined, and the over-swollen industrial population reduced to the severest straits.

And there was another charge levelled against Pericles' policy. It was said that he had pauperized the Athenians, providing free meals for the poorest, initiating public works to furnish them employment, using the state funds for their entertainments, paying them a fee for their attendance at the jury-courts, not to mention other "pensions and gratuities." [1] Now there can be little doubt that despite her commercial prosperity there was much real poverty in Athens. The Funeral Speech harps upon it more than once; and how low was the standard of life even for the middle-class citizen can be seen from Aristophanes' comedies. His meals, it has been said, seem to "have begun and ended with pudding." Sometimes it would be little more than a barley-cake eked out with garlic or a kipper; on festal occasions perhaps sausage-meat or a rich broth. An eel or a thrush was a luxury. The fresh fish-market was for the wealthy alone. [2] Houses were scantily furnished, and an inventory of the belongings of even that notorious spendthrift Alcibiades reveals an astonishing austerity. Nor was there any prospect of a rapid improvement. Commercial and industrial expansion had their limits. Vacant land for colonization—the old safety valve—was no longer available. From time to time, indeed, small bodies of indigent citizens were planted at strategic points in the Aegean; but this could be no more than an insignificant palliative. The population of the capital did not diminish, and the standard of life remained low.

Since then, like most democracies, the Athenian populace was impatient and headstrong, it was essential that they should be kept happy by some alternative means. Here lay the very kernel of Pericles' policy; and, like the far-sighted statesman he was, he had undertaken to solve it by *socializing the amenities of life*. So the Roman Emperors' policy of "circuses for the multitude" was anticipated at Athens on a far higher cultural plane. The architectural programme not merely provided

[1] These points are recorded by Plutarch, a historian of A.D. c. 100.

[2] Aristophanes wrote, it is true, during the war against Sparta, but in its earlier stages at least overseas commerce cannot have been much interrupted, else the traders would not have been so eager to continue the war. In one play the Council itself is represented as being won over by six-pennyworth of mayonnaise—a fantastic joke, but significant. Comedians of to-day might make similar play with a "banana." In any case, the elaborate organization for safeguarding and regularizing the food supply tells its own tale.

PLATE XI
The Theatre at Epidaurus in the Peloponnese, looking across the dancing ring (in which the chorus performed) to the stone seats of the auditorium. On the left are remains of the stage buildings.

PLATE XI

PLATE XII

employment, it gave the ordinary citizen something to talk about, and be proud of. The pageantry of the Panathenaic festival was given a new magnificence. Near the theatre an Odeon or Music-hall was built for the holding of choral competitions; and in the theatre itself the productions were more elaborately staged. These last were the most popular of all, and a generation later a fund was formed to encourage attendance by the payment of a small gratuity.[1] But even in Pericles' own time, there was just ground for his boast that they were "lovers of beauty," and (as he went on to add) that the beauty was given them "cheap." It was not the only time in history that "high thinking" has proved an adequate compensation for "plain living."

6. SOCIAL DIVERSIONS

At Athens provision for physical recreation was made by the State. Some small training-schools or "wrestling-grounds" were run by private enterprise; but the large sports-grounds or "Gymnasia," laid out at the public expense, were much more impressive affairs, covering a large area of ground and including baths, undressing-rooms, and so forth. How much time an average citizen could spare for daily exercise is difficult to determine. But Socrates, we know, always counted on finding his friends at one or other of such establishments; and they were by no means all members of the moneyed class. In any case, those who had the leisure followed a normal routine of taking athletic exercise in the afternoon, followed by a rub down and cold douche. In general, the Athenians were an active-bodied and active-minded race, and preferred the role of participants to that of idle spectators. Dancing was popular. Singing and lyre playing were part of the educational curriculum; and after supper every guest was expected to "oblige" with a song, generally to his own accompaniment.

But the great treats of the year were a different matter. In an age, when

[1] The object of this was in part, no doubt, to compensate the poor for loss of working time; but it also had the effect of helping to educate the masses—an interesting experiment in subsidized adult education.

PLATE XII

Above: Vase-painting. A boy listens to the pipes played by his older friend. The question. "were the ancients lovers of music?" seems here to receive an adequate answer.
Below: Vase-painting of a wild dance in honour of Bacchus or Dionysus the God of wine. It is well to remember that despite their habitual self-restraint the Greeks at times broke out into orgies of drunken revelry, especially at the season of the Bacchic festival. It is noteworthy that, while he makes the dance beautiful, he has given the dancers themselves coarse features. The Greeks were quite clear that drunkenness was bestial. All the same they probably regarded such orgies as Nature's safety-valve for "blowing off steam" from time to time.

the sabbatical rest was unknown, the occasional holidays, lasting often for days at a time, afforded much-needed relaxation, but they afforded also a feast for the eye, the ear, and the mind as well. Twice a year, at two festivals in honour of the wine-god Dionysus, dramatic performances were organized by the State. They were competitive; and some time in advance authors were invited to submit their work. From the applicants were chosen three comic playwrights and three tragedians. Each of the former were represented by a comedy apiece; but each of the tragedians by four plays, a group of three tragedies (known as a trilogy) with a serio-comedy to follow. The next step was to collect and train a chorus. Its members were drawn from private individuals, and the cost of their training, as of the costumes and other paraphernalia, was borne by some rich citizen or resident alien.

The origin of Greek Drama must be traced to some primitive form of ritual dance, in which a chorus, divided into two bands, danced and sang turn and turn about, as it might be a more elaborate grown-up edition of the game "Nuts and May." By and by had come a further elaboration. There was a "leader" of the chorus, and an "Answerer" [1] or actor was introduced to converse with him. Hence arose the dramatic dialogue. All performers wore masks (a relic, no doubt, of the original ritual), and the actor, by simply changing his mask behind the scenes, could reappear in a series of different roles. Eventually a second actor and then a third was added; and with this, drama, as the Greeks knew it, reached its full development. In the open-air theatre a curtain was scarcely practicable, and no change of scenery could be made between the acts. So it had become the function of the chorus to mark these intervals by a choric ode, sung and danced as of old by two bands in turn. During the main action of the play they remained as passive spectators in their dancing-ring or "orchestra" in front of the stage.

The conventions of such a drama may seem to us highly artificial, but in reality they were no more so than the conventions of opera or oratorio The actors (unlike the chorus) were professionals hired by the state; and much of the dramatic effect must have depended on their elocutionary powers. For besides masks, they wore club-soled shoes to increase their stature and enhance their dignity. Rapid or violent movement was therefore impossible. Nor in the absence of a curtain could death take place on the stage. Murder and suicide—the usual climax of a tragedy—was either heard from behind the scenes or more often reported by a messenger. Sometimes by a mechanical device the back-scene parted and revealed a tableau of the bloody corpse with the murderer standing by. Such

The Greek word "hypocrites" is the origin of our word "hypocrite."

A Tragic Actor (reconstruction of a statuette). Note that to increase his stature he wears a high mask and club-soled buskins, with padded clothes and gloves to match.

limitations, however, did not worry the Greeks. A playwright who knows his job can depict horror more effectively by the magic of words than by its visual presentation.

In tragedy the plots were invariably drawn from mythology, but in comedy the scenes and characters were those of everyday life; contemporary personages, politicians and generals, philosophers and poets, were mercilessly burlesqued. At the close of the performances, which occupied three days in all, judges carefully picked and further sifted by lot, awarded the prize—a bronze tripod or stool, the ancient equivalent of our silver challenge cups. Their verdict was no doubt influenced by the attitude of the audience, who expressed their views during the plays with considerable freedom, applauding or booing, or even pelting the stage. No audience could have been more attentive, quick to take a point or to mark any fault in the actor's rendering. To sit through a long spring day on a wooden or stone seat under a blazing sun was no mean test of enthusiasm; the more so when we remember the length of a tragic trilogy and the highly poetic language in which the plays were cast. Yet the Athenians certainly enjoyed the experience and talked of the plays long afterwards. Their conversation (as depicted by Aristophanes) was full of allusions to them—memories of the disappointment felt when a play by Æschylus was expected and the play of some inferior poet came on instead, or of the laugh which went round when an actor had been guilty of some comical mispronunciation. Judging, too, by the regularity with which the prize was awarded to plays of acknowledged genius, the standard of public taste must have been very high.

That the Athenians, then, had succeeded in democratizing culture, is abundantly evident. When Pericles said that the average citizen could carry anything off "gracefully," he was thinking in terms of the old aristocratic tradition of elegance and taste and dignified deportment. The best Greeks of all ages stressed the ideal of beauty to a remarkable degree. The very phrase which we have translated as "gentleman" was composed of two words—"agathos," which covered every shade of meaning between brave, public-spirited and good, and "kalos" which covered every shade between good, noble and beautiful. To have popularized this ideal by a process of levelling up rather than of levelling down was a wonderful achievement; and in fact there was among the Athenians little sign of vulgarization such as too often accompanies modern urban development. Wealth, as Pericles said, was not flaunted; and the poor man did not endeavour to ape a standard beyond his means. Crafts were peculiarly free from cheap standardized workmanship, such as defiled the walls of so many Roman villas. The beauty of the very houses, simple and bare though these must have been, served to cheer their occupants and redeem the drabness of life.

7. DEMOCRACY IN THE WORKING

In assessing the various compensations which lightened for the Athenian the hardships or drudgery of daily toil, least of all must we forget the satisfaction he derived from his share in political privilege. The responsibilities of self-government—when coming thus for the first time and in the fullest measure—must have been a tremendously exciting experience; and the Athenians certainly rose to their opportunity. Pericles was not exaggerating when he said that they could "fill any or every role" with success.

There was no permanent civil service at Athens. It was against the democratic instinct to trust professionals. So from top to bottom it was a government by amateurs. Sophocles the poet was once sent in command of a naval expedition. Thucydides the historian, though unsuccessfully, conducted another. A leather-merchant, who had criticized the handling of a campaign, was elected general out of hand, and told to finish it off himself. In the Courts no public prosecutor existed; every charge had to be brought by a private individual, and the idea of citizens arresting citizens was so unpalatable that slave-constables, imported specially from Scythia, performed the task under orders from the responsible magistrates.

Of the innumerable small posts in the local administration of Attica we have no space here to tell. In each "deme" or parish men had to be found to keep the civic registers, to collect the war-tax when needed, to organize the religious rites of the district and to supervise the election of State-Officials. These part-time jobs were performed by voluntary effort, much as are to-day the functions of school-managers, Justices of the Peace, or secretaries of cricket clubs. In the city or port market-wardens, dock-inspectors and collectors of harbour-dues were also needed. Their duties must have been more onerous, and they received no doubt some adequate remuneration.

But from time to time an average citizen might also be called upon to higher responsibilities in the State administration itself. Chief among these was membership of the Council of Five Hundred. Any man over thirty years of age was eligible for election, but, to spread its incidence as widely as possible, it was forbidden to hold the office more than twice. The Council's main duties, as we saw in a previous chapter, were to prepare the agenda for the sessions of the Citizen Assembly. Thus a great deal of important business passed through their hands—the reception of foreign ambassadors, questions of public finance, and so forth. A Standing

Committee of fifty councillors, acting in rotation month by month, was kept permanently in session, ready to deal with routine details or with any emergency that might suddenly arise. The Standing Committee also presided at the meetings of the Assembly; and, since its members took turns as chairman for the day, an average citizen might find himself once in his life-time occupying the proud position of "Speaker" at the Assembly's debate. Socrates, the philosopher, held this post on an important occasion when he tried (though unsuccessfully) to veto the illegal condemnation of certain unfortunate admirals. But neither the president of the Standing Committee, nor indeed the Council itself, had any real power to challenge or direct the policy of the Assembly. The will of the people was decisive and final in all major political issues.

From one of Aristophanes' plays we have an account of the proceedings, and it is so picturesque that it seems worth while reproducing some of it here. The Assembly met on the Pnyx, a broad auditorium levelled out of a hillside overlooking the town. At its top end was the speakers' platform hewn from the rock, and behind it were the seats for the Standing Committee. Sessions took place at stated intervals three times a month. When routine business was dull, attendance, it would seem, was unpopular; and officials dragged a robe well daubed with red chalk down the market-place till they had gathered a quorum. Punctuality, to judge from the play, was not a Greek virtue, but then there were no clocks or watches in those days. Proceedings began with a ceremonial purification of the site; a priest sacrificed a pig and then made a processional circuit of the Assembly. When the play opens, a solitary citizen is discovered awaiting the start of a session. His name may be roughly reproduced as Mr. Playfair, and the name of his friend and supporter as Mr. Godson.

PLAYFAIR: Of all the plaguy nuisances in life,
here's a morning fixed for Statutory Session
and the Pnyx empty. There the rascals gossip
down in the Market, till the scarlet rope
comes past to catch them; then they just skidaddle.
Not even the Chairmen in their places yet;
and when they come—tardy as usual—
what a wild rush and scrimmage there will be
to jockey for front benches. But for Peace
who cares a rap? Alas, my poor, poor country!
and here am I, the solitary first-comer,
ready, you bet, to shout and jeer and barrack
at any speaker who fails to mention Peace.
Ah mid-day gone and here are our good Chairmen—
just as I said, all jostling for front pew.

HERALD:	Pass on in front; gentlemen, pass on in front!
	Make way for the priest to pass.
GODSON:	Debate begun?
HER.:	First speaker, please
GOD.:	Well, here I am, and waiting.
HER.:	Your name, Sir?
GOD.:	I am Godson; and I've got
	special instructions from on high to open
	negotiations with the enemy.
	But, Godson though I be, I've not been voted
	travelling expenses by the Councillors.
HER.:	Ho, constables!
GOD.:	O Gods above, protect me!
PLAY.:	Hi, Chairmen there, I really must protest.
	It's sheer contempt of Parliament to arrest
	a man who merely wants to make a treaty
	and let us all go home and hang our shields up.
HER.:	Sit down.
PLAY.:	By God, I will do no such thing,
	unless the Chairmen "chairman" about Peace.
HER.:	Pray Silence for the AMBASSADORS FROM PERSIA.

Once the Assembly had heard the speakers and expressed its vote by a show of hands, it remained for the Executive Officials to put its decision into practice. Now since Cleisthenes' day, the Archons and War Minister, elected by a mixed process of popular vote and lot, had proved quite inadequate for the growing responsibilities and complexities of the high administration. They had therefore been left to the purely routine business of superintending religious rites, presiding in the Law Courts, and so forth. The real executive power had passed to a Board of Ten, in some ways comparable to a modern Ministry or Cabinet. Its members were known as "the Generals," but, like the President of the United States, who combines the position of commander-in-chief with the control of peace-time administration, their functions were civilian as well as military. They handled the Food Supply, administered State Finance, and, above all, dealt with the diplomatic side of Foreign Policy. At the same time they were not merely responsible for the organization of the Army and Fleet, they actually commanded in person whether at sea or in the field. Their political influence was naturally great. While they were responsible to the Assembly for all their actions and took their instructions from it, they also frequently spoke at its meetings, and had a large hand in shaping its policy. The fluctuations of public opinion were nowhere more clearly reflected than in the choice of the Generals. They were annually appointed by the direct vote of the Assembly. So, if for example a large section of voters tired of war and wanted peace, the more militant-minded Generals would fail for re-election, and a more pacifically-minded ministry would take their place. Not that they were of necessity a homogeneous body. There was no sense of cabinet responsibility, and men of diametrically opposed views might often serve side by side. There is, however, good reason for believing that one of the Ten presided over the rest, and he no doubt did something to hold them together. It is probable that Pericles himself owed his long period of power to an almost uninterrupted tenure of this presidential chair.

Thus from high office of state to the humblest parish clerkship, there was the widest possible scope for the individual Athenian citizen to enjoy the privilege of political responsibility, and to gain experience of administrative practice. One ancient authority asserts that at any given time no less than fourteen hundred persons occupied some sort of official post. Nor was even this the end of the citizen's public duties. During his nineteenth and twentieth year he underwent his military training in the Youth Corps called the Ephebes. As an adult he was liable for war-service, rowing in a galley, if he were poor, marching with the infantry if of moderate means, riding in the cavalry, if rich. His financial obligations, on the other hand, were light. The cost of the administration was not very great, since the higher officials received no salary beyond a subsistence allowance. There was no standing army apart from the Ephebes, who garrisoned the frontier forts. Funds for the upkeep of the fleet came from various sources, fines in the Law Courts, harbour-dues, the proceeds of the State silver mines, and, not least, the imperial tribute. So, except in time of war, no direct taxation was levied. There was, however, one method by which the resources of the very wealthy were tapped. Men of large fortune, including even the resident-aliens, were required to undertake various public duties, to fit out a state-galley, for instance, or to finance the training of a choir or the production of a play at the dramatic festivals. But there is good evidence that they took a pride in the performance of their duties. They boasted of their public spirit in the Law Courts, and, if their choir or play won a prize in the competitions, they would even put up a monument to record it.

One form of public service remains to be mentioned—the judicial administration. In antiquity, Justice was not, as sometimes is thought, the monopoly of Rome. Greek Law was planted in the Eastern Mediterranean by Alexander's conquests long before Pompey annexed Syria to the Roman Empire; and it required the genius of a clear-minded Greek to systematize and codify the tangle of Roman legal procedure. Roman judicial methods, however, lent themselves to systematization; and Greek methods did not; and there lay the difference. Under the Empire a Roman judge dominated the court, and his rulings upon any moot point were recorded, thus forming a body of precedents which his successors on the bench usually followed. In the Athenian Courts the presiding official was a cipher. The jury had the decisive voice, and not unnaturally they preferred to ignore any precedents and judge each fresh case on its merits.

Litigants, therefore, had to study the temper of their audience. In every suit, criminal no less than civil, the party-at-law was compelled to plead in person. He could, however, engage an expert to write his speech for him. One such expert was the Lysias above-mentioned; and we possess several of his compositions. Arguments often strayed very wide of the exact legal point at issue. Appeals were made to the political sentiments of the jury, to their patriotism, and above all to their emotions. Yet, to do the Athenians justice, strong emphasis was laid on the letter of the law. "This is according to law," "this contrary to law," is a recurrent theme of the speeches; and often to refresh the jurors' memory, the clerk of the court was required to read out the text of the law.

Juries were large, 201, 401, or even more; the odd number precluding a tie in the votes. A small fee was paid to jurors, and this attracted many who were old or infirm. Voting was by secret ballot; and, with juries of such a size, bribery was impracticable. Little restraint was placed on behaviour in court. The speakers sometimes complained of interruptions and hostile demonstrations. Mass-reactions rather than reasoned analysis of the evidence must normally have determined the verdict. Nevertheless, Athenians were shrewd judges of character, and we may well believe that justice was usually done. The worst aspect of the whole system was its effect on the people's character. The jurors found great enjoyment in the intellectual game of thrust and parry; and Aristophanes' picture of the elderly habitués of the courts is not a pleasant one.

8. THE NEW EDUCATION

The Athenians' outstanding qualities—their practical capacity, their æsthetic enthusiasms, their reasonableness and enterprise, and their quick adaptability to new situations—should not be allowed to blind us to their many shortcomings. In them, as in many civilized communities to-day, there was much of the savage still untamed. Superstition died slow. It was the custom for the Assembly to adjourn if a spot of rain fell or any other bad omen occurred. Men of high standing kept private astrologers; and an eclipse of the moon once caused a fatal postponement of military plans. Callousness and brutality were other symptoms of lingering barbarism. Infanticide was still the recognized method of birth-control. Torture of citizens was forbidden by law, but at one period the law was repealed; and even in normal times the evidence of slaves might only be taken under threat or application of the rack; so little, it was thought, could they be trusted to tell the truth against a revengeful master. Immorality and homosexuality went unrebuked and unconcealed. In the comic drama sex was shamelessly paraded; and, though Aristophanes considered this cheap, many of his own jokes would never be tolerated in ever the most licentious of modern societies. The best that can be said of them is that they were brutally frank, never salacious.

The truth is that, as so often happens during the adolescence of an individual, intellectual precocity had outstripped growth of character. Minds had learnt to run, so to say, before moral legs could properly walk. The mass of the people had begun to assimilate something at least of the Aristocratic culture; but the sane old ethical tradition, though still finding its "prophets" in Pericles and the contemporary poets, was far from being assimilated. The Athenians stood, in short, at a critical phase of their spiritual development; and just at this moment there came into play a new and disturbing educational influence which was to intensify still further the dangerous disequilibrium between mind and character.

One significant symptom of the times was a growing appetite for knowledge. An interest in intellectual problems had been awakened under the stimulus which democracy gave to free speech and free thought. Already discussion and argument were becoming a passion among a people who centuries later, in the days of St. Paul, never tired of "telling or hearing some new thing." Hitherto, it is true, Athens had produced no philosophers of her own. But Pericles, as we have said, was himself a student of philosophy; and among other intellectuals whom he attracted to the city was the Ionian savant Anaxagoras. For across the Aegean the spirit of enquiry was still alive. Heraclitus' doctrine of never-ending change had left other thinkers dissatisfied, and further attempts were made to discover the permanent reality which lay behind the shifting phenomena perceived by the senses. Anaxagoras had his theory. All things, he said, were compounded of "seeds," or, as we might say, "atoms." In each corporeal substance every kind of seed was present, though in varying proportions. Thus, bread, he argued, since it gives life and growth to the body, must contain all the elements to be found in the body itself—blood, bone, skin, hair, and so on. But behind all lay Mind. It was active Reason, not accidental Change, which governed the Universe and made things what they were. Yet even to Anaxagoras, Mind was itself a substance, more subtle and tenuous than all others, but a substance still; so unable were these early thinkers to imagine an immaterial reality.

It would be hard to exaggerate Anaxagoras' influence on contemporary thought generally, and more especially in Athens itself. He was a familiar figure in the streets of the city, and was popularly known by the nickname of "Nous," or, as we might say, "Mr. Mind." His writings were on sale in the market; copies could be had for little more than half a crown; and were eagerly studied, amongst others, it would seem, by Socrates himself.

A Teacher (from a vase-painting). On his knees is a writing-tablet, and in his hand a "stilus" for writing—the blunt end being used for erasures.

There was much, no doubt, in his unorthodox views of the Universe to shock the more conservative minds; but most of his readers must have been intrigued to learn that the Sun was a "red-hot stone," and that there were "ravines and valleys" and "houses" in the moon. Thus, Anaxagoras' ideas gave stimulus to a society already beginning to think for itself and to apply reason to practical problems. Like most Ionian thinkers, his main interest lay, it is true, in abstract speculation; but he was none the less prepared on occasion to come down to earth. His rationalistic confutation of superstitious beliefs made a great impression on Pericles, and, we may guess, on many others as well; and once, it is said, he dissected the skull of a one-horned ram to prove that the prodigy came from a purely anatomical cause. But, most significant of all, his insistence on the supremacy of Mind found an answering echo in a brand-new intellectual movement which at this time was sweeping like wildfire through Greece, and which was destined to revolutionize the whole temper and outlook of the Athenian populace.

More than ever the growing importance and size of the city were attracting to it outsiders whose skill or accomplishments might find employment and scope there. But the warmest welcome of all was now reserved for scholars, and scholars of a completely novel type, whose appeal was no longer in the main to a comparatively small circle of leisured aristocrats, but to the average man in the street. Anaxagoras and his fellow-philosophers had always been, first and foremost, what philosophers should be—independent and disinterested enquirers after truth. But these men came forward as professional teachers with all manner of technical and practical knowledge to impart; and with their advent an entirely new chapter in the history of Education began.

Elementary schooling was by no means neglected at Athens. The regulation made by Solon seems to have given the original impetus; and there were free-lance teachers in abundance. Attendance at some sort of class, if not compulsory, was now more or less universal. So from six to fourteen most boys received their grounding. They learnt to read, write, and count. They got much poetry by heart. They were taught singing and lyre-playing; and in the wrestling-school they underwent physical training. But Democracy had begotten a whole new set of activities for which this elementary course was no adequate preparation. The average man, as we have seen, might now be called on to take part in the public administration, cast his vote in the Assembly, perhaps even speak at its debates, and, as likely as not, plead his own case in the Courts. In addition to all this, the various professions were becoming more complex and a higher standard of efficiency was demanded.

It was to meet this new need and to train men for such functions that the new professors of learning came forward. They sprang up in almost all parts of Greece, and in Sicily too; but many of them, not unnaturally, gravitated also to Athens. "Sophists" or "Wisdom-mongers" was the name they went by, and their "wisdom" covered a wide field of subjects. They taught mathematics, which was useful for accountancy; geometry, which was essential in surveying and architecture; and astronomy, on which navigation depended. But above all, they dealt with the arts of verbal expression, logic, grammar and rhetoric. In a democratic state, the power of persuasion was the very foundation of a successful career, and oratorical skill the aspiration of the ambitious.

But though many Sophists were specialists and professed to impart particular and practical skills, the best of them took a much wider and more elevated view of their mission. Chief among these was Protagoras, whom we mentioned above; and he, and others with him, held an entirely new theory of education, the significance of which in world history can scarcely be over-estimated. Hitherto the precise aim of education had never been clearly defined. In the old aristocratic tradition the moulding of character to an ideal pattern of what the citizen should be, had been instinctive rather than rational. But the new school of thought aimed at developing personality, not by the inculcation of moral virtues, but by *training the mental powers*. In other words, the subject which these Sophists taught were not primarily of value for their practical utility, but for the mental discipline they provided. This conception of educational method was in due course adopted by the Romans; and from them it was passed on to Western Europe, where the subjects the Sophists had taught—grammar, logic, rhetoric, arithmetic, geometry, music and astronomy—became the Seven Liberal Arts of the Mediæval curriculum. Nor is the influence of the Sophists' theory by any means dead even to-day. It is still reflected in the modern conception of an "all round education" as opposed to a technical or purely professional training. In detail the original method has inevitably been modified to suit changed conditions; but the intention underlying the method remains the same—that is, so to develop the individual's mental powers as to make him a "full man," the sort of man that, as a member of society, he should be.

The popularity of these teachers was amazing. They carried all the younger folk by storm. In the gymnasia lads would leave their races and wrestling to listen to lectures on astronomy or grammar, or to trace geometrical figures in the sand. They would rise before dawn to attend the discourse of some newly arrived savant; and when their favourite lecturer left the city, they would follow him to his next destination. Gradually the educational craze came to permeate the whole life of the city; and the change that resulted from it was fraught with far-reaching and often disastrous consequences. An inquisitive and critical spirit, hitherto confined to some cultured few, now caught hold of the masses. Every Athenian, Aristophanes tells us, was eternally asking, "How's this?" and "What is the explanation of that?" In short, they were like children who have suddenly become aware of their own intellectual powers and who are learning to grow up. But there are many pitfalls in that difficult and hazardous process; and, though the Sophists must have their due of credit for the stimulus they gave to Democracy's education, it may be questioned whether they were the best people to give it. For, unlike the traditionalist teachers, they left one vital thing out of account—the moral factor. They set out to make good citizens simply by sharpening men's wits. But good citizenship is of little value if the aims of the state itself are bad; and what higher ends such mental training should serve they never stopped to consider. Perhaps the real root of the trouble was, however, that the Sophists, while protesting idealism, were themselves little better than intellectual adventurers, individualists with no communal aim. They did not, like the Ionian enquirers, seek knowledge for its own sake alone. They lived not *for* their profession, but *by* it. They charged fees for their tuition; and the fees were exceedingly high. Then again, they wandered about from city to city and so became in the last resort denationalized. They advertised their lectures by making the most extravagant promises. "Whoever completes my course," one claimed, "will be able to win any law-suit." In fact, it was an open boast among them that they could "make the worse appear the better cause." Some Sophists assumed arrogant airs, pretending to an omniscience which was quite contrary to the best traditions of Greek scholarship. Their individualist bias was at times even nakedly avowed. Protagoras himself declared that "man was the measure of all things." In other words, "nothing was immutably right or true. I stick to my ideas, but you may have yours; there is little to choose between them."

Individualism, no doubt, was already in the air. Democracy was bound to breed it; and the Sophists perhaps were merely giving expression to an inevitable and an essentially healthy development of human nature. Nevertheless, their teaching could scarcely have come at a more unfortunate moment. At Athens, as we shall see, it found the whole national temper embittered and unbalanced by the hideous ordeal of plague and the prolonged strain of war. As so often in times of crisis, factional interests and personal ambitions tended to take precedence over the good of the State; and men's minds were thus predisposed to grasp at any cynical theory or unscrupulous expedient. So it is hardly to be wondered at if in the immediate issue such, Individualist doctrine had a highly unsettling effect, among the rising generation especially. Many of the younger men lost their moorings and went completely adrift. Having learnt methods of criticism from their teachers they proceeded to try them out on their own. They pulled established beliefs to pieces, and made hay of the older folks' conventions. Some took to politics and argued on the platform that might was right, the strong must prevail and self-interest was the only possible motive of policy. Others broke into wild anti-social excesses. One notorious young aristocrat, Alcibiades, employed his brilliant wits for a career of pure self-seeking and eventually turned traitor to his country.[1] Such were the bitter fruits of this once promising movement. Under the leadership of men bred on the new-fangled doctrines, Athenian democracy was to plunge into follies and brutalities which not even the Sophists themselves would ever have approved.

9. THE DRAMATISTS

The trend towards individualism can nowhere be better traced than in the dramatic literature of the period. Fifth century Athens produced three great tragedians—Æschylus, whose career covered the time of the Persian wars and the two following decades; Sophocles, who wrote during the middle and closing years of the century, and Euripides, who was his younger contemporary. As a member of the generation which witnessed Marathon and Salamis, and himself a participant in both battles, Æschylus was regarded by posterity as the typical champion of the old morality, the spiritual heir of the Homeric tradition and the representative of all that was best in the past. But in reality Æschylus was much more than this. His poetry was couched in a sublime magniloquent diction, and its sublimity reflected the workings of a deeply religious mind. The orthodox belief in a plurality of gods he outwardly accepted as in duty bound; but it is clear that at heart he was himself a monotheist and held a profound conception of the deity. To him the supreme power was essentially righteous and just; and the problem which troubled him (as it troubled the Hebrew Psalmist and the author of Job) was the cause and origin of suffering, especially the suffering of the seemingly guiltless. In his plays he sought to probe the problem to its roots; and the answer he gave was this. Side by side with God there exists in the Universe a malignant power, the counterpart and antithesis of Good Fortune in which most ancients believed. This evil power lies in wait for man, and when by his pride or his folly some pretext is given, smites him ruthlessly down. Nor does its capacity to harm stay there. The father's sin of pride may even pursue his children and his children's children. This idea of the "family curse" forms the theme of Æschylus' masterpiece, the trilogy known as the Oresteia. King Agamemnon himself—so the trilogy starts—had inherited a legacy of guilt from a hideous crime of his father; and, to

---

[1] Alcibiades, it is true, was Socrates' pupil; but he was far too acute not to know all the Sophists' theories, and all that he did or said betrayed their influence on him. The Sophist, at his worst, is portrayed by Plato in his "Republic," though how far this is a historical picture is hard to say. In any case, Aristophanes in his "Clouds" (see page 103) makes a very damning attack on them and on their effect of their teaching.

make matters worse, his own vain-glory after the conquest of Troy delivered him into the power of the watchful demon. On his return he was murdered by Clytemnestra his treacherous wife. Blood called for blood; and his son Orestes haunted by evil spirits of Vengeance, then took his mother's life, and the father's sin thus found issue in the reluctant deed of the innocent soul-tortured son. "Man learns by suffering," was Æschylus' final message; and by this formula the ancients' superstitious dread of Nemesis was at last given its place in a rational view of the Universe. Truths are none the worse for being old; and it is worth remembering that in the mediæval Church pride was accounted the worst of sins. The experience of modern Europe gives no cause to reverse that verdict.

Æschylus was indeed a giant among dramatists. The characters of his plays, and the plots themselves no less, are cast in a titanic mould. There is no poetry in Greek literature so majestic as his; and, if we accept the Aristotalian dictum that the function of Tragedy is to evoke "Pity and Terror," then the Oresteia must be ranked among the supreme achievements—perhaps even as *the* supreme achievement—of the art. In it we witness men and women, not struggling, like Shakespeare's men and women, with problems and temptations to which in one degree or another all human flesh is heir; but rather caught, as it were, in some cosmic scheme of catastrophe, helpless yet still heroic in their helplessness, as Fate sweeps them irresistibly to their doom. Among the captives whom Agamemnon had brought home with him from Troy, was the Princess Cassandra, a prophetess whose destiny it was always to foresee the future yet never to be believed. Before she leaves the stage to follow her captor through the Palace door, the trance suddenly comes upon her, bringing a vivid premonition of the death there awaiting herself as well as him. Visions of horror rise before her eyes. The very walls appear to her as though running with blood. As she finally enters, she speaks these lines of moving simplicity, all the more effective by contrast to the playwright's usual style.

CASSANDRA: Now I must pass within to hymn the death-chant
             over my lord and me. I have done with life.
             Yet, friends, I'll make no idle whimpering,
             as a weak bird flutters at the brake. Hereafter
             be ye my witness how I spake true at the last;
             and when the day comes that a woman's life
             shall pay the price of mine and when a man
             shall fall for him whose wife was false, Remember!
             It is not much I ask who am to die.

CHORUS: Alas, poor maid. Thy weird is come on thee.

98

CASSANDRA: Hark yet once more to no dirge for my own passing,
              but a cry, my last cry under the light of the sun,
              calling vengeance upon these murderers
              for a poor slave's life so lightly taken. O
              the pity of man's lot! Dwells he with joy,
              'tis a vain shadow. Or with sorrow, blot
              but wet sponge over and so vanish all,
              nothing from nothing left—Fitter for tears
              the fate of such than is the fall of kings.

By contrast with Æschylus, Sophocles was more of an artist than a thinker. There was never a more consummate master of the playwright's craft. His plots move forward to their appointed climax with a matchless interweaving of circumstance and character. His choric odes expressed in lovely language the same old "prophetic" theme "Mêden agân," "Nothing in excess"; and he himself was a living embodiment of the sobriety he preached. He continued well past middle life to practise his favourite art of dancing, and he reached the unusual age of ninety.

It is in his delineation of character that Sophocles best displays the spirit of his age. The personalities of Æschylus' plays had been little more than types; they display no individual traits. Clytemnestra, for example, is an incarnation of lust and treachery, not a real human being with doubts or a sense of remorse. She would never, like Lady Macbeth, have been troubled to feel the blood on her hands. Sophocles' characters, on the other hand, are faithful studies of human nature. Each speaks, if not with an idiom of his own, at least in a different tone; and there is a rich diversity among them. In his play "Antigone," we have the picture of a ruler, called into power at a crisis, and nervously uncertain of himself. He is determined to govern strongly, so he threatens and thunders and blusters; then suddenly aware that he has gone too far, he stops short and retracts. His speeches are full of moral or political platitudes—the refuge of a man who knows his job only through hearsay, not by experience. "Honesty is the best policy," "All will be well if each does his duty," "The young must bow to their betters." The most significant character of the play, however, is his niece Antigone—one of the noblest heroines in literature. She is faced by a terrible choice. Her brother had turned traitor to his country and been killed. Her uncle had forbidden on pain of death the burial of his corpse. According to Greek ideas burial was a necessary passport to the underworld; and Antigone decided to defy her uncle's threat, and to follow a higher allegiance to Divine Law. This is what she says:

CREON: Yet hadst thou courage to transgress my law?

ANTIGONE: The Almighty hath not set his seal thereon,
          nor spake kind mercy for the piteous dead
          in that fell utterance. Thy writ, O King,
          hath not such potence as will overweigh
          the laws of God, not graven up on stone,
          immutable which whence they are none knoweth,
          not of today nor yesterday, but fixed
          from everlasting to eternity.
          What though man rage, I must obey that law
          and count it but a little thing to die.
          For death must come; and, if I die today,
          Why, I am glad to quit this world of tears
          where is the bitterness, far bitterer were't
          to leave my mother's son unsepulchred.

Here, then, starkly but most artistically portrayed, was the eternal
conflict between the authority of the State and the conscience of the
Individual; and, if anyone doubts whether the individualist spirit, which
first found birth in fifth-century Athens, has proved a blessing or a curse
to mankind, the answer lies in this drama of Sophocles. Lacking as it did
a moral objective, the Sophists' teaching may have done much temporary
harm. But at least it served the purpose of making the individual think
for himself. Greece made no greater contribution to human history than
by thus establishing the supremacy of the private conscience; and the
upward path of progress is paved with the decisions made by such martyrs
to a higher call as the girl Antigone.

Euripides even more than his two predecessors was the child of his
generation. The Sophist movement was then at its height, and he reflects
it at every turn. The speeches in his plays are perfect samples of the new
rhetorical art. His characters pit argument against argument in sound
logical order. Often, too, the arguments themselves are of the cold
calculating type derived from Sophistic training. But his thought went
incomparably deeper. His highly critical mind made him sceptical of the
established creeds and especially of the wildly emotional side of certain
religious cults. Even the myths he held up to question, and Aristophanes
frankly wrote him down as an atheist. But what made Euripides so great
a dramatist was his profound understanding of human nature, its littleness
and its greatness, its passions and fears, and above all its irrationality. He
was a psychological realist, and he treated the old stories as though they
were stories of contemporary life, reading into the minds of the mythological characters the thoughts and emotions of the men and women he
saw around him. Take the speech he puts into the mouth of Medea, a
woman brought from a foreign land to Greece and there jilted by a

faithless husband. It is an astonishingly intimate study of the feelings of a bride, written in an age when such feelings were little considered:

> Of all things living that draw mortal breath
> we women are the most distressful creatures,
> who first with a multitude of worldly goods
> must buy us husbands, lords over limb and life,
> running herein great hazard of freak chance;
> for to new home and habit unfamiliar,
> the young bride needs must use diviner's art
> to gauge untutored the temper of her mate.
> Be he indulgent and the twain harmonious
> life is all bliss; but falls it otherwise,
> far better 'twere to die. For a man hath vantage
> who may betake him, when the home-life palls,
> to mate with cronies and in companionship
> beguile his humour. But for us poor wives
> 'tis solitary communion with the one same soul
> for ever. O 'tis said that, while men fight,
> we women lead a safe snug life at home;
> comparison most false; rather I'ld stand
> three times in the battle-front than once bear child.

Such sentiments accorded ill with contemporary notions about the female sex; nor was it the elders alone who must have frowned. Men do not like to be shown the ugly side of their character, and Euripides, during his life-time, at least, was never popular. It was comparatively seldom that he was awarded the prize at the festival. But, if as a dramatist he faithfully portrayed the selfishness and cynicism of his age, this does not mean that he himself sympathized with them. He was a humane and sensitive soul, and had a strong fellow-feeling for the underdog. He loathed the atmosphere of a democracy gone bad; he became embittered and kept much to himself. Eventually he left Athens and took up his residence in Macedon. Yet his work had not been thrown away, and in the following century he was the most highly esteemed of all three tragedians.

It remains to say something of the comic playwright Aristophanes. Like Euripides, he belonged to the second half of the century and wrote during the prolonged war between Sparta and Athens. Fifth-century Comedy more resembled a revue than a play, though its scenes were loosely knit together by some sort of plot. Often the plot hinged on the interplay of two strongly contrasted characters—the peace-loving Playfair, for instance, and an extremely militant General—a tradition probably derived from some primitive dialogue of the "Punch and Judy" or "Clown and Harlequin" type. As we have already seen, too, comedy dealt with contemporary life; and the poet could give a remarkably free rein to his personal likes and dislikes; there was no law of libel at Athens. At one stage of the play, moreover, it was customary for the chorus to come forward and deliver outspoken political comment reflecting the author's own views. Thus the comic drama fulfilled the function now served by the leader-writers or cartoonists of the popular Press.

Aristophanes himself, though first and foremost a humorist, was also a serious political thinker. His views were conservative. He sided with the landowning class, rich or poor, who suffered from the war; and he made

A Lesson on the Lyre. (From a vase-painting.)

no secret of his dislike for demagogues. As a true patriot, however, he sought merely to curb the ways of democracy, not to abolish it. What was his attitude to the Sophist movement may easily be inferred. In one comedy called the "Clouds," he lampooned Socrates who, though not one of the Sophists, in some ways resembled them. In the second act of the play he was shown on the stage hanging up in a basket the better to "contemplate the sun," and on the ground below his pale emaciated pupils were studying geology with their nose to the earth and their rump in the air—"Doing astronomy all on its own." Towards the close of the play Aristophanes introduced two symbolical characters—"The Just Argument" representing the old education, and the "Unjust Argument"

representing the new. Here is the summing-up of the Just Arguments
views:

JUST ARGUMENT: Prepare then to hear of the Discipline rare
                  which flourished in Athens of yore,
                  When Honour and Truth were in fashion with youth
                  and sobriety bloomed on our shore.
                  First of all the old rule was preserved in the school
                  that "boys should be seen and not heard."
                  Then the lads took the road to the Harpist's abode
                  well-mannered in action and word;
                  not a cloak to their name, but they trudged just the same
                  through the snow and the wintriest weather;
                  and they sung some old song as they paced it along—
                  not shambling with legs stuck together—
                  "Lead on," it might be, "Pallas queen of the free;"
                  or it might be "Athenians wha hae,"
                  to some simple old chant which is all that we want
                  and was sung by their sires in their day.
                  But should anyone dare to "hot up" the air
                  with a newfangled quaver or trill,
                  he would soon get a whack for his pains on the back
                  who maltreated the Muses so ill.
                  None would then even dare such a stimulant fare
                  as the head of a radish to wish,
                  nor to make overbold with the food of the old,
                  the aniseed, parsley or fish,
                  nor dainties to quaff nor to giggle and laugh
                  nor his foot within foot to enfold.
UNJUST A.:   Faugh! this smells very strong of some musty old song
                  and of Grasshoppers mounted in gold,
                  and of sacrificed beasts and those old-fashioned feasts.
JUST A.:   Yet these were the precepts which taught
                  the heroes of old to be hardy and bold
                  and the men who at Marathon fought.
                  So you've nothing to fear, opt for ME, my young sir!
                  for mine is the method for you.
                  And then will you learn the Market to spurn
                  And dissolute baths to eschew;
                  and to rise from your chair, if an elder be there,
                  and respectfully give him your place.
                  and with love and with fear your good parents revere
                  and to shrink from the brand of Disgrace,
                  and deep in your breast bear the image impressed
                  of Modesty, simple and true,
                  nor resort any more to the chorus-girl's door
                  nor make eyes at harridan crew.
UNJUST A.:   Believe me, young friend, if to him you attend,
                  you'll be known as a mammy-suck there.

JUST A.:   Nay, nay, you'll excell in the sports you love well,
all blooming, athletic and fair;
not learning to prate as those idlers debate
in some argument ticklish and cute,
nor dragged into Court day by day to make sport
in some plaguy litigious dispute.
Instead you will fare to the playing-fields where
you may under the olives contend
in a trial of speed, crowned by wreath of plain reed,
with your excellent rival and friend,
all fragrant with woodbine and peaceful content
and the leaf which the lime-blossoms fling
while the plane whispers love to the elm in the grove
in the beautiful season of Spring.[1]

These lines were written with very obvious sympathy; and they show that Aristophanes was harking back, and, as it would seem, vainly harking back to the ideals of a very different age. It was the age in which his own elders and parents had been bred, the age of Marathon and Miltiades, Salamis and Cimon, when the old aristocratic tradition still lingered, somewhat stiffened perhaps by the Persian ordeal and with its code of nice manners and strict moral upbringing reinforced by a would-be Spartan athleticism. But Athens since then had moved far and fast. From the size, we might say, of a large market town, she had grown to what was then a metropolis; and this intensive urbanization had altered the whole complexion of the next generation. The very tone of Aristophanes' own comedies proved it. There was nothing of gentility here. Their problems and situations seldom strayed very far from the life of the ordinary man.[2] Their dialogue abounded in the coarsest vulgarities and in topical jests about persons of no special note. But they contained much subtle criticism too, many literary allusions and witty verbal conceits; and their appeal, it is clear, was to a serious-minded, highly intelligent but robustly popular audience, an audience of artisans, merchant-seamen and tradesfolk. Nor had the change yet reached its full conclusion. There was to follow a third and a most disastrous phase, in which a still lower stratum of the populace, and in particular the riff-raff of the port, came increasingly to call the political tune at Athens. Thus within the compass of a single lifetime this astonishing civilization passed through the full bloom of its perfection to an inglorious decay. In all history there is no parallel to the bewildering speed of the development, and it was bound to make the task of contemporary judgment more than usually difficult.

[1] Translation adapted from B. B. Rogers.
[2] Thus in the "Clouds," the hero—and victim of the visit to Socrates' "thinking-shop"—was a bourgeois bred on a farm and then married to an aristocratic lady of the city.

That he so early recognized the dangerous trend of the new intellectualism says much for Aristophanes' shrewdness: it was not the popular view, and the play was placed last on the judges' list. But it was sheer futility to dream of conjuring back the virtues of a vanished past. Had Athens preferred to stand still in that past, there might now have been less wild talk in her market-place, less argument in the gymnasium, and fewer "plaguy litigious disputes"; but her mental growth would have been arrested, and she would never have become the Athens of which the poet was himself so justly proud and which alone had made his own work possible.

To ourselves this much seems clear. During the period of Pericles' rule the City State had reached the summit of its achievement. Much as there had been to admire in the old aristocratic culture with its refinement of manners, its elegant drinking-songs and delicate statuary, its fine-spun speculations about the physical Universe, and, above all, as its finest flower, the tragic masterpieces of Æschylus, there was nevertheless something far more impressive about the democratic culture which succeeded it and which produced the stern magnificence of the Parthenon, the scientific austerity of Thucydides, Sophocles' matchless artistry, Euripides' psychological insight, and Socrates' profound moral teaching; and to these we may add the vivacious turbulent pageant of life with which Aristophanes himself has presented us. The idea of social Progress found no place in the Greeks' way of thought; indeed, while hoping for its ultimate return, they held mankind to have degenerated since the Golden Age of Legend. But Aristophanes' countrymen were the least likely people in the world to heed his advocacy of the past. They could no more have gone back to the "good old times" than our own generation could return to the uneducated days of the mid-Victorian squirearchy. Forward they had to go; and that way salvation could lie only in a wise intellectual leadership, the leadership, shall we say, of some second Pericles, who might appeal to their reason and convince them that the worse was *not* the better cause. But, as fate decreed, no second Pericles was forthcoming. False prophets, on the other hand, sprang up in plenty, and they did not lack for a hearing. So, by the time those lines of Aristophanes were written, the rot had already begun to invade public life. Athenian democracy, as our next chapter will show, was proving false to its own better principles, and listening more and more readily, as the strain of war with Sparta told, to the insidious enticements of the UNJUST ARGU-MENT.

CHAPTER VII

THE PELOPONNESIAN WAR

1. A DRAWN FIGHT

In the spring of 431, hostilities broke out between Athens and Sparta; and at once nearly all Greece was divided into two militant camps, ranged behind the one or the other protagonist. The war, known as the Peloponnesian War, formed the theme of Thucydides' history. It was a work of outstanding importance, the first attempt to treat the record of human affairs in a truly scientific spirit. By comparison with it, Herodotus' chatty narrative seems almost childish; and for insight, objectivity and sheer power of thought and language, it has no rivals in ancient literature, not many in modern. Its style admittedly is crabbed, at times even obscure. Prose-writing was then still in its infancy, and Thucydides was wrestling with novel and intricate ideas. Against this must be set his vigour of description, his flair for significant detail, and above all his sense of the dramatic. History to him was an art, not a mere compilation of facts; and in unfolding his story he never lost sight of the great tragic issues behind it. Favourite among his devices was to interrupt the narrative by speeches put in the mouth of this or that character. "They were drawn," he says, "partly from my own memory, partly from hearsay. But verbal accuracy was impossible; so I have set down what I thought the speakers likely to have said under the circumstances, keeping as well as I could to the gist of their words." But this technical device served a function beyond mere reporting. Thucydides used the speeches to analyse the motives and ideas which, in his view, had controlled men's actions and policies. Such analysis penetrated deep. He has been accused of exalting a series of insignificant border-raids into an important event in world-history. Shakespeare, too, when he wrote "Hamlet," was writing the story of an unimportant Dane; but in the process he has "written the story of every man's inner life." Similarly, the Greek historian, dealing with the microcosm of his own tiny world, has succeeded in laying bare the permanent forces which move human nature on its political side.

"What made the war inevitable," Thucydides says, "though no one openly admitted it, was that Athens was becoming too powerful and her opponents were afraid of her." So before the actual outbreak fears barely expressed on the one side and ambitions barely concealed on the other had produced a long period of tension. Several incidents had shown which way the wind was blowing. Corinth, more than most, had good reason for alarm. It was not twenty years since her vital traffic with Italy and Sicily had been gravely imperilled by Athens' encroachments; and she had no wish to be caught napping again. In 433 she had sought to strengthen her hold on the westerly trade-route by attacking Corcyra. Corcyra appealed to Athens, and Athens concluded an alliance and sent some ships to her aid. The sequel was that after an inconclusive engagement the attack on the island was called off. Next year, 432, Corinth tried a diversion. Potidæa, one of her colonies in the North-West Aegean, was a restive member of the Athenian Empire, and it needed little persuasion to egg her into revolt. Thus Athens was committed to a costly campaign and a lengthy siege of the town—a very serious drain on her strength at so critical a juncture.

It was now Pericles' turn to play his card; and he determined to give Corinth a warning of what sea-power, if ruthlessly handled, could achieve. Across the west Attic border, it will be remembered, lay the small commercial city of Megara. Apart from lending Corinth some aid in the attack on Corcyra, she had given no real provocation to Athens; but suddenly and without warning Pericles issued a decree that all Megarian produce should be banned from the harbours of the Empire. This cruel blow meant slow starvation for the little town, and a few years later Aristophanes, in one of his plays, introduced a Megarian farmer, desperate with hunger and attempting to sell his two daughters in the pig-market, suitably disguised in trotters and snouts. But if Pericles thus hoped to intimidate Corinth, he had miscalculated. He merely increased her alarm. Towards the end of the year, at her request, a Congress of the Peloponnesian Confederacy was called, and after much argument her delegates pushed the reluctant Spartans into a decision for war.

When by the spring of 431 diplomatic exchanges had ended and the war began in earnest, the strategic situation in Greece bore a striking resemblance to the European situation in 1940. On one side was Sparta, backed by her Peloponnesian Confederates, and, among others north of the Isthmus, by the Bœotian cities and Thebes—an invincible combination by land. On the other side was Athens with the financial resources of her Empire behind her and her equally invincible fleet. The city itself was impregnable; the two long walls secured its communications with the sea; and the Spartans, as their failure at Mount Ithome had showed, were no hand at assaulting a defensive position. Athens, in short, could hold out indefinitely; and, short of some major blunder, Pericles confidently asserted that the war could not be lost. But to what did he look for winning it, unless it were to sea-power? "The Peloponnese," says Thucydides, "could be encircled by war"—a somewhat vague statement; but a hint of his meaning may perhaps be found in one of the speeches he reports. There it is suggested that even inland states might feel the pinch, if imports by sea were cut off; but the maritime states (and by implication Corinth most of all) would be very hard hit. In other words, as we might guess, the clue to Pericles' problem lay on the trade-routes. Now Corinth's traffic with the West ran first through the narrow Gulf, and then northwards till Corcyra was reached, whence it crossed the Adriatic to Italy. Corcyra, as we have seen, was already Athens' ally; and stationed at Naupactus near the mouth of the Gulf was an Athenian squadron in waiting. Thus it was possible that Corinth's trade, if not strangled, might at least be interrupted [1]; and, if Corinth were once forced out of the war, the rest of the Peloponnesian Confederacy would very soon fall to pieces. There, so far as we can judge, lay Athens' best hope of victory. But on Pericles' own admission no speedy decision could be looked for; and patience, as later events unhappily proved, was not the strong point of Athenian democracy.

In the meantime neither of the combatants were disposed to risk a trial of strength in the element unsuited to them—the Athenians by land or their opponents by sea. All that followed, therefore, was a series of raids aimed (like the bombing-raids of modern warfare) at the destruction of the enemy's sources of supply—in this case food. Each year the Spartans invaded Attica, devastated the crops, cut down olive-trees, burnt farms, and departed home again. From the shelter of their walls the Athenians watched the havoc, restive at their own impotence. But Pericles would not risk a battle, and the best he could do was to send a naval squadron circling the Peloponnese and making occasional "commando raids" on coastal districts. In short, it was what the Americans would have called a "phoney war."

Then early in the second year came one of those unpredictable catastrophes which upset the best-laid plans. The city of Athens was crowded with refugees; even the space between the Long Walls was given up to them. The congestion was highly insanitary, and when plague broke out at the port, it spread like wildfire. Nothing worse could have happened; and so devastating were the effects in loss of life, lowering of physical stamina and still more of morale, that they must be counted among the major causes deciding the issue of the war. Thucydides' account of it is a

[1] Pericles actually forecast that the Corinthian fleet would be unable to venture out of port even for battle-practice.

masterpiece both for its diagnosis of symptoms and its psychological insight. It shall be summarized here.

"The Plague," he says, "came from Egypt; and starting at the Piræus it spread up to the city where the death-roll was soon very heavy. The seizure was alarmingly sudden. At one moment a man would be in normal health and the next moment sick of the Plague. It began in the head and worked downwards, first a burning forehead, blood-shot eyes, bleeding of tongue and throat, and a fœtid breath. Next it passed to the chest, causing hoarseness and a hacking cough. Finally it laid hold on the stomach, where it produced vomiting and convulsive retching. The skin went a livid pink and broke out in ulcers. Fevered patients could not endure the touch of even the flimsiest clothes, but stripped naked and often threw themselves into cold water. Their thirst was unquenchable. The strange thing, however, was that the body remained unwasted; and death supervened—usually after eight or nine days—from internal inflammation. Many who recovered lost fingers or toes, and some even their eyes. Others were left with memory blank, unable to recollect even their own identity. One uncanny feature of the whole visitation was that animals and birds of prey avoided the corpses or died after making their meal on them. Doctors were powerless. Friends were nervous of approaching the stricken, and whole families perished without any to care for them. Only the few who recovered dared make the venture; for a second attack never proved fatal, and such persons fondly imagined that they were now immortal and could never die of any other complaint.

"An added horror was the condition of intense overcrowding. No houses were available, and the refugees from the countryside had made their quarters in hutments stifling as ovens in the summer weather. Corpses lay in heaps; wretches lingering between life and death littered the roadways, crowded round the fountains or bivouacked in the temple-closes. All barriers of convention broke down. No one cared what was sacred or forbidden ground. Old funeral customs were ignored. Families which had already suffered many losses and so had run short of proper materials were driven to the most shameless shifts. Sometimes they would pile their own dead on a pyre prepared for another and set it ablaze. If too late for this, they would fling their burden on the top of the smouldering carcass and run for it.

"The moral breakdown was complete. Men felt free to gratify instincts which their hypocrisy had hitherto veiled. All around them they saw fantastic reversals of fortune, rich men dying and paupers stepping in their property. Now, they felt, was the golden chance to enjoy a good time, since neither life nor wealth could last long. What purpose in sacrificing themselves to an ideal, when before the world knew of their sacrifice, they might themselves be dead? So a reckless hedonism was the general mood; law was scoffed at; and the vanity of religion demonstrated by the mortality around them. The thought of retribution held no terrors when the sinner believed he had but a few days to live. The sentence of doom was hanging over him; and before it descended, he had best make the most of life's sweets."

The Athenians never recovered from the effects of the plague. It is estimated that a quarter of the population died. The survivors were warped and embittered. They resorted, as we shall see, to policies of brutal revenge incredible in earlier days. Their balance was lost and they veered erratically between moods of feverish optimism or sullen despair. Worst of all Pericles, the man who had so long held them together, had died; and without his guiding hand, they began to fall into two opposed factions. To call these democrats and aristocrats is to create a false impression. It would be more accurate to speak of the mercantile element and the landed element. The latter, both peasant and large proprietor alike, were hard hit by the Spartan raids. The destruction of their farms and orchards was more than they could swallow, and, like "Mr. Playfair" in Aristophanes' comedy, they clamoured for peace. The mercantile class, on the other hand, were evidently making a good thing out of the war. The chance of crushing Corinth was not to be missed; and they were bent on seeing the struggle through.

It was not the least tragedy of the plague that it must have removed men of promise capable of succeeding Pericles in the leadership of Athens. As things were, the choice was narrowed; and the leadership was disputed between two representatives of the opposing factions, each of whom typified the vices as well as the virtues of his class.

Nicias, the leader of the landed element, was the perfect "gentleman." "No man of his time," says Thucydides, "strove harder for an ideal." But, as no doubt the historian himself recognized, it was a very limited ideal. Nicias, so he tells us, "passed his life in the regular observance of religious duties, walking in the path of justice and giving provocation to no man." At the same time, as we happen to know, his social outlook, from a modern standpoint at least, was deplorable. He lived partly on the proceeds of a thousand slaves whom he hired out to the State and who were set to work in the Laureum silver-mines under indescribable conditions. Few men, however, have it in them to rise above the moral standards of their age; and our own ancestors with much less excuse lived on the sweated labour of infants drafted into industry from the public workhouses. Be this as it may, Nicias was greatly respected in his own day.

He was essentially a "safe man," honest, painstaking and cautious to a fault.

The mercantile or democrat spokesman, Cleon, was a man of a very different stamp. A leather-merchant by trade, he had received an up-to-date education, and was deeply imbued with the new Sophist doctrines. He employed all the most cynical arguments of pure self-interest, and played up shamelessly to the worst instincts of the mob. On the platform he was effective, but cheap. As he spoke, he would pace up and down, ranting and shouting and pulling up his cloak to slap a bare thigh. "He bellowed and roared," says Aristophanes, "like a torrent in spate." But he possessed a good business head. He knew what he wanted and he had drive; and since both Aristophanes and Thucydides entertained a personal grievance against him, it may be that they judged him too harshly.

As a commercialist, Cleon saw one thing very clearly. Without her grip on the Aegean, Athens was lost. It was not merely that sea-borne trade, and in particular the through-transit of corn from the Black Sea, was essential to her economy. Since the outbreak of war the tribute paid by the subject-states was more than ever needed to finance her fleet. A fresh movement of secession would therefore be fatal. This was the Achilles' heel of Pericles' whole strategy; and the enemy, too, were well aware of the fact. From the outset the Spartans had proclaimed their intention of "setting Hellas free"; and when in 428 the island of Lesbos came out in revolt, they sent a general over with promise of help to come. With Athens in command of the sea, that help never arrived, and Lesbos was reduced. The question of her punishment came up before the Assembly at Athens; and if only to give a warning to others, an example, it was felt, must be made of the rebels. Cleon did not as yet hold any official position; but it was he who moved the motion for the terrible sentence which the Assembly duly passed. A swift galley was dispatched to carry the order that every male in the island should be killed. Next day a fresh meeting was called, and the decision reviewed. Cleon stuck to his point, "If, right or wrong, Athens intended to rule, then Lesbos, right or wrong, must be punished. Treat her," he said, "as she would have treated you." Mercifully his plea failed. A second galley was sent after the first, and arrived just in time to countermand the massacre.

The war dragged on; when three years later terms might have been had, Cleon procured their rejection; and immediately after came the crowning chance to turn the tables on his opponents. It arose from an accidental military diversion. Demosthenes, Athens' ablest general, while on a cruise off the Western Peloponnese, put in his fleet for shelter at Pylos, a little bay on Spartan territory. It seems to have struck him that the place might be made a rallying-point for malcontent Helots. On the north side of the bay was an impregnable peninsula, and this he proceeded to fortify. The Spartans reacted promptly. They attacked the peninsula from the seaward, only to be driven off; but meanwhile most unwisely they landed a garrison on the island of Sphacteria which covered the mouth of the bay. The Athenian fleet, which had continued its cruise, then returned, and the Spartan garrison, some four hundred strong, was cut off on the island. Such, however, was the prestige of Spartan invincibility that the Athenians dared not land and attack them. The fleet simply blockaded the island, and it was hoped that starvation would soon finish them off.

Meanwhile at home the populace chafed at such dilatory tactics; and one day Cleon got up in the Assembly and declared that, if only he were one of the Generals, Sphacteria would soon be taken. Nicias, answering for the Ministry of which he was a member, replied, "Go then, and take it yourself." Cleon at first tried to back out, then accepted the post. He was no fool, and in undertaking the task he must have seen his way to its successful completion. In a recent campaign in the region of Naupactus, Demosthenes had gained some experience of mountain warfare; and it seems likely enough that he had let Cleon know that similar tactics might discomfit even the "invincible" Spartans. At any rate, preparations of a quite novel sort were at once set on foot. An enormous force of bowmen, slingers and other light-armed troops was collected; and when these were landed on the island, the Spartans were hopelessly at a disadvantage. When they charged, their nimble opponents took to the hills; when they retired, they were pursued with volleys of missiles. By the end of the day they surrendered. Cleon had boasted that he would have them back as prisoners at Athens within three weeks; and now to everyone's surprise he had kept his word.

From this time on, Cleon was the heart and soul of the Athenian war-effort. He put the screw on the subject-states to the point of trebling their tribute-assessment. Working closely with Demosthenes he abandoned the sound Periclean strategy of avoiding land-combat. First the two planned a surprise attack on Megara, by which, however, they succeeded only in capturing its port. Then they tried a full-scale invasion of Bœotia—intending perhaps to repeat the tactics by which Pericles had once gained full control over the Corinthian Gulf. Here, however, they overreached themselves; and the Athenian infantry was badly cut up in a pitched battle near Delium.

Meanwhile, in the same year 424, a dangerous unrest had been growing among the tributary-states, this time among the cities of the Chalcidic

Peninsula in the North-West Aegean. Here at least Sparta could send help overland; and Brasidas, her one audacious commander, hurried north with an army. Cleon went after him, and in the fighting which ensued both leaders were killed (422).

Negotiations had for some time been in progress between the combatants. Sparta felt keenly the capture of her men at Pylos; for so small was the number of her fully enfranchised citizens that even the loss of three hundred was a grave blow to her morale. At Athens Nicias, who on Cleon's death had regained control of the Assembly, cannot have omitted to underline the danger-signal of the Chalcidic revolt. So in 421 a Peace was arranged by no means unfavourable to Athens. But, as any eye could see, the real issue remained undecided; and the peace proved no more than a breathing-space before the struggle was resumed.

2. THE SYRACUSAN EXPEDITION

With Cleon gone, the popular party at Athens needed a new spokesman, and they were to find him in a man of very different antecedents. Pericles had left a nephew, by name Alcibiades. The young man had all the natural gifts and graces of an aristocrat. He was outrageously good-looking, with great personal charm, and wits as sharp as a needle. "When I was your age," Pericles had once lectured him, "I used to think myself clever too." "How I wish, dear uncle," was the quick retort, "that I had known you at your cleverest." Yet, vain and impudent as he was, Alcibiades fascinated everyone. He was Socrates' favourite pupil; but all the good he got from it was to learn the subtleties of argument, and he used such intellectual skill as he acquired for his own purely selfish ends. He played shamelessly to the gallery, and once, it is said, feeling himself somewhat out of the limelight, he cut off his dog's tail for no other purpose than to make folk talk of him. He knew exactly how to handle the Assembly. The mob idolized him; for, though at one time he was driven into exile and played traitor to his country, they received him back and replaced him in power. "They love him and hate him, but have him they must," was Aristophanes' verdict. "Charlatan and genius in one," he was to prove for the next fifteen years the evil demon of Athens.

In the aftermath of Nicias' Peace, Sparta's position in the Peloponnese was much weakened. Argos, never a member of her Confederacy, and hitherto a neutral in the war, was watching for the chance to pay off old scores. Among the Confederacy, too, there was grave dissatisfaction, especially among the Arcadians of the central plains. So the Argives and Arcadians got together; and looking round for an ally, they made overtures to Athens. About the same time, as it so happened, Sparta approached her too. Among the Athenians opinion was divided. Nicias favoured the old Cimonian policy of co-operation with Sparta. But Alcibiades saw the opportunity for a coup. By an unscrupulous subterfuge he persuaded the Spartan envoys to contradict themselves and then denounced them to the Assembly for playing a double game. This clinched the matter. The Spartan envoys were sent packing, and Alcibiades was empowered to lead an army into the Peloponnese and join hands with Arcadia and Argos.

In a pitched battle fought near the Arcadian town Mantinea, this formidable combination came within an ace of success, but at the last moment victory eluded them, and so Alcibiades went home with nothing to show for the audacious gamble. It was a sad reflection on the Athenian populace that they learnt nothing by the lesson. Next year his victory in the chariot-race at Olympia restored the young adventurer's prestige, and in 416 he was once more in power. The true character of his leadership was soon revealed by an act as mean and brutal as any in history. Lying east of the Peloponnese was a little island called Melos. It had never been a member of Athens' empire, but recently Cleon had included its name on the tribute-list—a pure fiction on his part; for, if Melos paid tribute to anyone, she had paid it to Sparta. On the strength of this, however, the unfortunate island was now denounced as a renegade. Its protestations were of no avail. The Athenians captured its capital by blockade, and then—horrible to relate—slaughtered all the male inhabitants and sold the women and children as slaves.

The motive of this stroke was doubtless to intimidate would-be rebels among the tributary states; but nothing can excuse it. Something must be put down to the effects of the Plague; and the intoxication of power was working on minds overwrought by that bitter experience. The Athenians had lost their poise, and next year on Alcibiades' instigation they undertook a fresh adventure of almost unbelievable bravado.

Sicily, as we have already seen, had long been a flourishing centre of trade. Its many cities—colonized in the first instance from Greece—were completely independent; and thanks to their favoured commercial position they had developed a brilliant and luxurious culture of their own. They enjoyed comforts which even Ionia might have envied. They had produced men of learning who had made important contributions to Greek intellectual life. They could be stout fighters, too, when the need arose. In 480—the year of Salamis—Carthage, the great maritime power of North Africa, had attacked the island; but, like the Greek states of the Motherland, the Sicilians had shown that they too could unite at a crisis, and they had driven the invaders back. But, the crisis once over, they had again fallen to quarrelling. Syracuse, the most powerful among them, had begun to domineer over the rest; and in 416, Segesta, thus threatened, appealed for Athens' protection.

It was not the first time that the Athenians had entertained the idea of interfering in Sicily. The island's wealth offered a strong temptation, and when Segesta's appeal came up for the Assembly's discussion, it was hotly debated. Nicias, cautious as always, discountenanced action. But Alcibiades took a different view. His uncle's strategy, as we have seen, had been aimed largely at crippling Corinth. Pressed to its logical conclusion, such a policy could best succeed by the conquest of Sicily and the destruction, once and for all, of Corinth's westerly trade. Commercial expansion, now more than ever, was a necessity to Athens' very existence; and with the Adriatic as well as the Aegean in her grip, she would be in a position to defy not Sparta and Corinth alone, but the still more dangerous enemy, her own economic stringency. Alcibiades, therefore, had little difficulty in persuading his countrymen to answer Segesta's call and send an expedition against Syracuse. He argued that most of the island could be won by diplomatic action alone. He even hinted that the conquest of Carthage might not be beyond the bounds of possibility. Above all, he painted a glowing picture of the commercial openings there awaiting the mercantile class; and when his advice was taken and the Assembly's decision made, many businessmen undertook to accompany the expedition and glean what profits they could. In their mood of giddy optimism the wealth of Sicily was already theirs.

Preparations were complete, and the expedition was ready to sail when an extraordinary event occurred in Athens. Lining the streets of the city were numerous stone pillars sacred to Hermes, the god of bounds and ways; and one morning the inhabitants awoke to find that all but one of these had been defaced during the night. Such sacrilege was a terrible shock to the superstititious populace. Who the culprits were, no one could tell. The likelihood is that they were enemy agents from Corinth or Megara. But, though he of all men had least to gain by the expedition's postponement, Alcibiades was suspected. Meanwhile, investigations proceeded, and various informers came forward. Alcibiades' enemies decided to hold their hand until he was safely out of the way.

So at last the great fleet of warships and transports was permitted to sail, and Thucydides has described its departure in a dramatic passage: "Early in the morning the men made their way to the Piræus and began to man the ships, and the whole population went with them. Some came to take farewell of a friend or a kinsman, some of their sons. Hope and sorrow filled their hearts as they passed down the road. The prospect of conquering Sicily gladdened them. But tears rose at the thought of the long voyage ahead and the doubt whether they would ever see their loved ones again. The imminence of the parting brought home to them perils of which they had never so much as thought when voting the expedition. Soon, however, the sight of the great armada in all its strength and brilliance revived their drooping spirits. It was a triumph of organization, and no armament so costly or so magnificent had ever before gone forth from any city in Greece. . . . At last the ships were manned and everything aboard was in readiness. Then silence was proclaimed by a bugle-call, and all with one voice offered up the traditional prayers— recited not ship by ship, but by the voice of a single herald, all the rest repeating the words after him. On deck men and officers brought out vessels of silver and gold and poured libations of wine to the gods; while on land a vast throng of citizens and friendly spectators also joined in the prayers. Finally the crews raised the war-chant; and, the ceremonial over, they put out to sea. For a while they sailed in single file, and then the ships raced each other as far as Aegina!" As Thucydides knew, when he wrote those lines, none of them would ever come back.

In its allocation of the high command the Assembly had arrived at a compromise, and it would be hard to imagine anything more foolish. Along with Alcibiades, as chief sponsor of the campaign, and Lamachus a plain non-political soldier, they had appointed Nicias who had made it abundantly clear that he disapproved of the whole adventure. The result was that when they arrived in Sicily, the three commanders could not agree on a plan of action. So the year 415 was frittered away, and the advantage of surprise was lost and with it probably the best hope of success. Meanwhile Alcibiades, the one brilliant brain among the three, was recalled to stand his trial for sacrilege. He took no risks, but fled to Sparta; and, worse still, when he got there, he gave the enemy the hint that they would do well to send a general of their own to Sicily.

In the spring of 414 the Athenians began the campaign in earnest. Their task was much facilitated by the geographical situation of Syracuse. Its famous roadstead—a splendid semi-circular bay with its entrance partially closed by a projecting peninsular—promised adequate shelter for their ships; and the city itself, lying north of the bay, was dominated from behind by a high ridge, known as Epipolæ. This ridge, when they landed, the Athenians quickly rushed by a surprise assault, and here they were admirably placed for pursuing the traditional tactics of siege—the circumvallation of the town. One wall they started to drive southwards to the harbour edge, another northwards to the sea-coast. If completed, these walls would have cut Syracuse off from supplies or reinforcement by land. The defenders, however, by cutting across the northerly wall with a cross-wall of their own, prevented if from reaching the sea; and, as things turned out, the gap thus left open saved the city.

For just at this moment a Spartan general, Gylippus, sent on Alcibiades' advice, had arrived in Sicily; and through the gap he and the army he had collected managed to slip in. His presence put new vigour into the defence, and it was soon the Athenians' turn to be cooped up in their camp near the edge of the Great Harbour. Their situation became very uncomfortable. Syracusan cavalry scoured the country behind them. Their forage-parties were constantly harried. Lamachus had been killed in the earlier fighting; and Nicias, now left in sole command, was a very sick man, suffering from a painful disease of the kidneys. He sent home a plaintive appeal for reinforcements, and, though Athens had already sent out the flower of her fleet, she answered the call. So soon Demosthenes, with another large squadron of ships and transports, was on the way to Sicily. His trained eye quickly took the measure of the situation. The heights of Epipolæ had been lost since Gylippus' arrival, and their recapture seemed the one hope. A night attack was launched, and the heights scaled by moonlight. All at the first went well; but in the flush of success the Athenians lost direction and, falling into disorder, were hurled back again. After this failure they were left with no alternative but to abandon the campaign. Preparations for departure were made, and all was in readiness when an eclipse of the moon occurred. Nicias' astrologers at once stepped in with a demand for postponement, and the superstitious general complied.

The days passed, and it soon became doubtful whether the Athenian host would get away at all. The enemy had now thrown a boom across the harbour mouth and were planning to give battle within the harbour itself. Here in the narrow waters they foresaw that the Athenian skill of manœuvre could not tell; and, to gain extra power for head-on ramming, they had specially strengthened the prows of their ships. Success in a preliminary skirmish encouraged their hopes, and they decided on an all-out effort to destroy the Athenian fleet. So the battle was joined, and Thucydides' account of it shall be quoted in full.

"As the battle swung both armies watched from the land, and their states of mind well reflected the tensity of the struggle—the islanders eager to add to their laurels, the invaders dreading yet worse things to come. The Athenians' solitary hope was their fleet, and the torment of their anxiety defies description. The ebb and flow of the conflict, too, greatly affected its aspect from the shore. The range of vision was so close that impressions of it varied as viewed from different angles. From one point they would see their own men winning, and taking heart they would offer up prayers for deliverance. Elsewhere matters might seem to go against them, and then they would moan and cry aloud, more unmanned by the spectacle than the combatants themselves. Where the battle seemed indecisive, it was worst of all. The prolonged suspense was agonizing. From moment to moment their salvation or doom seemed to hang by a hair, and they kept swaying their bodies this way and that way as their spirits rose or fell. So during this phase of the engagement, a strange medley of sounds went up from the Athenian Camp—shouts of victory, groans of defeat, and all the varied ejaculations of a great host in mortal peril. The state of mind among the combatants was not much different, till at last the long struggle ended. Bit by bit the Syracusans drove the Athenians back; then gathering themselves for a last triumphant onslaught, they hunted them to the land amid a hubbub of cheering. Crews that escaped interception by sea ran aground where best they could, and clambered out into the camp. The babel on shore ceased, and as one man the entire Athenian host gave vent to its dismay in a loud and desolate wail. Some rallied to the incoming vessels or ran to man the wall. But uppermost in most minds was the question how they now could get away. Their plight much resembled the plight of their own victims at Pylos. There the Spartans on the island had been doomed by the destruction of their ships, and now for the Athenians escape by land was equally impossible—short of some miracle."

So Nicias and Demosthenes led the army away overland. For some days they struggled on in a south-westerly direction till they were cut off at a river-crossing and all slaughtered or captured. The prisoners were taken to Syracuse and housed in the stone-quarries under Epipolæ. Many died a lingering death from privation and exposure; and after some weeks the survivors were sold as slaves.

3. THE LAST PHASE

With the Sicilian disaster the whole war-situation changed. The Athenians had lost the best part of their fleet, and, for the time being at least, the control of the Aegean had passed out of their hands. The subject-states began to revolt—Chios, Lesbos, Miletus, and, a little later, Rhodes. The enemy, too, were now in a position to render the rebels assistance. But their difficulty was to find ships and, still more, rowers, in adequate numbers. Corinth, of course, provided her share; but the Spartans themselves were not a seagoing race. Here fate, however, played into their hands. Persia had never forgotten her lost Ionian possessions, and she now saw her chance for their recovery. So the Great King once again entered the lists—not with fleets and armies, but with the more potent weapon of gold. His intention was to play off one group of Greek states against the other until both were exhausted, and for the present his cue was to finance Sparta and enable her to hire rowers and organize an adequate fleet.

Athens' position seemed desperate. "Whichever way they looked," says Thucydides, "there was trouble. They were overwhelmed by their calamity. Unutterable consternation seized them. The city had lost the flower of its youth and there was none to replace them. In the docks there was a woeful scarcity of ships; no crews to man them, no money in the treasury, and no visible prospect of deliverance." Worse still, the Spartans, acting on Alcibiades' advice, had again invaded Attica and built a permanent fort at Decelea scarcely a day's march from the city. This hit the inhabitants in more ways than one. Their slaves ran away to find sanctuary with the enemy. Their cattle, placed in Eubœa for safety, could no longer be brought overland. It was scarcely even safe to venture outside the walls unarmed.

But with astonishing resilience the democracy pulled itself together, and a permanent commission "of elder men" was appointed to advise the Assembly on policy. None the less the political atmosphere in Athens remained very tense; and under the surface trouble was brewing. The aristocrat reactionaries were restive, and secret clubs were forming. Here all the blame for the Sicilian débâcle was laid on the democrat mob, and discussions took place how best to end its intolerable mishandling of affairs. There was even whispered talk of a *coup d'état*.

Hitherto Athens had escaped those extremes of class faction which in some Greek states had led to violent struggles for power. But the impact of war, as Thucydides said, produces catastrophic results and his diagnosis of such internal stresses (quoted already at the beginning of this book) throws a vivid light on the mentality of the times.

"With the growth of the revolutionary spirit," he says, "stratagems became more ingenious and methods of revenge more extravagant. Words lost their familiar meaning. A new set of circumstances demanded a new use of terms. So now the reckless fanatic became the 'loyal party man.' Cautious statesmanship was 'a cloak for cowardice'; moderation 'the weakling's subterfuge,' and intelligence was written off as 'ineffective.' Act like a maniac and you were styled 'a real man.' Walk warily and your fellow-conspirators set you down as a renegade. The hectoring bully never failed of a hearing, and any criticism of him was suspect. Claims of party took precedence over family ties; for the partisan knows no restraints of conscience or decency. And how should he, seeing that associations of this type are based on anti-social ambitions, and their strength springs not from the moral law but from partnership in crime.

"So friendly advances from one party merely met with curt rebuff, and a pact, if made, could not last. Whichever side first summoned courage to strike, took a pride in the success of their treachery. To have triumphed in a battle of wits was a feather in their cap. For it is always more flattering to be thought an ingenious knave than a virtuous fool.

"The compelling motive behind all this was Power, pursued partly for notoriety's sake, partly for its material rewards; and the element of competition gave an added zest to the game. It mattered little what plausible slogans political leaders might adopt. One side might talk of 'Aristocracy's genius for compromise'; the other of 'Democracy's egalitarian principles.' But such lip-service could not disguise the truth. It was the control of the commonwealth that both sides coveted, and these rivals stuck at nothing in the struggle for power. In their lust for revenge all conventions of justice and patriotism were forgotten. It was enough if their party-spite could be gratified by some savage sentence or violent *coup d'état*.

"Religion had no hold, though cant might have its uses in white-washing their crimes. The neutral received short shrift at the hands of either party. Both alike resented his refusal to join them and share the risks they ran. Sincerity (which is no small part of idealism) was killed by mockery, and the atmosphere of general suspicion made conciliation impossible. Nobody would trust an oath and nobody would keep one. Nothing was taken for granted, and having lost faith in human nature, men took their own precautions. The second-rate intelligence usually came off best. Conscious of his inferiority as speaker or diplomat, such a man was afraid that his more adroit opponents would get their blow in first; so he struck ruthlessly. The abler man, disdaining practical precautions—as your intellectual will—was thus caught napping, often with fatal results."

Then follows a gruesome description of the scenes at Corcyra, where the faction-struggle seems to have reached its worst violence. No mercy was shown to defeated opponents. Some were slaughtered in temples where they had fled for sanctuary; others walled up and left to die of starvation. Finally, their corpses were flung "crosswise into waggons" and were carted away like lumber.

Thanks to the good sense of her citizens, such horrors were never enacted at Athens. But even there passions ran deep and there was much dark intrigue. So though Thucydides himself was not there to witness it,[1]

[1] He had been in command of a naval squadron during the campaign against Brasidas in Chalcidice; and he had arrived too late to save a town. For this "culpable negligence" he was sent into exile—probably on Cleon's initiative.

something at least of what he tells about class-antagonism must probably stand true of his countrymen.

The trouble started, it appears, with Alcibiades. He had tired of exile in Sparta, and crossing to Asia Minor had taken refuge with the Great King's satrap Tissaphernes. He was now anxious to get home again, but knowing that the Athenian democracy would not take him back, he decided to intrigue for the establishment of an oligarchic regime. He first approached some officers of the Athenian fleet then stationed at Samos, and through them got in touch with the malcontent aristocrats at home. There the leading spirits were the out-and-out oligarchist Antiphon and the more moderate Theramenes, an adroit trimmer nicknamed "the Buskin"—a boot which would fit either foot.

Plans were cunningly laid. The Assembly was summoned to meet at Colonus. This spot lay a mile or so outside the city walls where, with the Spartans at Decelea, it was unsafe to venture unarmed; and only the better-class citizens with full soldier's equipment would therefore attend. At the meeting a motion for reform was put forward, and it was resolved to set up a new Council of four hundred members. These were mostly drawn from the middle-class element, but among them were a number of the oligarch plotters. The same evening the newly appointed Four Hundred entered the Council House, and with armed men at their back evicted its constitutional occupants. The ostensible programme of the "reformers" was go back to the pre-Cleisthenic form of government from which the democrat rabble would be excluded. The Assembly was to consist of a limited number of citizens chosen on a property-qualification, and, in fact, a list of five thousand names was promised. But it was never published.

The real intention of the conspirators soon showed itself. They meant to let the Spartans in and to make peace—on condition, of course, that they themselves continued in power. Their first step was to secure, if possible, the control of the port. So, though other excuses were made for its building, work was begun on a fort near the Piræus-entrance. But now came a hitch. The crews of the fleet at Samos were staunch democrats to a man, and, when they heard of these doings at home, they came out in mutiny, deposed their officers, and threatened to sail back and overthrow the new regime. Alcibiades, seeing that such a step would leave Ionia at the enemy's mercy, dissuaded them, but their protest had served to brace public opinion at Athens. There suspicion of the new government's intention was growing. The promised Assembly had never been called, and even the more moderate men began to have their doubts. One day a prominent oligarch was assassinated in the market-place, and opposition suddenly gathered to a head. There was a rush for the Piræus. The half-finished fort was dismantled, and when a few days later the Spartan fleet appeared, its commander must have seen that the conspirators' schemes had miscarried, and it sailed away again.

A meeting of the Assembly was now called and it was decided to set up a democracy of limited franchise such as Theramenes and the more moderate section had all along intended—"The best administration," Thucydides says, "that Athens ever enjoyed."

Among the first acts of the newly constituted Assembly was the recall of Alcibiades—now the last hope of a despairing people. The outlook was undeniably bleak. Revolt was spreading. Eubœa had gone, and, what was worse, so too had Byzantium at the Black Sea entrance. Its recovery was vital, for there lay the corn-route, the life-line of Athens. So, when Mindarus the Spartan admiral moved up to Byzantium's aid, the Athenian fleet from Samos followed him. A couple of engagements were fought, and the Spartans completely destroyed. Thus the command of the sea passed decisively to Athens once more.

So the agonizing seesaw of fortune went on. At one moment victory itself seemed almost in sight. At the next the advantage was thrown away by the Athenian mob's incurable folly. For the government by limited franchise had been short-lived, and full democracy was now restored. The worst symptom of its demoralization was an inability to back up its leaders. With all his faults, Alcibiades was a capable strategist. He recovered Byzantium. He was pressing the naval campaign in Ionia; and there by a stroke of ill-luck, one of his lieutenants suffered a defeat. It was not a major reverse, but it was the first real success that the Spartans had won at sea, and the Athenians were furious. They vented their wrath by dismissing Alcibiades, and his place was taken by a new demagogue, Cleophon. This man was a lyre-maker by trade, a complete vulgarian, much less able than Cleon, but possessing something of Cleon's energy. An immense effort was made. New ships were built with feverish haste. Slaves were drafted into the rowing crews and even young aristocrats took a place on the bench beside them.

Hopes rose once more when the new armada put out. Here at last, it was felt, was a prospect of ending the struggle; and sure enough a victory, though not a decisive victory, was won off the Arginusæ Islands near Lesbos. Towards the end of the battle, however, a strong gale had sprung up, and the victors failed to save the crews of their disabled vessels. At Athens public opinion was deeply moved by their loss, and the admirals eight in number, were impeached in the Assembly for negligence. Evidence was not seriously considered, and it was proposed to pass the death-sentence upon all eight *en bloc*. This was a grossly illegal procedure, and Socrates, the philosopher, that day chairman of the presiding committee, raised objections. He was overruled and the sentence was passed.

Peace could now have been had for the asking. Sparta was ready to grant terms, provided Athens abandoned all claim to her lost dominions. Cleophon staggered drunk into the Assembly and defeated the proposal. Yet, even as things were, the war need not have been lost, had not Sparta discovered a leader of exceptional talent. His name was Lysander, a dour unpleasant character, but ambitious and determined. His skill as a naval commander had already been proved in the battle which led to Alcibiades' fall. What was still stranger in a Spartan, he was something of a diplomatist; and he won the confidence of the young Persian prince Cyrus, who had been sent down by the Great King his father, to keep an eye on the struggle. With Cyrus' financial assistance a better fleet had been built, and fresh rowers hired. Then Lysander struck. Like Mindarus, he made for the Sea of Marmora, and so threatened Athens' supplies. There the Athenians met him, and at Aegospotami or the Goat's River the decisive battle was fought. They were beaten.

All was now over, or as good as over. Cleophon, it is true, still refused to make peace, and it was left for Theramenes to go to Sparta and treat. Months passed, while the Athenians slowly starved. At length, in 404, they capitulated. Their Long Walls were demolished; all but twelve of their ships were surrendered, and not a remnant of their Empire was left them. Thirty pro-Spartan "quislings" were put in charge of the government. Thucydides himself, though he lived to see the tragedy, never carried his history to this point. Perhaps he had not the heart. The nemesis of power-lust—the nemesis which he must so surely have feared, and perhaps even foreseen—had overtaken his country. No need to write the final act; the drama was closed. Athens "was fallen, was fallen, that great city."

CHAPTER VIII

DEMOCRACY'S BALANCE-SHEET

I

If a people is to be judged by success or failure in solving its own particular problems, then the Spartans had doubly succeeded. It was not merely that they had won the war against Athens—more perhaps through good luck and their opponents' mistakes than through merit of their own. What in the long run was of far greater importance, they had attained through the Lycurgan system a stability both economic and political which was without parallel among other Greek states. But this they had done by deliberately sacrificing what most Greeks chiefly prized—all intellectual activity, all cultural amenities, even family life itself. It is always well to ask at what cost security is worth while.

The Athenians had pursued a very different road. From the moment when Solon launched them on the course of commercial and industrial expansion, they were committed to living by their wits. Democratic development was the inevitable sequel, and with it the need for higher standards of mental efficiency. The intellectual activity of the preceding aristocratic age had been speculative and theoretic, scarcely touching the realities of everyday life. But, when the Sophists undertook to educate the average man and to bring intellect to bear on practical problems, the highly sceptical spirit of Ionian enquiry was automatically transferred to the realm of affairs. It was an easy step to cast doubt on traditional ethics, and the cynical appeal to self-interest was glibly employed to justify whatever policy the need of the moment might suggest. So during the course of the fifth century the temper of the Athenian people steadily hardened, and in the attempt to solve their economic and political problems they were forced to a progressive abandonment of their liberal ideals.

How Athenian Democracy had exploited the tributary members of their Empire, requires no further emphasis here. But within the city itself there were classes whose contribution to the national economy was no less essential and who in one degree or another were similarly sacrificed to the interests of the citizen-body.

It is not always sufficiently recognized how large a part in the life of Athens was played by her resident aliens or "metics." Yet, in the first instance, we should remember, it was their exceptional skill or ability that had been the *raison d'étre* of their invitation or admission to the country. Some, like Lysias, took a high place in its cultural activities. Others were teachers or musicians or artists. In industry and business generally, they were indispensable. Among the contractors for one State-undertaking (listed in an extant inscription), less than a third were Athenian born, and among the craftsmen employed the proportion was lower still. Metics had a virtual monopoly of the grain-trade. Some kept factories which in part must have contributed to the vital production for export.

Now originally, as we have seen, Solon had attracted these foreigners to Athens by promise of full citizenship, and their presence was thus a valuable asset both of man-power and finance. They served in army and fleet. They paid the war-tax or capital levy, and, if specially rich, they were liable for such burdens as the outfit of a warship or the production of a tragedy. To what extent they were *in practice* admitted to political rights is hard to say. What seems certain is that naturalization in the full sense was rare and grew rarer as time went on. The Athenians, in fact, became increasingly exclusive, and this illiberal tendency reached its climax in the year 451. In that year a law was passed which removed from the citizen-roll any man whose parents were not both Athenian-born. The motive of this harsh measure can only be guessed. It seems likely that the rapid growth of the citizen population had overtaxed its food-supply, and that some check to further immigration seemed prudent; and beyond this, it is not improbable that there was a real danger lest the Assembly might be swamped by the alien element, and that the masses were jealous of sharing their valued privileges with outsiders. Be that as it may, the resident aliens, while still liable to all the duties of citizenship, were hence-forth debarred from any hope either of enjoying its privileges themselves or even of their descendants enjoying them. They could neither vote in the Assembly, nor hold office, nor take any part in public life. Only under special licence were they even permitted to carry their case into the Courts. It speaks well for Athens that despite this one-sided arrange-ment the metics still continued to value her commercial and cultural advantages, and that in the course of the next century their number actually increased.

But the effort of citizens and metics alone could not have sufficed to balance Athenian economy, had it not been supplemented by the labour of slaves. Of these, we may distinguish two classes, both in their different ways essential to the community's life. First there were the menials kept in the homes of the well-to-do. Such domestic staffs, composed mostly of females, but including some males, were often large. A very rich man might keep fifty. The average citizen might have three. By the performance of the household tasks they set their master free for business or political duties. Some were more directly helpful. The more intelligent acted as copyists, secretaries or accountants. Others played the part of "pedagogues" conducting their master's sons to school and back again.[1] Along with this type of slave may perhaps be grouped those skilled in some handicraft—building, carpentering, vase-painting, or what-not. Such valuable assistants often worked side by side with the free artisans.

A Young Labourer. (From a vase-painting.)

The other class were engaged on mass-production in industry; and, as the city's trade grew, the number of these "factory-slaves" increased. Cephalus, the resident alien from Sicily, kept a workshop for manufacturing shields in which seven hundred hands were employed. About their treatment little is known; but in the silver mines at Laureum conditions must have been appalling. Into these were drafted slaves of the rougher and more intractable type. The underground galleries along which they had to crawl have been discovered. They measure little more than two feet square. Iron shackles, too, have been found, and hand-

[1] See Illustration, page 127.

lamps calculated to last for a ten-hour shift. The working of the mines was leased by the state to contractors. Private individuals would hire out slaves, for whom they had no personal use, to work in the mines—branded, like cattle, with their owner's name. In one Court-speech a litigant describes how he got up before dawn one morning to walk down to Laureum and collect the rent due to him on such a slave. Nicias, we know, owned a thousand of them; and in all it is reckoned that twenty times that number must have been employed. But the condition of these and other industrial drudges troubled nobody's conscience. They were regarded—in the famous phrase of the philosopher Aristotle—as "human

An elderly slave acts as "pedagogue" to a boy on the way to
a music-lesson.

instruments"; and indeed they performed in antiquity very much the same function as is performed by the modern machine.

Not that the treatment of slaves at Athens was worse than elsewhere in Greece. On the contrary, it was better. One Athenian writer said: "Here slaves enjoy very considerable licence. They may not be struck. They will not even make way for you in the street. Yet, if it seems odd that we allow them to live in comfort—and I might put it even higher—there is none the less good reason. It is that for a maritime power economic considerations make it essential to humour slaves. For, if a slave fears you (as in Sparta he did), look what violent lengths he will go to. Rather than that, it pays us to treat him more or less as one of ourselves." Though punishments inflicted on slaves were often harsh, exceptional brutality, especially if resulting in death, laid the assailant open to prosecution. Manumission, if rare, was by no means unknown. Certainly, if we may judge from Aristophanes' plays, the cheeky household slave was no down-trodden creature. An epitaph on a slave-girl, written at a later age, shows a further humanization of domestic relationships:

> In body but in that alone
> She was a slave in days agone,
> But now her body too is free
> To match her spirit's liberty.

Yet, even when viewed in the most favourable light, the institution remains a hideous blot on ancient civilization. The Greeks themselves were under no illusion. They knew what loss of liberty meant. "Half manhood goes when slavery's day sets in" was a well-known saying among them. But they drew a racial distinction. The great majority of slaves were of barbarian origin, kidnapped by raiders either from Thrace or from the southern coasts of Asia Minor. This appeared to the Greeks right and proper, and Aristotle bluntly declared that barbarian peoples were "by nature slavish"—the argument of the "Herren Volk." The enslavement of Greeks by Greeks, on the other hand, was always regarded as something of an outrage. Later on, in the time of Aristotle, a law was passed forbidding the purchase of Greek prisoners of war. But in the fifth century unhappily, the tendency was all the other way, and the deterioration of Athenian democracy's principles was nowhere more clearly marked than when Melian islanders were condemned by the Assembly to be sold into bondage. Hard as it is for the individual to rise above the social standards of his age, it remains astonishing that among all the thinkers and poets of Greece none ever seriously questioned the necessity for slavery. But then not even St. Paul himself would appear to have contemplated its abolition, and the mediæval Church acquiesced in the institution of serfdom.

One other class of person remains to be described. Women, needless to say, took their full share—according to their ability—in the country's economic activities. They were not much employed in agriculture except at harvest time, and possibly the vintage. Occasionally, however, they worked at crafts such as shoe-making. They kept inns, too, baked bread and served as barmaids. Above all, they were the mainstay of the market. There they stood at their booths, selling wine, figs, honey, vegetables, perfumes, garlands, knick-knacks, and so forth. The corn-sellers were notorious for the sharpness of their tongues, which would have done credit to Billingsgate. But women's chief accomplishment was the making of cloth. They spun wool and wove it interminably in their homes. There is an amusing description of one harassed householder with whom fourteen peevish female relatives had taken up their quarters as war-refugees. On someone's advice he set them to cloth-making, and the result, we are told, was excellent. "They took their dinner while they worked, and did not sup till all was over. From glum they became cheerful; instead of scowling at one another, they had a glad look for all; and they ended by loving their patron and he loved them for being so

A lady at her toilette, mirror in hand. (From a vase-painting.)

useful." Dressmakers existed, but only for the smart lady's benefit. In general, it was unnecessary. The Greek's ordinary garments consisted of two oblong pieces of cloth, one pinned round the body shirtwise and caught up at the waist with a girdle, the other of thicker material thrown over the shoulders like a Scottish plaid.

All that we have said about woman's life—with the exception of spinning and weaving—applied only, however, to the working-class. The wives and daughters of the gentry were actually in a worse position than their poorer neighbours. This, oddly enough, was a direct result of the law passed in 451. Previous to that, marriages with alien women had been common enough, and Ionian ladies were notoriously attractive. But, since under the new law the children of such marriages were debarred from citizenship, these alien women sank into the position of courtesans. They continued, as they had done in the past, to "go into society." They mixed freely with the festive gatherings of males; some of them, like Pericles' famous mistress Aspasia, won a high reputation for their charm and their wit. But the legitimate wives were no longer able with propriety to attend at these mixed gatherings. "The less heard of women in male company the better, whether for good or for ill," was Pericles' harsh advice. In other words, the respectable lady's position was henceforth to be that of the "haus-frau" pure and simple. In the female quarters of her home—well away from the front door—she lived a life of almost oriental seclusion. It was not even thought decent for her to be seen out shopping. If she ventured into the streets, she must have an attendant.

Meanwhile in the eyes of the law a woman had no independent status. She was always the ward of some man—father, brother, or husband. Marriage came early, at fifteen or sixteen. It was a strictly business arrangement between bridegroom and parents. Love-matches were as yet unknown. It was the typically Greek view that a marriage based on a cool and deliberate choice was better calculated to prosper than one undertaken under the influence of passionate emotion. As mistress of the house, the wife's days were spent in supervising the slaves and in other domestic duties. One writer depicts the attempt of a liberal-minded husband to educate his young wife. "When she came to me she was not yet fifteen. She had been brought up, so to speak, in blinkers, and taught to ask no questions. It was scarcely an education to learn how to weave or to weigh out the yarn for her maids, though I am bound to say she was very well up in cooking," and his first lecture ended as follows: "Prove yourself my superior and nothing could please me better. I shall be your faithful servant, and age will not diminish your influence over me. On the contrary, the better companion you make to me and the better you look after our home and our children, the more we all shall think of you. Everyone will admire you, not so much for your handsome looks as for your sound practical ways."

The life of women was a dull life clearly, and from time to time protests were raised. Euripides displayed real sympathy, and Plato, the philosopher, discussed the employment of women on an equal footing with men, and their right to a share in the government. In one of Aristophanes' comedies, too, we find an amusing skit on a "Women's Parliament"—which would appear to have lacked point, had not some talk of Feminism been in the air. But these were solitary voices, and even if the stricter conventions were gradually broken down, female emancipation, for the richer class at least, made no real headway. On the other hand, it is not to be supposed that all women were unhappy, and a deep devotion between husband and wife is often recorded, as in this touching epitaph.

O Atthis, who didst live for me,
 On me thy last didst breathe
Source of my joy in days gone by
 Now likewise of my grief—
Thou in sad slumber leav'st me lone
 To mourn thy spirit blest,
Whose faithful head was never laid
 But on thy husband's breast.
Without thee, Atthis, I am done,
 For, when death took thee home,
Then every hope we shared in life
 Went with thee to the tomb.

2

From what has been said it should be abundantly clear that Democracy at Athens was, in fact, a minority rule. Leaving women aside, the adult population of the city has been estimated roughly as follows:

50,000 citizens,
25,000 resident aliens,
55,000 slaves.

On this showing the enfranchised element represented considerably less than one-half of the whole population, and, judged by present-day standards, ancient democracy was thus subject to very grave limitations. But history must be viewed in its true perspective, and within these limitations there can be no doubt that the Athenians pursued and to a large extent achieved, the democratic ideal. Freedom of speech and thought was certainly their normal practice. Criticism of authority was unhampered. Aristophanes could speak his mind frankly on policy and make what fun he liked of politicians.[1] When Cleon on one occasion protested, he met with no sympathy. Occasionally, it is true, exception was taken to unorthodox religious beliefs. Shortly before the outbreak of the Peloponnesian War, the philosopher, Anaxagoras, was arraigned for impiety: had he not said dreadful things about the Sun—that it was "a red-hot stone much larger than the Peloponnese." He was heavily fined and retired from Athens. The real motive behind the accusation, however, was political. It was part of an attack upon Pericles' circle of which

[1] It is hard to admire sufficiently the liberality and courage of those who *selected* the plays for the Festival. What censor of to-day would permit, let alone promote, the production of a play that advocated peace in the middle of a war or lampooned the commander-in-chief?

Anaxagoras was a member; and Phidias the sculptor also suffered. Conservative-minded opponents, frustrated in the political field, had adopted this mean method of having their revenge. After the close of the war, Socrates, too, fell victim to a similar spite. Yet against this must be set the fact that already for the better part of a life-time the pertinacious old critic had been allowed complete freedom to carry on his discussions and call in question every belief of contemporary society. Toleration was, in fact, better understood in fifth-century Athens than at any epoch until quite modern times.

In how many ways and with what genuine devotion the citizen of Athens served the state has already been fully described; and it is here more pertinent to enquire what he received in return for his service. Chiefly, no doubt, the satisfaction of belonging to what he justifiably believed to be the finest city in the world; but there were more material benefits too. The State guaranteed and safeguarded the importation of his food. It provided much employment, especially to men in the building trade. It controlled all religious ceremonials and pageants. It organized dramatic and other popular entertainments. The gymnasia were built and laid out at the public expense; so too were the baths which adjoined them.

Social services were then, of course, as yet in their infancy; and under Pericles' rule, as he himself boasted, their tendency was to reward individual merit, not to subsidize failure or misfortune. Benefactors of the state, among them successful athletes, were often voted free meals in the Town Hall for life; and the sons of war-victims, as we learn from the Funeral Speech, were brought up at the public expense. Humanitarianism, however, was not wholly lacking. Cripples were assisted by a dole; and we possess an entertaining speech delivered in defence of his claim by a lame man who was taxed with the needless extravagance of making journeys on horse-back. From quite early days, too, the State hired doctors; one practitioner was bribed away from a neighbouring island by the offer of a rise in his salary. As the masses, moreover, learned to exert their political power, they used it to make the rich pay for the poor. We have mentioned already how a public fund was started, out of which a gratuity was forthcoming for those who attended the theatre—a privilege highly prized by the more indigent; and the fee paid to jurors served after the manner of a pension to the aged and infirm. But after Athens' defeat, when her Empire was lost and the pinch of poverty became severe, there was a growing tendency to extort less justifiable concessions; and even attendance at the Assembly was rewarded by a small payment. Money was distributed, too, at other festivals besides the Dionysia; and any surplus that accrued to the public exchequer was made over to the Theoric Fund from which all such gratuities were paid. The rich complained bitterly that the proletariate was becoming pauperized.

Yet it would be wrong to think of Athens as a Socialistic state. Nowhere was individual effort and self-reliance more deliberately encouraged. In education, especially, this principle was strictly observed. All instruction—intellectual, musical or gymnastic—was left to the initiative of free-lance teachers, and choice of schooling appears to have lain entirely with parents' good sense. Yet the results were, to say the least, remarkable. The enthusiasm aroused by the Sophists' lectures was no mere flash in the pan. Intellectually the Athenians must have been the most acute people who ever existed. A single incident is enough to prove it. In one of Aristophanes' comedies there was a famous scene in which Æschylus and Euripides were represented as engaged in a poetic dual. Each criticized the other's works, parodied his style, discussed obscure passages and, above all, bandied quotations with him. Yet it was by far the most popular of all the dramatist's plays, and by an exceptional mark of approbation a second performance was given.[1] What modern audience would sit through a play in which Lord Tennyson and Mr. Eliot discussed each other's poems; or, even if they did sit, how many would recognize the quotations and appreciate the point of the criticisms. Furthermore, none but a people, among whom a high standard of intelligence was widely diffused, could have produced such a crop of literary, artistic and intellectual genius in so short a space of time. There is no parallel to it in history.

Consider the names that this tiny community produced within the space of two generations—Æschylus, Sophocles, Euripides and Aristophanes in drama; Thucydides, the "father of history"; and Socrates, the founder of moral philosophy; Phidias, the sculptor of the Parthenon, and Ictinus, its architect. Besides these must be counted many other dramatists who at times won the prize over the heads of their better-known rivals, sculptors and architects whose works still testify to the justness of their ancient reputation, to say nothing of the numberless vase-painters whose consummate draughtsmanship has remained for the most part anonymous. When we come to assess the measure of Athens' failure or success, that record is by no means irrelevant.

Whether it is better to live dangerously, like Athens, and fail, or to play for safety, like Sparta, and succeed, must obviously be a matter for

[1] It has been argued that genuine appreciation of plays was confined to a comparatively small intelligentsia. But this play was produced on the very eve of Athens' final collapse, and it seems incredible that at such a crisis the democratic populace could have been put off with a play which they were unable to understand. In another comedy (from which a quotation was given above) Mr. Playfair makes great talk about his experiences in the theatre, and he was clearly a very average citizen.

individual taste. But for Athens, once she had chosen her course, there could be no final or permanent solution of her problems. It was impossible for her to stand still. Her whole history was a succession of crises, and her national economy moved perpetually in a vicious circle. The more she strove to multiply her exports, the more hands were needed for their manufacture. More hands employed meant more mouths to feed; and this in its turn demanded a larger volume of exports to pay for the food. Her position, too, as an imperial power, inasmuch as it forced her increasingly to belie her own democratic principles, was by the nature of things precarious. It was the signal triumph of Pericles' statesmanship that for so long a period of years he was able to tide over these problems with such continuous success. Yet, as soon as one problem was surmounted, another took its place; and it can hardly seem surprising that, once his guiding hand was gone, the Athenian democracy grew bewildered or that in its bewilderment it committed the long series of blunders which brought about its ultimate ruin, choosing bad leaders, making over-hasty decisions, and taking refuge in desperate gambles or ill-considered barbarities. When the end came and Athens fell, it was natural enough that contemporary Greece wrote her democracy down as a failure. But this was a short-term view. Among the great men of history many have appeared failures in their life-time; but posterity, perceiving their influence to grow with years, has reversed the contemporary verdict. To apply the same criterion to a people would seem only common justice. Greek civilization, says Professor Toynbee in his "Study of History," was the most brilliant that has existed up to the present day. The civilization of fifth-century Athens represented its peak, and her influence—literary, artistic, philosophic, and even in some degree political [1]—is with us still.

[1] The political thought of the seventeenth century, when Parliamentary government was taking shape, was much influenced by the study of Greek writers. It may be recalled that Milton's well-known pamphlet on Free Speech was named after the Athenian Areopagus.

CHAPTER IX

CHANGING TIMES

1. SOCRATES

The rule of the thirty quislings, set up by Sparta to govern Athens, did not last many months. Democrats, gathering in countries across the border, came home and turned them out; and the Spartans, feeling Athens to be no longer militarily dangerous yet difficult to control, accepted the *fait accompli*. So a democracy was again established—but an embittered democracy conscious of past failures and eager to find scapegoats on whom to set the blame. One was found in the person of the philosopher, Socrates. Very many in the city felt that teaching such as his was in part responsible for the rot among the rising generation; and after all, Alcibiades was notoriously his pupil. So in 399 they brought him to trial on the double charge of impiety and of "corrupting the youth." He was convicted and sentenced to death by drinking hemlock.

Socrates, though he rose far above its standards, was the creature of his age, just as Plato his pupil was in a somewhat different sense typical of the age which succeeded it. It is to his writings that we owe most of our knowledge about Socrates (who never himself wrote anything), and to disentangle from the Platonic Dialogues what ideas belong to the master and what to the pupil is no easy matter.[1] But from a study of the contrast between the two men, we may glean something of the changing temper of the times as well as of the Athenian contribution to Hellenic thought.

Born in 469, Socrates was a proletarian, and an ugly one at that, with a stout stocky figure, large earnest bulging eyes, and a snub nose. He worked as a sculptor, married to a shrewish wife; and, since he possessed no private means, it meant, as he said, "myriad poverty" when he came to devote himself entirely to the life-long mission of philosophic enquiry. Fairly early in life he seems to have been interested in the New Learning, and to have studied the theories of the Ionian school of which Anaxagoras was a member. But he grew dissatisfied with their continued emphasis on Matter as the prime reality of Creation. He felt convinced that behind all the sense-perceived phenomena of cause and effect lay something of infinitely greater importance. Anaxagoras had called it Mind, and left it

[1] See footnote, page 144.

at that. But Socrates called it "soul," and with this daring venture of intellectual imagination he brought into being the concept of spiritual existence independent of matter [1]—a concept which has governed all subsequent thought.

When he was forty, there came a curious but crucial episode which changed Socrates' whole life. What happened shall be told in the words which, by Plato's account, he himself used at his trial. "Everyone here, I think, knows Chærephon," he said, "he has been a friend of mine since we were boys together; and he is a friend of many of you too. So you know the eager impetuous fellow he is. Well, one day he went to Delphi, and there he had the impudence to put this question—do not jeer, gentlemen, at what I am going to say—he asked, 'Is anyone wiser than Socrates?' And the Pythian priestess answered, 'No one.' Well, I was fully aware that I knew absolutely nothing. So what could the god mean? for gods cannot tell lies. For some time I was frankly puzzled to get at his meaning; but at last I embarked on my quest. I went to a man with a high reputation for wisdom—I would rather not mention his name; he was one of the politicians—and after some talk together it began to dawn on me that, wise as everyone thought him and wise as he thought himself, he was not really wise at all. I tried to point this out to him, but then he turned nasty, and so did others who were listening; so I went away, but with this reflection that anyhow I was wiser than this man; for, though in all probability neither of us knows anything, he thought he did when he did not, whereas I neither knew anything nor imagined I did." And so the search went on, Socrates visiting other folk among whom he hoped to find real knowledge, poets and handicraftsmen and the rest, but always with the same negative result.

Thus, as time went on, the tough old philosopher abandoned himself entirely to what he considered his divinely appointed quest after truth, pursuing it in company with anyone whom he could draw into conversation, but particularly with a group of young followers who soon gathered round him. Outwardly, therefore, he resembled the Sophists; but, in fact, his whole method was a conscious protest against theirs. He took no fees. He made no pretensions to omniscience; on the contrary, he affected a half-humorous pose of complete ignorance ("Socratic Irony" they called it). Unlike the Sophists, too, he never wandered about from city to city. He was a true son of Periclean Athens, a "lover of that fair mistress," and he conceived it as his mission to goad his fellow-countrymen out of their complacency, "like a gadfly stinging some sleepy

[1] The conception of "Soul" as a moral entity—i.e., as something of supreme importance to the individual man—was certainly Socrates' discovery, though Protagoras and his school had already assigned to it a central place in the cosmic mechanism.

old horse," and to persuade them of the paramount importance of "bettering their *souls*." His main quarrel with the Sophists, indeed, was that they professed to train men by intellectual discipline to the ideal pattern of manhood and citizenship, but when asked to define that ideal, they could give no satisfactory answer—Nazis can manufacture "good citizens" of the National Socialist state, but the "good citizens" of a brigand state must needs themselves be brigands. For his own part, Socrates was convinced that it was the ideal of Justice and Moral Righteousness—a harmony between all the human instincts and faculties; and that, if only men could but *know* where in such a spiritual state consisted, then nothing would be easier than to attain life's goal of happiness. But, until it were known, how could it be taught?

So he pursued the enquiry day in, day out, through a series of endless discussions, posing people with questions and cross-examining their opinions. The discussions led to no positive conclusion. For Socrates' method was highly critical, and, whatever theories were put forward, he always succeeded by his ruthless logic in knocking them down. Judging from results, many of his pupils absorbed the destructive element of his teaching and missed its real point. For Socrates' true greatness lay in his unshakable faith that, however baffled he might be in his attempt to discover their nature, Truth and Goodness were a reality—the permanent reality which the Ionian physicists had so often discussed, but which even the best of them still held to be material. Of the spiritual nature of the soul and of its immortality, too (though he was not prepared to say that he *knew* about this), he was absolutely convinced.

So far, therefore, from abandoning the moral conventions (as Alcibiades and his sort were only too ready to do), Socrates clung to them most determinedly in his practical everyday life. He was punctilious in the performance of his civic duties. He served in the army with a pluck and ferocity which, in one battle at least, scared off the pursuit of a victorious enemy. He was elected to the Council, and stood out, as we have seen, in heroic isolation against the illegal procedure of the Assembly. Even after his condemnation, when he might have escaped from prison, he refused to do so because it was against the law of the State.

In Socrates this unswerving moral integrity was, in the last resort, part and parcel of his *intellectual* faith; and of this a word of explanation is required. When the Pythagoreans discovered what they took to be the mystical significance of numbers, they based their theory on the fact that mathematical truth is the one element of reality which the mind can fully comprehend. Now we know that under any circumstances two and two make four, or that the square on the hypotenuse of a right-angled triangle is equal to the square on the other two sides. Such knowledge, though it may require some education to make the individual aware of it, is none the less self-evident, pre-existent in the mind, not put into it from outside. Similarly, Socrates appears to have believed that there exists in man's soul from birth a *knowledge of the good*, and that it should be the function of education to make that knowledge explicit. We moderns might call it conscience; and Socrates himself was inclined to think it came from God (for like all the more profound Greek thinkers he was at heart a mono-theist). But the perception of Goodness, thus innate in the soul, was to him something very different from instinct or inspiration. An intel-lectualist to the core, he was convinced that all moral problems, like mathematical ones, were susceptible of rational explanation, and that through hard thinking alone could man discover the key to virtue and happiness. In other words, the knowledge he sought was not the spiritual certitude of the saint, but the positive proof which the sceptic demands and which, though it for ever eluded him, Socrates still pertinaciously believed to be awaiting discovery. Meanwhile he very obviously enjoyed the quest and found in the use of the intelligence—to him the supreme function of our mortal nature—the noblest and the most repaying of all life's activities.

Yet in Socrates' make-up there was also a mystical element which at times seemed to conflict with his intellectualist creed. He often fell, we are told, into long trances of contemplation from which he would awake with a start, mutter a prayer, and be gone. Often, too, as he himself said, a "divine voice" warned him (and it was always negative) against some act he was contemplating.[1] At his trial this "voice" was undoubtedly one of the counts in the charge of impiety. The defence he set up—as reported by Plato—did nothing to better his case. He simply reiterated his belief that he had been "called" to convert his countrymen to a more serious consideration of their "souls," and he could do no other, not if they were to condemn him a thousand times over. When after conviction he was asked (as was customary in some legal suits) to nominate the penalty he thought fitting to his case, he jokingly suggested that as a benefactor of the state he should receive free meals at the Town Hall for the rest of his life. Subsequently he proposed a fine. His accusers asked for the capital sentence, and, perhaps not unnaturally, they got their desire.

[1] That there was no real inconsistency between Socrates' mystic experience and his intellectual standpoint, is clear from the extract of his final speech given below. When his "Voice" checked him over trifling matters, he evidently humoured it, much as Dr. Johnson humoured his idiosyncrasy for touching alternate posts on a paling. But when at his trial great issues were at stake, then he sought to understand and rationalize the "Divine Sign." Its warnings, in other words, were in his view based on some principle, the truth of which could be proved by Reason.

When the sentence was passed, Socrates took leave of the jury in a final speech; and this speech so significantly combined the various elements in his character—the sceptical and the mystical, the half-playful and the deadly serious, and above all the calm assurance that everything in the world was planned for the best—that its closing passage shall be quoted here [1]: "Stay a moment my friends," he said, "for so I would call you; we still have time to romance a little together, and I feel that the inwardness of to-day's events requires some elucidation. There is one very odd fact. In the past, as you know, my familiar 'voice' has repeatedly checked me whenever I was on the point of making some blunder, no matter how small. Well, you might think that what has come to me to-day is as bad a thing as could possibly be. Yet, when I left my home this morning, the 'divine sign' made no protest. Nor did it when I entered the court, nor when I was engaged in my speech; though commonly enough it will check me when the words are on the tip of my tongue. No, throughout the whole of this affair it has never once intervened, whatever I might do or say. How is that to be explained? I will tell you. It looks to me as though what has happened were a blessing in disguise and that we are all quite wrong in regarding death as something bad. And the strongest evidence of it is that my familiar 'sign' could not possibly have failed to intervene had I been on the wrong road. In this belief I am greatly strengthened by the following reflection. There are only two possibilities about death. It may be total extinction and loss of all sensation, or alternatively there is the traditional view, and it may be a spiritual change, a migration of the soul to some other world. Well, suppose it to be a loss of sensation like dreamless sleep, what a grand thing that would be. Why, you need merely to pick out one such night of dreamless sleep and compare with it all the other nights and days of a lifetime and then consider how many of these have brought more pleasure or profit, and I will wager that the Great King himself, let alone any average man, would find it no difficult sum. So if that is what death is like, good, say I; eternity would be one endless night.

"Or let us suppose that death is what we may call a change of residence, and that the tales they tell us are true and the dead are all gathered yonder; could anything be better than that? Just think of arriving in Hades—farewell to the mock 'Judges' of this world; instead, there would be the great tribunal of which we have so often heard tell, those four true Dispensers of Justice, Minos, Rhadamanthus, Æacus and Triptolemus; not to mention all the other heroes of old who lived just lives in their

[1] The speech is one of the three given by Plato in his "Apology, or Self-defence of Socrates." But it seems reasonable to suppose that he reproduced the main gist and tone of his master's words.

day—no wasted journey that! What would you not give, I would like to know, to make the acquaintance of Homer or Hesiod, or Musæus or Orpheus? Personally I would be glad to die many times over, if such a thing were true. For me, in particular, what a red-letter day it would be to encounter Palamedes or Ajax or others of the ancients whose deaths came about through a miscarriage of justice. We could compare our cases together, and that, I fancy, I should rather enjoy. But best of all would be to examine the good folk down there, as I have examined them here, and find out, if I could, which were really wise and which merely self-deceived. It would be worth a good deal, would it not, to question the leader of the Trojan Expedition or Sisyphus, or Odysseus? Indeed, there is no end to the men and women whom it would be the height of bliss to cross-question down there—in Hades, I take it, there is no capital sentence for that; besides, amongst other advantages, their lives never come to an end, if the tales, that is, are true.

"No, my friends, we must take a hopeful view about death; and you should bear one truth in mind. Alive or dead, no ill can touch a good man. His affairs are in the gods' keeping. So what has come to me is no accident. To be dead and quit of this troublous life is quite clearly for my good. That is why my 'sign' did not seek to divert me and why I have no serious quarrel either with those who brought this charge or with those who passed this verdict. Something different, of course, was in their minds. They thought to do me a mischief, and there they were wrong. But one favour, please. Some day my sons will grow up and they may well show signs of caring for money or suchlike more than they care about character. Then will be the time to have your revenge. Be as hard on them as I have been on you; and, if they fancy themselves when really they have nothing to fancy, you must abuse them just as I have abused you, for setting their heart on the wrong things and misconceiving their own worth. We shall then have no cause to complain of our treatment, I and my sons. But enough. It is time to be going—I to death, you to your lives; and which of us goes to the better part, no one but God can tell."

Looking back we can see that in Socrates were blended the two spiritual currents of the past. On the one hand, he had the moral outlook of the old aristocratic tradition. In his personal life he fully conformed to its code, by his courage and courtesy, by his fidelity to the state, and not least by his austere self-mastery. No one ever saw Socrates angry. He could endure great privations; and when the other diners were all under the table, he alone would keep a clear head. At the same time in his teaching he always set character first. The word most frequently on his lips was "Aretê"—a word which is commonly translated as "Virtue," but which to the Greeks combined all the moral and social qualities which go to the making of the perfect man and citizen. On the other hand, Socrates had the intellectual outlook derived from Anaxagoras and the Ionian school of thought. His whole philosophy was an attempt to rationalize Aretê—a conception long moulded by the narrow requirements of a small political community, hitherto in the main instinctive, more or less blindly accepted, never clearly thought out. He rightly insisted that so far from accepting such a ready-made code, each man must seek to understand for himself what the goal of life should be. But he was mistaken in believing that to understand is in itself enough, or that intellectual freedom and social morality could be so easily harmonized. To all appearances his life-work ended in failure. Many among his pupils became dangerous Individualists. And by following the dictates of his own personal creed he found himself at the last branded as a rebel and a traitor to the society he had so earnestly striven to serve, and with no alternative but to abandon his teaching or to die a martyr's death. But the apparent failure was short-lived. Socrates had set something going in the world which, so long as men have minds to use, will never die out. In the immediate issue it was Plato's task to continue his master's enquiry and try to complete, so far as it ever can be completed, the educational synthesis of Intellect and Character. This he did not by divorcing the two, but by insisting that character is formed by mental habits, and sound character, above all, by right mental habits.

Meanwhile the tragic end of his mission left Socrates, as we have seen, quite unperturbed. He died as he had lived, in buoyant optimism. Nothing ever daunted him. "Let us follow where the argument will lead," he would say, as he went on to demolish yet another of his contemporaries' most cherished convictions. He had a robust faith in human nature. He had an immense devotion to Athens. No doubt he was greatly saddened by her fall; but we may feel sure he was not dismayed. Plato was; and therein lay the difference between the two men and between the two ages to which they severally belonged.

2. PLATO

Plato was barely twenty-four when Athens fell. So the better part of his life was spent in a changed world. Thirty years of war had left their mark both materially and spiritually. The havoc to economic life was terrible, and such havoc was then less easy to repair than in our modern mechanized society. Agricultural recovery was painfully slow. Olive-trees do not grow again in a night-time, and the farms which the Spartans had gutted removing even the roof-tiles, took long to rebuild. Trade had been badly dislocated; and, though Athens managed to recover her mercantile lead in the Aegean, the mass of her citizens remained in the direst poverty. The ancients were little given to describing economic conditions. They accepted them as they accepted the weather, thinking neither worthy of mention until they became catastrophic. There is, however, one fourth-century writer who has left us some sketches of contemporary types, and these tell a significant tale. It is a tale of scraping and cheese-paring, of quarrels over a lump of salt or a lamp-wick, of folk who use a dinted measure to weigh out the family rations, borrow cloaks and refuse to return them, and "move furniture, beds and wardrobes about" in the hunt for a three-farthing piece. It was not lack of public spirit alone which necessitated the payment of a fee for attendance at the Assembly. Unemployment was widespread, and vast numbers of men were driven to seek a livelihood as soldiers of fortune, selling their services to whatever Greek or barbarian state would hire them. Ten thousand such mercenaries, among them many Athenians, enlisted with Prince Cyrus in a campaign against the Great King, his brother, and were led right into the heart of Mesopotamia itself. A Spartan King died fighting other folks' battles in Egypt, and Alexander in his eastern campaign had to meet a large Greek force ranged under the Persian command. Many states became seriously depopulated, and one town founded with high hopes in the middle of the century under the proud title of the "Great City" dwindled again so disastrously that it was nicknamed the "Great Desert."

All this distress served to intensify the spiritual change which was coming over Greece. The City State was rapidly breaking up. The old zest for co-operative effort was no longer the mainspring of men's lives. They were cutting adrift from their moorings, going their own ways and thinking their own thoughts. Even Plato abandoned the political career he had planned for himself at Athens, and at one period of his life he went out to Sicily to assist a tyrant-prince with philosophic advice To imagine Socrates in that role would not be easy. But men's whole outlook was changing; so much that they had hitherto pinned their hopes on was vanishing and life seemed empty of purpose. The most thoughtful began to despair of society and lose faith in human nature. The Cynic philosopher, Diogenes, retired contemptuously to live in a tub where he could be independent of humanity and all its silly ways. A note of disillusionment and pessimism crept into the temper of the ancient world,[1] and even when Rome by her imperial rule restored

---

[1] The theory has been advanced that among the prime causes which led to the Hellenic decline was the spread of malaria. The evidence is not conclusive.

stability and cohesion, that note persisted. It is reflected in the literature of successive ages, where its cynical tone finds an ultimate echo in such lines as this sour little epigram:

> Like swine we all are fattened up through life—
> mine author saith—
> under the careful eye and careless knife
> of Farmer Death.

Plato, even if disillusioned and dismayed, was not the man to accept these symptoms of decline with resignation or despair. From his master Socrates he had learnt to believe that life draws its meaning from something deeper than the changing fashions of social convention or individual choice, and he was to devote his life to upholding that belief. But whereas Socrates' dialectical method had been largely destructive, aimed at divesting men's minds of preconceived notions, and so clearing the path for the recognition of the truth, Plato for his part sought to build up a constructive system of thought, piecing together the threads and drawing out the ideas of those rambling discussions which at the time may have seemed to lead nowhere.

The literary medium he adopted was the pedagogic method of his master—the Dialogue. His style was unique—the greatest perhaps of all Greek styles, combining with amazing elasticity the colloquial and the sublime, the jocular and the serious, as Socrates himself had doubtless combined them. It is difficult, as we have said, to determine what theories are those of his master and what are his own. In the earlier dialogues it is thought that he reproduced Socrates' teaching more closely than in the later. But in general his task was to give formal expression to what was already latent in that teaching and to render explicit the ideas towards which his master had been groping. So out of Socrates' mysticism he constructed a theology and out of his day-to-day discussions a philosophy.[1]

That the difference between Right and Wrong is something fundamental in life Socrates most firmly believed. But, though easily said, this is not so easily squared with the facts of human experience. The story is told of a certain Persian monarch that he once summoned before him a group of Indians and a group of Greeks. He then enquired first of the Greeks if they would be willing to eat their deceased parents—as the Indian custom was; and the answer he got was an emphatic denial. He next asked the Indians whether they would burn their dead as the Greeks did; whereupon the outraged creatures set up a dismal howl. So what

[1] An analogy has been drawn with the Fourth Gospel, the author of which, in expressing the profoundest truths *implicit* in Jesus' teaching, has given them an *explicitly* doctrinal form, very different from Jesus' utterances as recorded by the Synoptists. They are couched, moreover, sometimes in monologue, sometimes in dialogue form.

seems good to one people or one age, may seem bad to another; and it looks as though the difference between Right and Wrong were a mere matter of fashion or convenience.

Plato's solution of the problem was this.[1] Just as Heraclitus had maintained that all natural phenomena perceptible by the senses are shifting and mutable, so he declared that whatever appears to our mortal vision as good, just or beautiful, is equally illusory and unreal. These appearances are, in fact, no more than pale reflections of the ultimate "Idealities" ("Ideas" was Plato's word, but by this he meant something quite different from mere mental concepts)—the Idealities, that is, of Goodness, Justice and Beauty, "laid up in heaven" and perceptible only to the "eye of the soul." Once, however, man has learnt to perceive them, he should be able to recognize at its true value their reflection in the work-a-day world of time, space and sense.

Plato's philosophy must not be thought of as a rigid system. His views were always taking fresh shape, and though their basic content remained the same, his expression of them never attained finality. In his search for the Good Life his enquiry very naturally led him to an examination of educational methods; and in his most famous Dialogue the "Republic," he set out to formulate their ideal pattern. With great boldness of vision he recognized that no educational reform can avail very much unless accompanied by a reform of social institutions. In a communist state, alone, can you educate for Communism or in a Nazi state for National Socialist ideals. So Plato's project led him on to work out the pattern of the Ideal State—a Utopia. Not a democratic state; far from it. For Plato put down all the evils of his day to the follies of Democracy. If he took his model from anywhere, he took it from conservative Sparta; but it was to be an intellectualized Sparta. The mass of the people he felt to be incapable of governing: their job was to plough, manufacture or trade. The state, meanwhile, was to be managed by what we should call Civil Servants. He called them "Guardians." They were to be carefully selected and bred on the best eugenic principles. For this purpose communism of wives was essential; indeed, Communism was to be the keynote of the Administration's whole existence, and all individual ambitions were to be ruthlessly suppressed. The Guardians then were to be an aristocracy of

[1] Some critics consider that Socrates, not Plato, originated the theory of the Idealities. But Aristotle (who should have known) says: "Socrates interested himself in ethical matters, neglecting the world of Nature, seeking the Universal in the ethical sphere and fixing thought for the first time on ethical definitions"; and "some make out that the Idealities are something apart from sensible things; but Socrates, *though he gave impulse to the theory*, did not himself separate the Idealities from the particulars of sense." This might conceivably mean that Socrates believed in moral Idealities, but not (as Plato seems to have done) in Idealities corresponding to objects in the physical world. But Aristotle was a master of clear definition; and if he meant that, he might have been expected to say so categorically.

intellect, combining the moral virtues of the old-fashioned "gentleman" with the intellectual capacities of the New Thought. Their education was so planned as to lead them up to the eventual contemplation of the permanent "Idealities," Goodness, Justice, Beauty, and so forth; and, since nothing within man's mental scope is so demonstrably permanent as mathematical truths, Plato, like the Pythagoreans, laid great stress on this abstract form of educational discipline. Once they had attained to its ultimate goal and the true nature of the Idealities had sunk into their souls, the Guardians were then to return to their task of governing the Ideal State under the inspiration of their newly-won knowledge.

In such a system, however, there remains one awkward problem: who is to choose the Guardians and upon what principles? And in the last resort Plato was driven to the conclusion that an Autocracy would be necessary—the rule of a Philosopher King. Even so, we are faced with another question. What would the Autocrat's philosophy be? If the philosophy of Mr. Wells, let us say, we should have a Civil Service of scientists. If of Hitler (and even National Socialism after all is based on some sort of philosophy) we should then have a Constabulary of Thugs. So once again we are compelled to enquire: Who would choose the philosopher King? To this there would seem to be no final or satisfactory solution; and Plato's fundamental distrust of human nature, and above all of the average man, thus leaves a disconcerting question mark over the whole lofty edifice of his political castle-in-the-air.

Yet we must be fair to Plato. He was not, after all, of the stuff out of which Totalitarians are made; and if his quest for human perfection led him to envisage a somewhat fantastic society, he knew all along that his Utopia was a visionary city—"never likely to exist upon earth," as he said, "but capable," as he added, "of being founded within a man's self." For indeed, though his treatise was called the Republic, constitution-building had never been its primary purpose. The State in his view was nothing more than the human personality writ large; and whatever principle makes for Justice in the state, must also, he argued, be the principle making for Righteousness in the soul. In both he distinguished three corresponding elements: in the State, first the *intelligent* rulers; second, the *"spirited"* warrior-class whose duty is to fortify the rulers' authority; and lastly, the common herd whose main preoccupation is to satisfy their *bodily* needs. To these three—in what must be considered the first genuine attempt at psychological analysis on record—Plato then compared the three human faculties or forces: Reason, Will-power, and the Desires of the Flesh. And his conclusion was this: Let the two grosser elements in either case be subordinate to the Rule of Reason, and thence will result that harmonious condition of State or of Soul which politically is termed Justice and morally Righteousness.[1] Look where you will, it would be hard to find a better definition of the moral ideal—a harmony or synthesis of all the human faculties and passions, akin to the intellectual synthesis which we call Truth; and, though the individual conscience (as we ourselves should put it), must in the first instance take its pattern from the prevailing social code, yet a conscience, thus limited, is not enough, and the true pattern, as Plato acknowledged, must be looked for elsewhere than on earth. Some of his last words on the subject are worth quoting here, even if in a greatly abbreviated form.

SOCRATES.   So these worthless and ignorant folk whose lives are given up to indulgence can never find real satisfaction. Their pleasures are impermanent and impure. They sit guzzling at table with heads down and eyes fixed on the earth, like so many cattle; and in their greediness they kick and gore each other with hooves and horns of steel, vainly seeking to fill with that which is not, the nullity of their souls.

GLAUCON.   Your account of the common herd, Socrates, would do credit to an oracle.

SOCRATES.   How then can its pleasures be anything else but ghostly imitations of genuine pleasure? For these simply take their colour from the pains with which they are bound to alternate. It is purely a matter of contrast.

GLAUCON.   Inevitably.

SOCRATES.   Then again take the type we have called the man of ardour and spirit. If he likewise neglects to *think*, and allows passion, ambition and love of success to betray him into temper and violence and spite, the result will be equally futile, will it not?

GLAUCON.   It is bound to be so.

SOCRATES.   Then we may say with confidence that the types we have spoken of can attain their maximum satisfaction, *if and only if they take knowledge and reason for guide*.

GLAUCON.   That is so.

SOCRATES.   Now, if we are agreed what difference Right and Wrong make in the matter of pleasure and pain, we will proceed, I think, by simile. We may perhaps liken the Soul to one of those fabulous monsters which combine several shapes in one; and for our first shape let us imagine a complex protean creature with a multitude of heads and capable of assuming the aspect of any animal-type wild or tame.

GLAUCON.   It would need a clever artist to model a creature like that.

SOCRATES.   Now take as well two other shapes, the one a lion and the other human. But the first creature must be larger than the lion and the lion than the human being.

GLAUCON.   An easier job for our artist.

SOCRATES.   Finally, join all three together in one to form a single whole; and let the external appearance of the combination be that of a man.

GLAUCON.   Done! . . .

[1] In Greek the same word is used for both.

146

SOCRATES.   Now, if we hold that to do the Right is in a man's own interest, this means that whether in word or deed the human element within us should have the mastery over our entire self. That element must tame and look after the many-headed monster; and it must make an ally of the lion; and finally, it must encourage both lion and monster to live at peace with each other and with itself as well.

GLAUCON.   If we hold a brief for the Right, that must follow.

SOCRATES.   So a man of sense will never commit his bodily functions to the irrational pleasures of the brute beast within him. He will not even make health his primary object, nor value strength or beauty except as aids to moral perfection. To him physical harmony will, in fact, be merely a stepping-stone to a harmony of the soul.

GLAUCON.   Yes, that is the harmony to which true musicianship must look.

SOCRATES.   And, when it comes to questions of money, there too the whole man must be in like accord. He must never be dazzled by the popular notion that wealth means happiness, nor seek to pile up limitless riches which bring limitless cares in their train.

GLAUCON.   I should think not.

SOCRATES.   No, the spiritual polity, established within him, must never be lost from view. Neither superfluity nor penury must cause disorder there; and with that goal to steer for, he will regulate, as best he may, both his saving and his expenditure.

GLAUCON.   Exactly.

SOCRATES.   So, too, with honours and office—whatever will make him a better man he will accept and nothing loth; but whatever in public or in private life may mar that inner harmony, he will have none of it.

GLAUCON.   Then he will never take a hand in politics, if that is his chief concern.

SOCRATES.   Nay, by the Dog of Egypt, in his own private polity he most certainly will, but not perhaps in his country's politics, unless Fate is uncommonly kind.

GLAUCON.   I see. You are thinking of our Ideal City, our philosophic "Utopia"; for I do not think it can exist on earth.

SOCRATES.   Perhaps, though, somewhere in Heaven its pattern is set, and whoever wishes may see it and then found it within his own self. But whether it exists or will ever exist is beside the point. For by the rules of that city alone he will live or else by none at all.

GLAUCON.   I expect you are right.

From these heights, none the less, Plato, like his own Guardians, could come down, if need be, to earth; and it stands much to his credit that even at the age of sixty he did not shrink from the challenge of applying his ideas to practical affairs. In 367 he was invited to go over to Sicily and there help to instruct a young tyrant-prince of Syracuse. He went, and he wasted much valuable time in trying to teach the young man geometry. It was not a success. He failed to convert his pupil into a "philosopher-king," and came home to Athens greatly discouraged.

On his return he devoted much thought to even deeper problems about the Universe—not the physical problems of Ionian enquiry, but metaphysical speculations about the nature of God and the Soul. Here the resources of logical thought proved ultimately inadequate; and in the attempt to express the inexpressible he fell back on allegorical myths, much as the author of the Revelations sought to describe the wonders of the Heavenly Jerusalem in terms of harps and precious stones and pavements of gold. One problem, however, baffled him. His belief in the illusory character of the material world inclined him to hold a contemptuous view of the body. Like the Pythagoreans before him, he seems to have regarded it as a clog or impediment to the spiritual growth of the soul—a doctrine which certainly influenced the mind of Augustine and which throughout the Middle Ages led to harsh ascetic practices and an unworthy shame of man's physical instincts. His philosophy, in short, contained within itself a dualism which was never resolved.

Plato's influence on posterity has been incalculable. A Roman statesman, contemplating suicide, sat all through the night over his famous dialogue on the Immortality of the Soul; and Elizabethan ladies experienced ecstasies of emotion in the study of his ideas. For he stands, so to speak, above the ages; and his hold on men's minds has lost nothing through the passage of time. In periods of perplexity when the spread of Individualism or the break-up of long-established traditions seem to threaten the world with moral anarchy, they inevitably turn back to the sturdy Platonic doctrine of the bed-rock Idealities or, following the Platonic educational model, declare salvation to lie through authoritarian inculcation of spiritual verities.

Yet in another sense Plato was essentially the product of the age in which he lived. For, if the current of life was then taking a new direction, there can be no doubt at all on which side of the water-shed he stands. He could scarcely have thought, still less published, what he did, as a member of fifth-century Athens. He belonged to something much more closely akin to our own self-conscious world with its doubts and introspection and spiritual malaise; and, even if his whole philosophy was directed to answering such doubts, the malaise was none the less real because it took the form of distrusting human nature itself. And apart from his more abstract speculations, he raised for the first time many practical problems which still puzzle mankind to-day. He questioned, as we have seen, whether woman should not be thought capable of performing the same jobs as a man "except fighting." He discussed economics and in particular their relationship to political power. He laid the foundations of psychology. Above all, he taught that for the solution of human problems character and goodwill are not in themselves enough unless accompanied by clear scientific thought. That truth the modern world is learning through its own bitter experience. And, needless to say, the world of Plato's own day did not listen. It mattered little what diatribes on Democracy he might write on what Communist Utopias he might envisage; the instinct of Individualism, once awakened, was not to be thus easily suppressed. Whatever it cost them in spiritual perplexity or social disorder, men recognized that humanity had at last come into its birthright, and posterity at least in innumerable ways was to reap the benefit. For without the vital force of individual initiative and, if need be, individual defiance of established convention and authority, the emancipation of mankind from bigotry, superstition and despotism would have been impossible. But Individualism of its very nature is an explosive and disruptive element; and, as in many subsequent epochs, so too in the epoch and country of its birth, it brought trouble in its train.

The change which was coming over fourth-century Greece took many forms, some regrettable, and some the reverse; but nowhere can the change be better observed than in the literature and art of the period. Portraiture—hitherto seldom attempted, or, if attempted, strongly idealized—now became a regular vogue; we possess some copies, at least, of works dating from this epoch, and their sculptors did not shrink from a realistic portrayal of individual traits and poses—Socrates' bulging eyes, Demosthenes' frown, or the handsome voluptuous curves of Alexander's features. In drama, too, there was a similar change. Fourth-century Comedy—mainly represented by the plays of Menander in the next generation to Plato—is very different from the Comedy of Aristophanes with its knock-about burlesque of contemporary savants or soldiers. Its life-like studies of human psychology more nearly resemble the realism of Euripides, though, needless to say, more shallow. Among the characters appear the gay young spendthrift and his fast young mistress, the unscrupulous go-between, the smart-witted slave and the stingy tyrannical father. Types, if you will, but types highly individualized and clearly differentiated one from the other.

Literature is a faithful mirror of an age, and it is evident from such plays that men and—now at last—women were beginning to live their own lives and follow their own instincts untramelled by social conventions. Boys and girls were even beginning to make love-matches, though these were not as yet what we should call highly respectable. It is scarcely too much to say that the germ, out of which the novel would one day be born, was already present in the later stages of Hellenic life. Love-poetry—and love-poetry of a very different tone from anything to be found in Sappho or other earlier writers—at length makes its tardy appearance; and it may not be amiss to close this chapter by quoting one charming little epigram written soon after the end of the fourth century B.C. For this, after all, is the way the world goes, not in the lucubrations of a philosopher's study, but in the meeting of two lovers at a street-corner on a windy night. Socrates would have approved, and Plato too, for, intellectualist though he was, he was at heart very human, and he wrote the greatest treatise on Love that has ever been written.

> Sweet melts the snow in summer on parched lips;
> and sweet for mariners long by winter pent
> to espy Spring's Blossom-Crown.[1]
> But sweet beyond compare, when one cloak wraps
> a pair of Lovers, and two true hearts chant
> Love's praise in unison.

[1] An allusion to the constellation which the Greeks called the "Garland."

CHAPTER X

THE BREAK-UP OF GREECE

The century which was now to witness the dissolution of the whole Hellenic system was not an inspiring period. The great days were over. The City State's vitality was swiftly ebbing. With one possible exception, it produced no more great leaders; and, theorists apart, this was to be an age of small men. Even the distinction between aristocrats and proletarians vanished. There were just rich and poor people, and the successful politician was the financier who could balance accounts. Democracy itself had lost its creative impulse. Plato was the sole literary genius that fourth-century Athens gave to the world. Even the brilliant improvisation of the amateur in State service was now a thing of the past. Instead, we find a society of professionals—professional politicians, professional soldiers, professional bankers, even professional pugilists. Specialization was the order of the day. The growing complexity of technical detail demanded it, and the exigencies of the struggle for existence kept every man intent on his job. He had little leisure or interest to spare for public affairs. Politics became venal. Gold, filtering in from Persia and elsewhere, proved a potent weapon of intrigue, and charges of bribery were freely bandied across the public platform. True patriotism was at a discount. Yet war for its own sake continued to make a sinister appeal. Its excitements were welcomed as a respite from humdrum toil. To mercenery and citizen-soldier alike, it brought prospect of plunder, or, if he were lucky, a prisoner to capture and sell as a slave. Even the rich were under the illusion—not confined to ancient times—that somehow or other war paid.

So the quarrelsome City States, grouped and regrouped in bewildering combinations, still continued their futile struggle for supremacy. And, as years passed, it became ever more clear that by their suicidal competition they were sealing their doom. But, apart from the certainty that sooner or later they must succumb to some external conqueror, there were no great or clear-cut issues such as had marked the course of the preceding era, no great issues, that is, save one—the eternal antagonism between the East and the West.

For the real victor of the Peloponnesian war was Persia. By diplomacy alone and without striking a blow she had recovered all that she had lost through Xerxes' débâcle nearly eighty years earlier. For, needless to say, her financial assistance which had tilted the scales in Sparta's favour, had not been given for nothing. Ionia had been the price she asked; and, when the war was won, the Spartans stood by their bond. So once again the close proximity of the Great King's Empire cast its ominous shadow across European Greece. Military aggression, it is true, was no part of his purpose. The lessons of Salamis and Platæa had been too well learnt; nor, indeed, had he the strength for such an enterprise. But Athens' Aegean supremacy had taught him that, if united, even the small Greek States might be dangerous; and he was resolved that, if he could help it, such a union should never recur. So he continued his diplomatic game of encouraging discord among them, throwing his weight now on this side, now on that, till by their interminable wars they completely exhausted their strength. It was beyond his power, of course, and indeed beyond anyone's power, to foresee that their very weakness would one day expose them to conquest by an obscure little kingdom called Macedon, and that then the tables would be fatally turned against Persia herself.

Meanwhile, after Ægospotami, whatever Ionia's fate, the control of the Aegean had passed automatically into Sparta's keeping; and, as was only to be expected, she mishandled her opportunity badly. The states, who had looked to her as a liberator, soon discovered their error. The regime established by Lysander, her victorious commander, proved infinitely more oppressive than Athens had ever imposed. The island cities were placed under Spartan governors, each with a garrison at his back, and the democracies favoured by Athens were replaced by pro-Spartan oligarchs. But, like the thirty quislings whom Lysander had set over Athens, these unpopular administrations very speedily collapsed, and the admiral's high-handed methods having proved a dangerous failure, he was recalled and deposed.

Now, however, there occurred an episode which brought about a complete *volte-face* in Sparta's foreign policy. In 401 Prince Cyrus collected his army of ten thousand mercenary Greeks and, marching up into the heart of the Persian Empire, came within an ace of winning its throne. But, though he was killed in the moment of victory, his campaign had a great and unexpected significance. The military weakness of Persia was nakedly disclosed, and the Spartan authorities were quick to see that they had made a needless as well as a mean bargain and that the re-liberation of Ionia might well be within their power. Agesilaus, the man to whom the crusade was entrusted, most certainly viewed it as such. He was more high-spirited and chivalrous than most Spartan Kings. He knew his Homer, and he appears to have pictured himself as a latter-day Agamemnon, setting forth to do battle on the Asiatic shore against the hereditary foe of his race. So successful were his tactics that at one time he threatened Sardis itself and even pushed his campaigns still deeper into the heart of the northern hill-country. The Great King grew alarmed, and after his manner undertook a diplomatic diversion. An agent, primed with fifty gold talents, was sent over to Greece with orders to stir up trouble among Sparta's neighbours at home. Thebes fell to the bait and declared war against her one-time ally. She was joined by Corinth, Argos and Athens; and soon a large "Foreign Legion"—a motley but efficient collection of Greeks hired with Persian money—was operating round the Isthmus. Sparta's whole position in Greece was thus placed in jeopardy, and Agesilaus' campaign in Ionia was promptly called off. The Great King's diplomacy had triumphed once more.

To make doubly sure, however, he resolved to drive Sparta altogether from the Aegean. He placed an Athenian soldier of fortune named Conon over a squadron of ships, half his own and half Greek; and their combined strength made short work of the Spartans in a battle off Cnidus. But the result of the victory was scarcely what the Great King had expected; for with his ill-judged permission Conon sailed some of the ships to the Piraeus; and Athens, with her fleet thus reinforced, slipped back into her old place as the leading maritime power. She even began to gather round her the nucleus of a new confederacy. The Great King again took alarm; and, again shifting sides, he lent his fleet to Sparta. Following the now familiar strategy, an attack was aimed at Athens' life-line, the Black Sea entrance. The stroke was shrewdly timed. For nearly ten years the inconclusive but devastating war had been raging round Corinth, and everyone was sick of hostilities. Overtures were made for a settlement, and in 386 the Great King achieved the crowning triumph of his subtle tactics. He summoned a congress of the warring states to meet at Sardis and the summons was answered. Never in all their history did the Greeks sink lower than when their delegates stood in the presence of the Persian satrap and humbly listened as he read them the terms dictated by his imperial master—"I Artaxerxes deem it right . . ." The terms were simple. His claim to Ionia was to be formally recognized. For the rest, all other Greek states were to be free and independent. Athens, in short, though permitted as a sop to retain three insignificant islands, was warned off from any renewal of her old maritime Imperialism. As for Sparta, on the other hand, it seems to have been tacitly understood that she might use her arms as she liked in mainland Greece. In that there was no peril to Artaxerxes it suited him well.

So at least Sparta herself interpreted the terms of the Great King's settlement. She began by bullying her smaller neighbours; then by a peculiarly treacherous coup delivered without even a declaration of war, she seized the citadel of Thebes. But here she had gone too far. Her unprovoked aggression had awoken a spirit of national resistance throughout Bœotia. A band of patriots got together; and one night, disguised as women they entered the Spartan governor's residence, where they murdered him in cold blood. The citadel was recovered and the garrison surrendered. A Spartan attempt to repeat the tactics of surprise upon the walls of Athens brought her, too, into line against the common enemy. So another miserable war began its weary course. In 371, it was interrupted by a move for conciliation. A Congress, at which a Persian envoy attended, met in Sparta; but at the last moment negotiations broke down. The Spartan King refused to sign; and within a month a Spartan army delivered against Thebes what was clearly intended to be a knock-out blow.

The battle which followed was to mark an epoch in military history. Hitherto the Greeks, for so intelligent a people, had been curiously conservative in their tactics. The pattern of battle seldom varied. Two solid formations of heavy-armed warriors, each presenting a continuous shield-line, simply charged one another front to front, and endeavoured by sheer weight of brute force to break through the opposing line. This "phalanx" formation was normally massed to the depth of eight or twelve ranks, ranged one behind the other to lend weight to the charge. But when the Thebans now met the Spartans in the neighbourhood of Leuctra, they increased the number of their ranks on one wing to fifty—a weight of impact against which not even the "invincible" Spartans could long stand. After a tremendous tussle they broke.

Her unexpected victory brought Thebes at one stride into the forefront of the Greek world. Her commander, Epaminondas, was not merely a military genius, but a statesman and man of culture as well, and he was determined that the hideous menace of Spartan supremacy must be ended. Three times he invaded the Peloponnese, even marching into Spartan territory itself. His main objective, however, was to build up a league among Sparta's nearest neighbours the Arcadians, and so form them into a counterpoise to her military strength. As capital of the League he founded Megalopolis—the "Great City" mentioned above. But some of the League members proved fickle allies, and a fourth expedition was called for. So once again, near the Arcadian town of Mantinea, Epaminondas found himself face to face with the full Spartan host. As at Leuctra, his handling of the massed phalanx succeeded; but in the very hour of his victory he himself was mortally wounded. With his death the whole impetus of the Theban effort collapsed. Sparta, it is true, never again recovered her old predominance. Her man-power was dwindling, and her military prestige broken. But such a result had been bought at a high price. Greece's powers of resistance had been fatally weakened, and this at the very time when those powers would be sorely needed.

Meanwhile Sparta's preoccupation had at least left Athens free to develop her revived maritime supremacy. Despite the Great King's peace terms, though indeed without strictly violating them, she had drawn under her protection a number of island-states as well as some mainland cities in the North-West Aegean. A fresh Confederacy had been formed— this time on much more equitable and liberal lines. As in the original Delian League, representatives sent by its members assembled in regular conference; and instead of the detested tribute a voluntary contribution was levied. This spontaneous, though limited movement towards Pan-Hellenic Union was perhaps the one bright spot in the whole confused and gloomy outlook.

No feature in fourth-century history is more astonishing than the rapidity with which Athens recovered her trade. To this, no doubt, several circumstances contributed. The Spartans were not a commercial people, so could not seize the opening. Corinth, Athens' likeliest rival, suffered severely by the devastating war stirred up by the Great King's agent, and at one time her ports were captured. But beyond this Athens' knowledge and experience was her greatest standby. It was not for nothing that for the best part of a century the carrying-trade of the middle seas had been largely under her control and direction, and the benefits of such control must by now have become almost indispensable to others besides herself. True, gold—brought from the East, the Black Sea and the Northern Aegean—was beginning to replace her silver currency; but she, too, had taken to issuing gold coins, minted in the first instance from the ornaments of her temples. The whole financial technique of commerce, moreover, was further developed by the introduction of banking. Money-changers, who sat at their tables in the Athenian market, had begun to advance loans to merchants and ship masters. Such trans-actions could only be made for voyages to or from Athens; but in days when seafaring was still hazardous, it was an immense stimulus to trade; for the bankers would insure vessels or cargoes by the method of advanc-ing a loan, on the security of either. If the vessel went down, the lender suffered a total loss. High rates of interest were charged, often amounting to 30 per cent. and the money was collected within three weeks of the termination of the voyage.

This highly lucrative business was almost exclusively in the hands of resident aliens. The most famous of all bankers, Pasion by name, was by origin a slave. In general, they held a high reputation; but smaller money-lenders, imitating the big firms' methods on a more modest scale, got themselves a bad name. An entertaining description of one such usurer has come down to us. "There I found a wrinkled old man, with a scowl on his face and a musty moth-eaten document in his hand. He addressed me in an offhand manner as though it were all waste of his time. My letter of introduction said I wanted a loan; but he began to talk in sums far beyond my ideas, and when I expressed surprise, he spat with marked irritation. I got my money all the same, at a high rate of interest, of course. What a plague these people are with their counters and crooked fingers! Heaven preserve me from setting eyes on a usurer or a wolf!"

Large fortunes were undoubtedly made by both traders and bankers. Pasion died leaving a fortune, which in our days would be worth at least £100,000. One orator remarked on the sad change from the good old days when public buildings alone had attracted the eye. Now, while his poorer neighbours next door might be half-starving, the rich man would live in a sumptuous mansion, furnished with rugs and tapestries from the East, and adorned with sculptures and paintings.

At the same time Democracy saw to it that men paid heavily for the privilege of financial success. In a dozen ways, some in theory at least voluntary, but many compulsory, a man of substance was called on to put his hand very deep in his pocket. Here is a list of public services rendered, taken from the speech of a certain litigant who boasted of them in court. He had financed a comedy and several tragedies, a boys' chorus and a men's chorus (for which he won the prize), a sword-dance display and a naval race in the regatta; for seven years he had spent large sums on the upkeep and outfit of warships; twice he had paid the war-tax or capital levy, besides a great deal expended on "sacred missions and pro-cessions." It was perhaps natural that one writer of the day declared that "to be rich is more dangerous than to break the law; no wonder men try to conceal the size of their fortune."

By such exactions, of course, the poorer citizens to a large extent benefited. The gratuity for attending the theatre was more highly prized than ever, and even when the Theoric Fund, out of which it came, should in prudence have been devoted to military needs, the Assembly would not hear of the suggestion. During the century, too, fresh pensions were instituted for persons incapacitated by old age, accident or disease.

Among the rich there was much outcry about their burdens. Listen to the philosopher Aristotle: "Men's vice is insatiable. At first the dole is enough; then, when they get used to it, they ask for more, and so on *ad infinitum*. Such pauperization is like trying to fill a jug with a hole in the bottom." If this appears a somewhat partisan statement, the fact remains that Athenian finances were in a poor way. Since the loss of the tribute gathered from the subject-states, the public income had dropped, on an average, by one-half at the very least, and in some periods by considerably more. Yet the cost of living measured by the price of corn had very nearly doubled. Little wonder that the State was always on the verge of bankruptcy. About the middle of the century a statesmanlike Minister named Eubulus did something to restore financial soundness; but for all that the city was in no position to fight a war of even modest dimensions. She was compelled to hire mercenaries (for the man in the street, if conscripted, could no longer compete with the highly-trained professionals of the day); but as often as not, when she had hired them, she could not find money to pay them. Such a condition of things does much to account for the Athenians' impotence and lethargy even at a time when, as we shall presently see, their very existence was at stake.

From what we have shown of the considered views of Plato and others, it is clear that in their opinion the only remedy for this state of things lay in constitutional change. Democracy was out of favour with the few who cared to think; and like Plato, some of these were beginning to turn to the alternative of the Autocrat—a strange conclusion, you may say, for freedom-loving Greeks to arrive at; but practical experience seemed to them to corroborate their theory. In the world around them they could point to more than one highly successful monarchy. There had been Dionysius of Syracuse, for instance, the father of Plato's young pupil. This man had saved Sicily when threatened with utter catastrophe from Carthaginian invasion. He had built up a strong army, kept a fine court, patronized poets and philosophers, and he even wrote tragedies himself. A still more successful prince was Evagoras of Cyprus. He too had similarly saved his island from absorption by Persia; and he governed it so well, promulgating such sound laws and lending such encouragement to literature and art that Isocrates, an Athenian professor, wrote him a highly eulogistic biography. Times were changing indeed. To the political pamphleteer it was no doubt refreshing to turn from the drab incompetence of fourth-century Democracy to the brilliant efficiency of these autocrats; and the time was not far distant when this same Isocrates would hail as the potential saviour of Greece a semi-barbarian aggressor from Macedon. It did more credit to his foresight perhaps that he further regarded submission to Macedon as a necessary prelude to a Pan-Hellenic crusade against Persia. None the less, it would have been a sad end to the Hellas we have known, had not even at the eleventh hour a manlier view prevailed, and a final, though unsuccessful stand been made in defence of her liberty.

CHAPTER XI

MACEDON AND PERSIA

1. PHILIP

North of Thessaly, and in the hinterland of the three-pronged Chalcidic peninsula, lay Macedonia. It was a rough mountainous country, and to the Greeks its inhabitants seemed little better than barbarians. They were a wild folk, habitually carrying arms, much occupied in clan-feuds and vendettas, and great drinkers, with a most un-Greek habit of taking their liquor neat. Their monarchs, however, made some pretensions to culture. They had learnt much from their more civilized neighbours of the south; and Euripides was not the only learned visitor to find a welcome at their court. Towards the Greek communities on their border their attitude had varied between friendly intercourse and occasional hostility; but now the relationship was to take a more sinister turn.

In 359 the Macedonian crown passed to a young man of three-and-twenty named Philip—a maker of history, if ever there was one. In boyhood he had spent three years in Thebes as a hostage. There he had seen something of the disunion and weakness of Greece, and he meant to profit by it. His first step was to create a strong national army, so he set to work to discipline his rough clansmen. Experience was gained in conquering the hill-country westwards to the Adriatic, and its highlanders, too, he drafted into his army. During his stay at Thebes he had had opportunity to study Epaminondas' tactical innovations; and now in training his own troops he adopted the new-model phalanx, rendering its spear-front even more formidable by giving longer lances to the rear ranks. A cavalry corps he found already in existence; it was drawn from the aristocracy and known as the "Companions." Under his leadership it became the best in the world.

Philip's intentions were obvious. He meant to make his country a first-rate Power. But a first-rate Power needs a port; and between Macedon and the sea lay a line of Greek cities, dotting the Chalchidic peninsula and the adjacent coasts. Of these the more prominent were Pydna, Potidæa, Amphipolis, and above all Olynthus. Some were dependencies of Athens; and, as the leading Aegean Power, she was bound to take interest in all. Nevertheless, Philip meant to have his way. He first seized Amphipolis for the sake of its gold-mines, a valuable asset in financing his army. Then he took Pydna, which gave him a port. Meanwhile he cast dust in the eyes of Athens, promising to relinquish this city or exchange that— promises which, once her protests died down, he conveniently forgot.

But this was only a beginning. Philip meant to conquer all Greece; and, once set on a project, he was not the man to draw back. His character was a curious blend of barbaric toughness and fine intelligence. He admired Greek culture, and he had a soft place in his heart for Athens. He even engaged the philosopher Aristotle to tutor his son. But he would stick at nothing in achieving his goal. In the course of his wars he had "an eye put out, a shoulder broken, an arm and a leg rotted away"; but he counted all these well lost. Historical parallels are admittedly dangerous, but Philip's resemblance to Hitler leaps to the eye. In diplomacy he was a complete opportunist, breaking pacts and duping ambassadors without shame. He kept paid agents in whatever country he coveted. "Pass me a mule's load of silver through the gates," he boasted, "and I will take any town." He struck, when he did strike, with lightning rapidity. But, unlike Hitler, he possessed inexhaustible patience. He would spread his tentacles southward till serious opposition was met; then would switch his attention elsewhere and wait sometimes for years till suspicion died down. Above all, he desired that the Greeks should themselves accept him as their champion—but champion against what? He needed some bogey to use much as Hitler used Bolshevism. The Persian menace was too remote. He wanted something nearer home; and Fate supplied his want.

In 356 a startling event occurred. A band of Phocian marauders, dwelling in the mountains west of Bœotia, swooped suddenly on Delphi and made themselves masters of the shrine. Greece was aghast at the sacrilege, and there was something else besides piety in the outcry. As with the fear of Communism in our own day, so then material interests reinforced men's religious alarms. At Delphi, as we have mentioned, there was a vast accumulation of treasure. Most Greek states kept there a store of silver and golden vessels, a legacy from past benefactions and employed on occasion to swell the pageantry at Apollo's festival. This treasure was now at the Phocians' disposal, and they used it to hire mercenaries. Very soon they became the terror of their neighbours; and in 353 a Thessalian town thus threatened, appealed for Philip's protection.

Here then was his chance to act the champion against the enemies of Greece; and he lost no time in marching his army down. The Phocian resistance was stout, but eventually he forced his way southward through Thessaly and made for the key-pass of Thermopylæ. Here lay the road, not to Phocis alone, but to Bœotia and Thebes, and beyond them to

Attica itself. Little wonder that the news startled the Athenians. For once they threw off their complacency and decided on action. So, when Philip reached Thermopylæ, he found the way barred by their army. The last thing he wanted at this stage was a collision with Athens. So he tactfully withdrew.

The Athenians sank back into lethargy. Resistance to Macedon was by no means a popular cry. It found one spokesman, however, in the orator Demosthenes. He was a grim, pessimistic character, embittered by an unhappy boyhood and political frustration, and hardly a real leader. Nor did he at this date hold any official position. The technicalities of warfare were now beyond the scope of amateur strategists, and the direction of campaigns was left to hired professional captains. All Demosthenes could do was to agitate; and in season or out he reiterated his warning, pouring forth appeal or invective with passionate earnestness in hard, dry, well-reasoned periods—the classical model of patriotic oratory.[1] He even toured other cities in the attempt to rouse public opinion. It was a brave stand; but nobody listened. The old spirit of self-sacrifice and pugnacity was dead, and even had Demosthenes been twice the man he was, it was now too late to save Athens or Greece.

For three years after his rebuff Philip lay low; and, when next he struck, it was at Olynthus, the leading Greek town on his border. Treachery hastened its capture; and to the universal dismay he sold its inhabitants into slavery. Olynthus was Athens' ally, but she had been painfully slow to act; and even when on Demosthenes' plea an expedition had been sent, it was turned back by storms. Now there was no alternative but to swallow her humiliation and reach, if possible, some understanding with Philip. So a deputation of ten—Demosthenes among them—was sent to Macedon on a mission of appeasement. Philip flattered them. He assured them that all should be settled; even against Phocis, he declared, he harboured no evil designs; but he would swear no oath to a treaty. Presently he moved south, taking with him the dupes of his procrastination. On reaching lower Thessaly he sent them home, still protesting that all would be well. But barely had the envoys arrived back in Athens when news came that a Phocian traitor had sold the pass of Thermopylæ, that Philip had slipped through, entered Phocis and razed all its towns to the ground.

The Athenians were horror-struck. But the rest of Greece applauded the restoration of Delphi to its priests and the punishment of the sacrilegious marauders. The Arcadians set up a statue to Philip's honour. Argos voted him a golden crown. He was complimented by the

[1] The younger Pitt always studied Demosthenes when about to address the House.

Amphictyonic Council, an ancient body recently revived by states adjacent to Delphi. What must have pleased him still more, he was even invited to become a member of the Council, and a few months later to preside over the celebration of Pythian Games.

Philip was now within striking distance of Athens. But he held his hand. He still had hopes that she might become his willing vassal; and he was already forming projects in which the co-operation of her fleet might prove invaluable. For, once Greece were his, Philip meant to lead a Pan-Hellenic crusade against Persia. The idea was not new. The trail had long ago been blazed by the Ten Thousand Greeks who had marched with Prince Cyrus. Agesilaus' crusade for the recovery of Ionia had followed; and at this very moment Isocrates was urging its resumption. During the next six years, therefore, Philip pushed his campaigns along the Thracian coast towards the Dardanelles, and attacked, though un-successfully, the key-fortress of Byzantium. The road for his projected invasion of the East was thus being prepared.

In 339 he returned to the affairs of Greece. And now with a short-sightedness that baffles belief, the Amphictyonic Council played straight into his hands. A trifling border-dispute had arisen near Delphi and they summoned their recent champion to settle it. Once on the spot, Philip threw off pretences. In the spring of 338 news reached Athens that he was moving on Thebes. Amid scenes of panic desperate efforts were made to put the city on a war footing. At the eleventh hour even the Theoric Fund was converted into a military chest. Old quarrels with Thebes were forgotten, and the Athenian army was rushed to her assistance. Demosthenes, now the hero of the hour, marched in its ranks.

Near Chæronea the decisive battle was fought. Philip won; and Greece lay at his feet. He posted garrisons in key-towns, then called a Congress at Corinth and dictated his terms. They were generous. The various states, though permitted a local autonomy, were to be organized in a League over which Philip, of course, would be master. So Greek liberty was dead. Yet next year, when Philip announced his plan for the invasion of Persia, the League Council received it with enthusiasm, and arrangements were made to provide a Pan-Hellenic army and fleet. Not many months later, as the result of a family quarrel, Philip was murdered, probably by an agent of his own wife. His young son Alexander reigned in his stead.

2. ALEXANDER

Alexander at twenty was everything a Greek would admire—strikingly handsome, athletic enough to have entered for Olympia had he cared to train, a great huntsman and a rider who had never known a horse he could not master. His intellectual gifts were exceptional and he had been educated by the wisest man in the world. He had imagination, too. He was a great lover of Homer, and slept always with an Iliad by his bed. But chief of all his qualities was his personal magnetism; he was the sort of leader that men will follow anywhere—the ideal captain, in short, for the great adventure to which, in accordance with his father's intentions, he meant to lead the Greek world.

Yet at the outset the Greek world remained sulky and restive. Twice there were risings—once during the first weeks of his reign, and then again when his death was rumoured during a campaign against some tribes in the north. On the second occasion he made Thebes an example and destroyed the town utterly. After that there were no more revolts. Though lukewarm at first, enthusiasm for his eastern campaign grew with its mounting success; and finally he was accepted as a national hero. It is not without significance that in contemporary portraiture sculptors affected a type which reflected the young man's well-modelled features.

When in the spring of 334 Alexander crossed the Dardanelles he probably envisaged little more than the conquest of Asia Minor. But in the battle fought nearby at the Granicus River he won a crushing victory over the Persian advance-guard, and this may well have decided him to strike at the heart of the empire itself. For such an undertaking his forces seemed small, not more than forty thousand at most, part Greek and part Macedonian. Yet it was no madcap venture. Apart from a few picked corps and a body of Greek mercenaries the Great King had no first-rate troops. His oriental levies, though inexhaustible in number, were of poor quality. Darius himself was no leader. His satraps were unreliable; and, given a swift blow at its vitals, the unwieldly Empire was ready to fall in pieces.

Alexander moved deviously on through Asia Minor, freeing the Greek cities as he went. At its eastern limits the main Persian army was awaiting him; and in the coastal plain near Issus a stubborn battle was fought. But the staunchness of the phalanx and the impetuous charge of the "Companions" carried the day. Darius fled; but Alexander did not pursue him. Before advancing further, he meant to secure his southern flank. So he marched down through Syria, captured by seige the Phœnician naval base at Tyre, and then passed on to Egypt, where he was hailed as a deliverer. While wintering in the Nile valley, he chose the site for a new commercial centre to take the place of Tyre. His choice was good; Alexandria, as it was to be called, occupied a highly favourable position for linking the trade, not merely of Mesopotamia and the Mediterranean, but, when these too were opened up, of India and the Far East. Yet what would be its chief role in history, not even its founder can dimly have guessed. As a result of his conquests, the world's centre of gravity was shifting—culturally no less than economically; and in the not distant future, Alexandria was to replace the cities of the Aegean basin as the focus of Greek intellectual and artistic life. Thus, unknown to himself, the major part of Alexander's work was already accomplished.

In 331 the eastward march was resumed. Mesopotamia was crossed, and near Arbela on the upper Tigris, Darius was again brought to battle, and this time decisively. With him was now a vast array of tribal levies drawn from all parts of his empire; and in the open plain Alexander's inferior numbers were under a handicap. But the old tactics of phalanx and cavalry again carried the day. Darius escaped, later to be murdered by his own followers; and meanwhile Babylon, Susa, and the old Persian capital Persepolis passed in quick succession into Alexander's hands.

Common prudence would have dictated a pause and the consolidation of territories won. But Alexander's appetite had been whetted, and there was no stopping him. At Persepolis and Susa vast treasure had been taken. He could afford to send home such of his Greek volunteers as wished it. Those who remained, together with his own Macedonians and some native recruits whom he now drafted in, could be kept indefinitely on the proceeds of the loot. Thus his army was no longer representative of any truly national cause. It owed allegiance to its master alone—the ready instrument of his will or his whim. And by this time, indeed, Alexander was becoming a despot in more than name. Power had gone to his head. He took to oriental habits of pomp and luxury, wore Persian robes and tiara, and ordered even his European subjects to prostrate themselves in his presence. And, like a second Cyrus or Darius, he began to covet conquest for conquest's own sake.

So in 329 he pushed his march eastwards again into the furthest dependencies of the crumbling empire. First he threaded his way up through Afghanistan and overran the provinces of Bactria and Sogdiana, staying a while at Samarcand, the capital of the latter, to marry Roxana, a princess of noted beauty. Then, turning south again through the passes of the Hindu Kush, he penetrated the Punjaub. As befitted a pupil of Aristotle, his scientific interests were strong, and exploration was no doubt in part his motive. Ancient ideas of geography were crude, and very likely he imagined he was approaching the extreme limits of the Eastern world. But after crossing the Indus his troops refused to go further, and Alexander had no choice but to lead them back, suffering terribly from thirst and heat, along the shores of the Indian Ocean.

Once back in Babylon, he began preparations for the conquest of Arabia; and, while these were in progress, he turned to the somewhat neglected task of organizing his empire. His practice had been, where practicable, to maintain the existing administrative machinery, leaving Greek cities, for instance, to govern themselves and satraps to rule their old provinces. Some readjustment, among the satraps especially, was needed. But beyond this it was clearly Alexander's ideal to fuse, so far as possible, the East and the West. His European soldiers were ordered to marry native wives; and meanwhile the Hellenization of Asia was already proceeding apace. Towns on the Greek model had been planted along the routes of his march. Seventy-five such foundations are known to have existed, some as far east as Samarcand. The more distant soon decayed and disappeared; but others remained, like Alexandria, to become flourishing centres of Hellenic culture. Greeks from Europe, attracted by the prospect of trade, poured out to inhabit them, and the civilization which they brought with them was to work, like a disturbing leaven, on the drowsy conservatism of the East.

Alexander's fame was now spreading wide, and during his two year's stay at Babylon, ambassadors eager to stand well with the new conqueror, arrived from all quarters of the West—from Ethiopia, Carthage and Italy, and even from the chieftains of Gaul and Spain. So he had much work on hand, and the strain on him began to tell. A fever, caught on campaign, had already undermined his constitution, and oriental habits of self-indulgence were getting the better of him. He was drinking heavily. One morning, after a banquet held to celebrate his impending departure for Arabia, he awoke on the verge of delirium. He lingered for some days, but never really rallied. He was still in the prime of life, and never perhaps in all human history did a single man's death send so great a shock through the world.

3. THE SUCCESSORS

Without Alexander's leadership men felt bewildered and helpless. He had left no instructions about the disposal of his Empire. His only son, born by Roxana after his death, was never even considered; and his generals and viceroys divided the territory among themselves. There was much quarrelling and some fighting, and frontiers remained fluid. But the broad lines of the division were these. Macedon and Greece went to Antipater, son of Alexander's viceroy in Europe. Asia Minor and the bulk of the old Persian Empire went to Seleucus and his successors the Seleucids. Ptolemy, the Governor of Egypt, continued to hold it, and similarly passed it down to his line. So things remained in unstable equilibrium until Rome appeared on the scene and one after another made the three dominions her own.

In Greece true political independence was dead. The ruler of Macedon watched her states jealously, ready to intervene. Locally, however, a shadow of liberty remained. Athens, though losing much of her trade, survived as a centre of learning, to which in Roman days young men still flocked for their University training. In the rest of the country two leagues were formed: one, the Ætolian League, composed mainly of states north of the Isthmus; the other, the Achæan League, in the Peloponnese. These experiments in federalism were remarkably successful; and thus, when it was already too late, the quarrelsome Greeks achieved some measure of unity. It is easier for even animals to live at peace when once their claws are drawn.

The Seleucid monarchs were not long able to maintain their Empire intact. Its more easterly provinces fell away, and Asia Minor too was lost. The capital from which the remainder of their realm was governed, was situated at Antioch—near the head of the Syrian coast—an enormous city built with every refinement of Greek architectural skill, and rich in every luxury the East could provide. Its rulers were staunch upholders of Hellenism; but with one of them, Antiochus Epiphanes, it became a positive craze. Early in the second century B.C. he tried to impose it on his Jewish subjects by force. In the Temple precinct at Jerusalem he set up a statue of Olympian Zeus—the "abomination of desolation spoken of by Daniel the prophet"; and during a lengthy but fruitless campaign against the Maccabean guerillas he also destroyed Jehovah's shrine at Samaria. Despite Antiochus' failure, Hellenic culture slowly crept into the life of the exclusive Hebrews. By the time of Christ a Greek gymnasium and theatre existed in Jerusalem. Greek dress became the fashion, and most inhabitants of Palestine could speak Greek in a debased colloquial form—the language of the Gospels. Even the rigorous application of the Mosaic Law began to be tempered by the rational outlook which Hellenism inevitably bred.

But Antioch was outshone by Alexandria. Far more than the Seleucids the Ptolemies of Egypt were genuine enthusiasts for literature and the arts, and this great waterside city was a monument of all that was best which could be salved from the wreck of Greek civilization. Nothing like it had ever been seen in the world before. It measured ten miles in circumference. Its streets were laid out in the approved rectangular pattern with a main parade a hundred yards broad. A mole had been built under Alexander's orders linking the city with the island of Pharos and its famous lighthouse; and on either side of the mole was a spacious roadstead. Within the walls stood a magnificent group of buildings—a Hall of Justice, government offices, warehouses, and so forth. Outside lay a Hippodrome and Stadium. A canal brought water from the Nile, which was distributed by conduits to cisterns in private houses.

By the beginning of the Christian era the population of Alexandria stood at a million. Every race in the world was represented, each with its separate quarters. Among them was a large Jewish colony, whose scholars produced the Greek version of the Old Testament, known as the "Septuagint" or "Work of the Seventy." The city swarmed with Greeks, traders and bankers, artists and architects, students and scientists. From them were drawn the administrative officials who superintended building, public health, and other municipal services. In the Law Courts a Greek code was followed and adapted, as time went on, to meet the needs of non-Greek residents. There was, however, no Town Council. The ruling Ptolemy—after the manner of Egypt—was absolute monarch.

Ptolemy the First was a man of great enlightenment, and it was mainly due to his efforts that Alexandria became the new home of learning. He built the famous Museum or Hall of the Muses, where a great company of scholars and scientists worked in collaboration at the royal expense. Nearby was the great Library containing at one time some half a million papyrus-rolls. Here scribes were employed to copy out classical master-pieces; critics annotated them and divided them into books and chapters. Others compiled dictionaries and grammars. Thus Alexandria became, as she was long to remain, the intellectual centre of the Mediterranean world.

Enough has been said to show how Hellenism flourished in the new soil where Alexander's conquests had planted it. In all history it would be difficult to find any single event which had done so much to revolutionize the outlook of so large a number of the human race. This is not to say that Jewish peasants and the cosmopolitan loafers by the Alexandria quayside all became scholars and philosophers. But that the more educated classes were deeply influenced is certain. Herod the Great was an ardent Philhellene. The priestly caste at Jerusalem adopted a wholly new attitude towards the interpretation of their scriptures. Even the man in the street must have assimilated something from his familiarity with Greek customs, with Greek legal and political methods, and, above all, with the Greek language. When Jesus spoke of the Pharisees as "hypocrites" or "actors" [1] his hearers cannot have failed to interpret the word in terms of the theatrical performances which the Pharisees themselves so greatly abhorred.

[1] Jesus almost certainly spoke Greek as well as Aramaic; and it is at least possible that he did so on this particular occasion.

Thus from the valley of the Nile and the Syrian hinterland to Greece, Sicily and Southern Italy, there was now a more or less homogeneous culture. When all these countries presently passed under the rule of Rome, that fact not merely helped to facilitate the task of imperial administration; it was also to exercise a growing influence on the mind and character of the Romans themselves. Not least did it affect the spread of the Christian Faith. For St. Paul and other missionaries could never have accomplished their task, had they not been moving in a world which spoke the same language and in some degree thought the same thoughts. More important still, it meant very much that, when later the great theological controversies were raised, the terminology of Greek philosophy was available for the use of the early Christians, and they were thus able to formulate in clear and precise terms the doctrines of the Church. A strange sequel indeed to the ambitions of an impetuous young man, who liked to think that he was treading in the footsteps of his hero Achilles, and waging, as it were, a second Trojan war against the hereditary foe of the West.

CHAPTER XII

HELLENISTIC CULTURE

With the Hellenistic [1] Period we are leaving Greece in more than a literal sense behind us; and historically as well as geographically the scene now shifts and expands. For the passing of the independent City State marked the close of an epoch; and in the wake of Alexander's conquests the Greeks found themselves launched upon a new and larger world. There, politically and economically, problems were awaiting them which concerned not diminutive valleys occupied by a handful of men, but vast and populous continents; and the solution of those problems lies beyond the scope of this book. For it belongs rather to a new phase of human history which merged almost imperceptibly into the era of Roman Imperialism.

Culturally, on the other hand, there was no such break. The old classical spirit received a new lease of life, and its tradition not merely survived; it was very sedulously nursed. Hellenistic authors and artists worked, as one might say, self-consciously looking back over their shoulder at the past. Poets could still shape language into lovely patterns and express delicate shades of mood or fancy. But the old sublimity and profundity were gone. Sceptical habits, engendered during the period of the Greek decline, had checked the spontaneous flow of the imagination. Literary criticism was a more characteristic feature of the age than literary creation. More still was men's intellectual energy concentrated on the abstract sciences. Brilliant discoveries were made in mathematics, mechanics, biology and astronomy. Some found an application to practical uses, but only to a very limited degree. Their final importance lay less in ancient than in modern times, for they were ultimately to form the starting-point for our own scientific research.

Any account of Hellenistic thought must inevitably begin with the work of a man who belonged not to the transplanted civilization of Alexandria or Antioch, but to the decaying civilization of European Greece—Aristotle. He was of Ionian stock, but born at Stagira on the borders of Macedon. He moved early to Athens, and there became a pupil in Plato's Academy. Thus, as he rose to the height of his amazing

---

[1] "Hellenistic" is the term applied to the period during which after the collapse of Greek political independence, the centre of Greek civilization shifted eastwards.

genius, it was his task to continue and to develop the philosophic tradition which Plato had founded. But the new trend he gave to it was of immense significance. Plato, as we have seen, had been drawn by his theory of the Idealities into a Dualistic view of the Universe. For according to him there exist two worlds—the world of permanent reality perceptible only by the eye of the soul, and the world of physical phenomena, illusory, impermanent, perceptible only by the senses. The gulf thus lying between the two Aristotle set himself to bridge. According to his view all "forms" of existence derive their permanence from the operation of Mind. Thus a cat *is* a cat, because Mind, distinguishing in it certain physical characteristics, differentiates the "cat" form or "cat" type from all other types of animal. Ultimately it is the Mind of God—the prime cause of all things, the "unmoved mover"—which has so organized the Universe out of chaos. But the principles of differentiation and causation, which have made the world what it is, are no longer something *outside* it like the transcendant Idealities of Plato; they are *inherent* in material things as perceived by Mind. From this it follows that man's reason and observation can discover what those principles are. So Aristotle undertook with exemplary thoroughness to explore the entire realm of human and animal life, discriminating, defining and systematizing the various types of character, of behaviour or of physical attributes which he found in them.

The treatises which he wrote—summaries in the first instance of lectures to be delivered to pupils—covered an incredibly wide field. They dealt with Logic, Metaphysics, Physics, Biology, Rhetoric and Poetry, Ethics and Political Theory. In all these his principal purpose was the formulation of accurate and scientific definitions. Thus in his "Ethics" he defined the various virtues as a mean between two extremes; the right use of wealth, for example, as lying midway between stinginess and prodigality—an interesting rationalization of the old Greek doctrine of the Golden Mean. In his treatise on Poetry he laid it down that the function of Tragedy is to "purge" the soul by an experience of "pity and terror"—a purgation productive of the calm elation which results from witnessing such a play as, say, "Othello" or "Hamlet."

At first Aristotle's methods were rather those of a logician than of a scientific observer. He would argue that things must be so because *reason* required that they should be. Thus, finding that the hypothesis of four elements—Earth, Air, Fire and Water—did not account for the "circular" movement of heavenly bodies (since Air and Fire only move upwards and Earth and Water downwards), he proceeded to postulate the existence of a fifth element, Ether, which, possessing itself a rotatory motion, carries the heavenly bodies along with it.

Later in life, however, Aristotle progressed—especially in biology—to a more scientific technique. He was now the Director of the Lyceum, a rival school to the Platonic Academy, and here his studies were aided by a large band of collaborators. Careful observations of animal life were made and the results tabulated—the habits of fish, varieties of insects, and so forth. Animals were classified—those, for example, which contained blood and those which did not, those that breathed air and those that breathed water. One member of the school wrote a treatise on botany. To give more than a hint of Aristotle's encyclopædic research is here impossible. It was to exercise a vast influence on posterity; and though without the aid of microscope or telescope its conclusions were often superficial and even fallacious, it gave a vital impetus to further enquiry more especial from the Renaissance onwards.

After Aristotle's day interest in science waned at Athens, but it was reborn in Alexandria. There under the patronage of the Ptolemies it flourished exceedingly. Attached to the Museum was an Observatory, a zoo and a botanical garden. In these a large staff of scientists and students carried on their work at the royal expense—a classical example of what subsidized research can achieve. It is not unlikely, too, that the practical bias of the native Egypt had some influence. The earliest Greek thinkers, as we saw, were ready enough to learn from foreigners. But since Thales' day a more exclusive habit of mind had set in, and with it a tendency towards abstract speculation very much divorced from real life. In the less rarified atmosphere of the Near East the Hellenistic thinkers were more willing to come down to earth, and some of their discoveries were even put to a technical use. Thus in mechanics a certain Heron invented an automatic device which opened and shut the doors of a temple by steam-power; and Archimedes of Syracuse, who also at one time studied in Alexandria, constructed a spiral pump for drawing water up from the Nile.

Far more important, however, was the advance made in medicine. Greece had always been famous for her doctors, one of whom, Herodotus tells, had been carried captive to Persia, and there cured King Darius of a dislocated ankle which had baffled the court-physicians. Most notable of all had been Hippocrates, the "father of medicine," who late in the fifth century had founded a school on the island of Cos. In this school the symptoms of various diseases had been closely observed—epilepsy, tapeworm, and what was probably typhoid among them. Hippocrates' general doctrine was to dominate the medical world, not merely of his own day, but for many succeeding ages. Taking the current theory of the four elements—Fire, Air, Water and Earth—he declared that all illness results from an excess or deficiency of one of the four which he renamed Hot and Cold, Wet and Dry. The curative process should therefore consist in restoring the natural harmony of the body, by a hot diet if there were a deficiency of one element, or by blood-letting if there were an excess of another. As late as the seventeenth century A.D. this doctrine still held the field, and even to-day its influence is not wholly extinct.

First-aid on the battlefield. (From a vase-painting of a mythological scene.)

It was among the chief tasks of Alexandrian scientists to collect the writings and apply the theories of the Hippocratic school; but in one respect they were even able to make an advance on these. Post-mortem dissection of the human body had been impossible in Greece, where the dead were invariably burned; and hence the knowledge of the internal organs had remained rudimentary. In Egypt, where the dead were mummified, there was no such religious obstacle to dissection. Indeed, there is a tradition that Alexandrian doctors were allowed to practise vivisection on condemned criminals; and, although it is probably false, the tale none the less shows they were interested in the workings of the living organism. Be that as it may, anatomical research certainly went forward and valuable work was done. Alexandria long remained the leading medical centre of the Mediterranean world; and under the Roman Empire its great pundit Galen was accounted the chief authority in antiquity.

But the practical value of Hellenistic science must not be overrated. Greek intellectuals had a deep-rooted contempt for manual labour—a heritage, no doubt, of the aristocratic epoch. Mankind, in their view, was divided into workers and thinkers; and for the thinkers knowledge was something to be pursued for its own sake not for any ulterior end.

A young doctor operates on a working-man's arm. (From a vase-painting.)

So the work done in Ptolemy's Museum was mostly of this abstract character, and very brilliant work it was. We need only think of the geometry of Euclid (c. 290 B.C.) or of his younger contemporary Aristarchus, the astronomer, who anticipated Copernicus' famous discovery by announcing that "the sun remains unmoved and the earth revolves about it in the circumference of a circle." This startling approximation to the truth seems, however, to have made little permanent impression on Aristarchus' contemporaries or successors. By the end of the third century, indeed, Alexandrian science had seen its best days. But work continued. It received a grievous setback when during Julius Cæsar's Egyptian campaign a part of the great library of books was burnt; yet still the Museum struggled on, and from start to finish its remarkable career covered a period of six hundred years.

The scientific pre-eminence of the Alexandrian school is apt to overshadow its literary achievements. Yet the Hellenistic writers were far from negligible. Much of their energy went, it is true, into a pedantic study and slavish imitation of the classical masterpieces. But some names stand out without which no list of Greek poets would be complete. There was Callimachus, for example, at one time keeper of the Ptolemaic library, and the author of the poem best known by Cory's translation, "They told me, Heraclitus, they told me you were dead." Far greater was Theocritus, the parent of pastoral poetry, an "escapist" as we should call him nowadays, whose imagination, dwelling on the happy scenes of simple rustic life, conjured up a fanciful picture of an idealized Arcadia where shepherds piped beside murmurous mountain rills and love-sick swains neglected their flocks to tell the story of their passion or die of broken hearts. Such fantasies were a strange departure from the directness and sincerity of fifth-century poetry; and stranger still they were couched in the archaic medium of the Homeric hexameter. Yet for sheer artistry Theocritus' idylls are inimitable, melancholy and gay by turns, yet always filled with a haunting, wistful music. Not that they have had no imitators. The Roman Vergil followed them in his Eclogues, Milton in his Lycidas, and many others before and since. Translation can give no hint of their beauty, but there is a fragment of Theocritus' work in a very different vein—a conversation between two Alexandrian ladies—so striking in its modernity that it seems worth quoting here.

GORGO.   Praxinoe at home?
PRAXINOE.   Why, Gorgo dear,
          of all the wonders! So at last you're here.
  (to a slave) A chair, Eunoe! put a cushion on.
GORG.   It's nicely, thank you.
PRAX.   Please to sit you down!
GORG.   Oh, dearie me, the job to reach your door!
          such swarms of people, four-in-hands galore,
          top-boots, frock-coats; and then the distance, dear!
          Whatever made you come and settle here?
PRAX.   The other end of nowhere—just his game
          (the spiteful creatures; men are all the same)
          to buy this hole—well, who'd call it a house?
          to stop us two from living nice and close.

A lady of the Hellenistic period. (From a statuette.)

GORG.	Hush! do be careful and not talk like that
	of your good man in hearing of the brat.
	See, how his eyes are starting, Bless the lad!
(to child)	So, so my beauty! Mummy not mean Dad.
PRAX.	My, but you're right. He's looking.
GORG.	Nice papa!
PRAX.	"Papa" went shopping for Vinolia—
	oh, well! we'll call it 'tother afternoon—
	and brought home salt, the six-foot simpleton.
GORG.	Mine's just the same—to make the money fly.
	He paid a pound for leather yesterday
	and all he got was filthy second-hand
	odd bits and pieces. Troubles never end.
	But come, my dear, take up your cloak and shawl.
	Let's to the palace to see the Festival . . .
(to slave)	Eunoe, take the wool and put it down—
	there on the floor, you good-for-nothing loon!
	Always asleep, the pussies. . . . Hurry up!
	A wash, please! Idiot, what's the use of soap
	without the water? Pour away! don't waste!
	Stop! now you've wet my dress.
GORG.	How very chaste,
	Praxinoe! I do admire that fold.
	How much a yard?
PRAX.	Don't ask me. Untold gold.

Another literary genre very popular with Hellenistic writers was the epigram. This poetic form—a short highly wrought stanza normally of half a dozen lines or less—had been used by Simonides and others for inscriptions on tombs.[1] It was still employed for that purpose, often expressing deep emotion with great simplicity of language.

> This small stone tells that we loved greatly. Still for thee
> I seek and shall, until I find thee, seek no less;
> But thou—if dead men may remember—O for me
> drink not of the Dark River of Forgetfulness.

But gradually the scope of the epigram had been enlarged. It was used for humour.

> Mr. Funk thought fit to be
> Sober in drinking company;
> So to the drinkers, Mr. Funk
> Appeared to be the one man drunk.[2]

But the greatest of Hellenistic epigrammatists was Meleager, born at Gadara near the Sea of Galilee more than half a century before Christ performed his miracle there; and in his hands the love-poem reached its perfection. Though somewhat voluptuous in tone, their delicacy of

---

[1] "Epigram" originally meant "inscription."
[2] Translation by a scholar of Winchester College.

phrase and variety of cadence give his lines an unrivalled quality of richness, impossible to reproduce in English. This poem in a less passionate vein may give some idea of his delightful, though sophisticated, style.

> Oyez! lost, stolen or astray!
> Love the madcap boy has flown;
> He left his bed at crack of dawn
>   And stole away;
> A saucy will-o'-the-wisp young sliver
> Grin impish; tongue awag; and tears
> To melt a stone with; Item, wears
>   Wings and a quiver:
> Father unknown—'tis understood
> That neither Sea nor Sky nor Earth
> Admit to knowledge of his birth
>   Or parenthood.
> His loss indeed will not be mourned.
> This very moment, I dare swear
> he's laying springes for souls. Beware!
>   you have been warned.
> But hist, my masters! there he lies
> Snug in his nest. Our quarry's found;
> And you, Sir Bowman, run to ground—
>   in Helen's eyes!

One impressive feature of Hellenistic literature was the purity of its Greek. The colloquial Greek, now widely spoken round the Eastern Mediterranean, had been greatly affected by outside influences. As found in the New Testament, it is loose in syntax and contains many borrowed words, some Latin, some oriental. It is the more remarkable, therefore, that the Hellenistic authors avoided such foreign contamination; and, except to the trained eye of a scholar, there is little to distinguish the Greek of Simonides from the Greek of Meleager or Callimachus.

On the other hand, when the shadow of Roman domination fell over the East, the impetus to free thought and free expression soon faltered and died. During the second century B.C., Macedon and Greece were incorporated in the Empire. During the following century Pompey conquered Asia Minor and Syria; and not a generation later Egypt, too, became a province. The example of the Greek genius inspired, it is true, a great literary efflorescence at Rome. During these two centuries and the first century A.D., Ennius, Lucretius, Vergil, Cicero, Horace and Tacitus, were all in one degree or another imitators of the Greeks. But after them the creative faculty seemed to vanish. Under the later Empire mental energy was diverted to the discussion of theological problems; and the great controversies raged—not least at Alexandria—out of which emerged the doctrinal formulæ of the Christian Creed.

In the intellectual labour, which such formulation entailed, Greek (as we have said) supplied the leaders of the Church with a ready-made medium of philosophic thought and expression. No Jew out of his own resources could have written the Creeds. Still less could any Roman. And, when we pass on down the centuries, it would still be impossible to overestimate the debt which Europe owed to the pioneer work of Greece. Even when Rome herself was becoming effete, Alexandria remained a centre—though a decaying centre—of learning. It was not until A.D. 500 that the city finally fell before the invasion of Persian hosts from Mesopotamia. And by now the focus of Hellenism was shifting once more. When in A.D. 323 the Emperor Constantine had founded Constantinople on the site of the ancient Byzantium, he had intended it to be a Roman capital with Latin for its official language. But in the sixth century under the Emperor Justinian the city took a new lease of life, and more and more it became the home of Greek learning and art. It was a vast metropolis—the largest ever seen in Europe until modern times, and to it gathered scholars from Egypt carrying with them precious manuscripts from Alexandrian libraries.[1] So the old Hellenistic tradition lingered on, still vigorous even in the days of its decline. Byzantine art, though stereotyped and conventionalized, retained at least the old Greek sense of formal decorative design. Superb churches were built; and the influence of Byzantine architects and sculptors even spread to the West. The labour of scholars was unremitting. Annotation and commentary was carried on with pedantic enthusiasm; and from time to time a spark of the old creative spirit even flickered up among the writers of the Imperial Court. Here is one little epigram, the work of Rufinus, one of Justinian's civil servants. It is written with all the old purity of taste and diction—a swan-song, we might say, not altogether inappropriate to the passing of the Ancient World.

> Of flowers in such sweet grace arrayed,
> as my poor art might lend to them,
> I fashioned for my lady's head
>   this simple diadem.
> For here with chaliced rose are met
> the weeping wind-flower's fairy bell,
> lilies and blue-eyed violet
>   and hang-head daffodil.
> Forget your vanity an hour,
> and wear them, lady, while you may!
> Beauty, which blossoms as a flower,
>   as flower must fade away.

[1] It is to this fact in a large measure that we owe the survival of the classical masterpieces.

CHAPTER XIII

THE GREEK GENIUS

I

In a famous choric ode, written for his play the "Antigone" in the year 441 B.C., Sophocles sketched in outline what we may call the life-history of mankind. Individualism had at that date barely begun to raise its head; and if a poet's vision was ever prophetic, it was here. Man, he says in effect, is a miracle of resource; he has learnt first to till the soil, harness wild horse and mountain-bull and navigate the seas. "Speech and wind-swift thought" next taught him City-life, wisdom of mind, skill of hand and the healing of disease; and "the subtle ingenuity of his devising leads him now to Good, now to Evil." Yet so long as he takes Religion and Justice for guide, both he and his city will prosper; but there remains an alternative—and "never may such an one share either my home or my thoughts"—the "Cityless Man." And this is what the Greek in the last stage of his decline actually became, a man without roots or national loyalties, a sojourner in strange lands, a wanderer on the face of the earth.

He was to be found everywhere, not only in the half-oriental cities of Alexandria or Antioch, Gadara or Tarsus, but also in the Roman West. The Imperial capital swarmed with Greeks. Unnumbered thousands reached it as slaves; and to the not too intelligent Roman master their varied accomplishments made such menials especially useful. They could keep his accounts, write letters at his dictation, copy out books for him, read aloud as he lounged or sauntered, and entertain him after dinner with recitations or songs. In the administrative sphere they proved themselves indispensable, serving as clerks or secretaries to imperial officials. Some, even despite a servile origin, climbed into high posts at the Palace. As doctors too they were much in request; and under the Empire they held a virtual monopoly of the arts, planning its buildings, painting its frescoes, carving its portrait busts, or copying famous statues for the salons of its rich. Juvenal, the second century satirist, complains with great bitterness of the ubiquity of the "hungry Greekling"—"schoolmaster, elocutionist, surveyor, painter, masseur, doctor, conjuror and astrologist."

Hellenism's most powerful agent at Rome, however, was its philosophy. It was no uncommon thing for the gentry to hire Greek tutors for their sons; and at the same time they were not above employing them as their own moral mentors. One man of affairs records in a letter the great debt he owed to a certain Euphrates, an impressive old savant, with flowing beard and long hair, whose lectures he had attended in early youth and whom even in middle age he gladly took every chance to consult. It was from such men's teaching that the educated Roman acquired his philosophy of life; and he had before him, broadly speaking, two choices. For shortly after Aristotle's death a sharp cleavage had occurred in Greek thought. One school, founded by the Cypriot Zeno,[1] used to hold their discussions under a "portico" or "Stoa" in the Athenian market-place, and for this reason they were known as the Stoics. The other school were the followers of Zeno's contemporary Epicurus. The outlook of both Epicureans and Stoics was at root individualist; for their prime concern was the quest of personal happiness. Both, furthermore, were agreed that the word was an unpleasant place to live in. But they differed radically in their view of its metaphysical origin, and consequently too in their prescription for making the best of it.

The Universe, according to Stoic belief, was permeated and controlled by a Divine Power or World Soul—clearly a leaf taken out of Plato's book. From this Divine Power were derived Justice, Law and Morality; hence to live in harmony with its principles was the one sure road to happiness. So Duty before all else was the Stoic's rule. From that path nothing must turn him. All honours and riches he must scorn, all passions, emotions, even family affections he must ruthlessly suppress. Thus in complete detachment, serving society but indifferent alike to its applause or its threats, he might grimly face whatever life should bring, master of his fate and captain of his soul, and happy "as a king" even though tortured on the rack.

To the Epicureans the Universe was not a system but an accident. It had come into being, they held, by a purely fortuitous collision and combination of atoms—an echo of early physicist doctrines and of the Platonic view of the illusory world. From this it followed that Law and Morality sprang not from divine and permanent principles, but from the mutable conveniencies of mankind. Religious fears and inhibitions—chief source of human misery—were mere legendmonger's fancy. The gods, if they existed, held entirely aloof. Right and Wrong were therefore to be determined by self-interest alone; and the individual would best find his happiness in "escapist" pleasures—some peaceful rustic retreat, intellectual activity and the society of friends. The less high-minded interpreted the prescription more grossly: "Let us eat, drink and be merry: for to-morrow we die."

[1] Zeno was reputed to be a Phœnician which may account for the strong fanatic element in his teaching; for the Phœnicians, as may be learnt from the Bible, were notorious for this quality.

Between these two opposed views of life the puzzled Romans veered. Stoicism, it is true, produced some notable heroes among them. But weaker characters more often contrived to combine the two views simultaneously. Pliny, the writer of the above-mentioned letter was just such a man. While in town he followed his mentor's precepts and stuck to his uncongenial public duties with a conscientious tenacity. Once, however, his favourite country mansion was reached, he surrendered himself to the Epicurean pleasures of a literary dilettante.

Such spiritual sterility stands in gloomy contrast to the uniquely creative vitality of the Greek prime. It is no explanation to put the fault on the Romans. The psychological change went far deeper than that. It was part and parcel of the political change which had come over the Ancient World. The Greek City State, with its intense communal enthusiasms and passionate civic idealism, had given to men's lives an inspiration and a driving-power which were inevitably doomed to vanish with it. The Roman Empire was too vast and unwieldy a unit to excite the same un-selfregarding loyalties. The rigidity, too, of its absolutist and often tyrannical rule discouraged a free use of the mind. The Democratic spirit and all the vivid life that went with it were dead.

On the other hand, the Intellectual Awakening, which was the City-State's supreme achievement, had come to stay. The civilized world was henceforward to become increasingly a battle-ground of ideas—ideas which in one degree or another found their ultimate source in Hellenism. From the analytic and critical spirit that Hellenism bred, arose the fierce theological controversies which were the major preoccupation of early Christendom and from which finally emerged the formal doctrines of the Faith. The political issues of the Middle Ages, again, turned largely on the effort of kings to establish the supremacy of Law—an instrument of government which the Romans had forged but Greek methods of thought had tempered. Meanwhile, the leaders of the Mediæval Church, in their endeavour to add an intellectual to a spiritual authority, relied almost slavishly on the forms of Aristotelian philosophy. Finally, at the Renaissance the rediscovery of the true Hellenic spirit, with its lively impulse to Freedom of Thought, aroused a ferment of new ideas—cultural, moral and intellectual—which has never since died down. Wars have been fought for them and countries plunged into revolution; and our own generation has been witness of a culminating struggle between the blind forces of a retrograde barbarism and the ideals of human dignity and individual liberty which are the heirlooms of Ancient Greece.

Thus over a period of time, which almost certainly has not yet seen its end, Hellenism has retained an unfailing capacity to direct and canalize human effort towards a richer and worthier life, the precise content of which it has not been the function even of Christianity to define [1]; and we are bound to ask ourselves what it was in the Greek Genius that has made it so vital a force in the evolution of Western Society. This chapter is in the main an attempt to answer that question.

2

Pericles well expressed the Greek Genius when he said of his country-men that they were "at once critical and constructive." Through all their history the Greek people continuously strove to bring order out of chaos; and this they did by a twofold process, first by analysing, sifting and, so to say, picking to pieces, then of building up out of the pieces a coherent and rational whole. By such a process was evolved out of a medley of primitive superstitions the Homeric conception of the Olympic gods, each with a separate character and well-defined function. The same process led the Ionian philosophers from their critical observation of natural phenomena to the infinitely daring conclusion that all sprang from a single prime source. So again with the "prophetic" ideal of Moderation, Justice, and Reason; for this equally was an attempt to *integrate* human life—individual or communal—by eliminating its extremes of passion, its social tyrannies, and its logical inconsistencies, or, as Plato would have said, by harmonizing the discordant elements of the soul. Thus in religion or science, ethics or metaphysics and, we may add, in art and literature too, the same end was kept always in view—the creation of an ordered synthesis in which every detail should fall into its place, first things rank first, the less essential be subordinate to the more essential, yet all make their appropriate contribution to the common whole.

Nowhere can this principle be more clearly observed than in the Greeks' own language—always a faithful mirror of a people's mentality. In style and structure Greek linguistic methods were a complete contrast to our own. The easy-going, loose-minded Englishman will express his ideas in a series of independent sentences ranged side by side, as it might be a row of single-room huts. The Greek preferred to build a more complex and more comprehensive edifice. Viewing a group of ideas as a logical unity, he would bring them all together into one long period in

[1] It would be easy to draw up a long list of questions on which Christians have hitherto never agreed: Is Capitalism right or Socialism wrong? Where should a precise line be drawn between the rights of the Individual and the claims of the State? What are the ethical effects of compulsory military training? Should the State subsidize the arts? On what principles should the censorship of plays be conducted? and so forth. For the solution of such problems goodwill may certainly be needed, but still more clear thought in distinguishing between means and ends.

which through the subordination of clause to clause he was able to bring out explicitly the interconnection between idea and idea—"a lot of little pieces of string," as the schoolboy ruefully put it, "all tied together in one enormous knot." But literary knots, when skilfully tied, serve a valuable purpose. By their very complexity they focus the mind on the logical interplay of ideas; and it was to their precise grasp of logical relationships that the Greeks owed the unique clarity of their thought.

"An uncriticized life," Socrates was fond of saying, "is scarcely worth living at all"; and long before Socrates' day the Greeks, being anything but drifters, had begun to ask themselves what life was all about and what in it should be considered most worthwhile. A good tale is told by Herodotus about the philosopher-statesman Solon. In the course of his travels abroad Solon, it seems, paid a visit to Croesus the "millionaire" King of his day. He was duly shown round the royal treasure-house; but at the end of the tour Croesus observed him with surprise to be little impressed. So he put him the point-blank question (which he himself felt could admit of only one answer), "Whom do you consider the most enviable man in the world?" "Tellus, an Athenian," was the unexpected reply; and, as some further elucidation seemed called for, Solon continued—a man of modest but adequate means, Tellus had enjoyed the satisfaction of seeing his country prosper, his sons turn out well, all their children grow up, and finally, to crown this exemplary life, he had died with distinction on the field of battle. In sum, Solon said, give me a man free from illness and deformity, immune from major disaster, the father of satisfactory children, and (with a characteristic Greek touch) a fine fellow to look at; then, if all goes well to the end, you may consider him happy. The philosopher's verdict had the merit, at least, of putting the millionaire in his place; but it also serves to show how thus early in their history the Greeks set themselves to consider what really counted in life. The ideal scale of values was a favourite theme for discussion among later philosophers; and Aristotle for one drew up a list in order of merit. At the top he placed Intellectual Activity; and at the bottom Wealth, "if properly used." A little ahead of wealth came Health, Beauty and Athletic Skill; and ahead of them again certain recognized manly virtues. The priorities, of course, may be matter for opinion; but to have formulated a clear scale of values at all was certainly no bad thing; it is more than most of us do. The Greeks were the first people to attempt it; and in this they were following their usual practice and trying to look at life *as a whole*, just as in education they strove to develop the full man by training all his powers and faculties, physical and emotional, no less than intellectual and æsthetic.

The same principle, as we have indicated, applied to their Art. With them Unity of Design was the first condition of Beauty; and therein lies the main difference between Classical and Romantic technique. In Gothic architecture, for example, the details are seldom thus related to the whole. More often than not the mediæval cathedral or church is a haphazard agglomeration of styles, built, rebuilt, altered or enlarged at half a dozen different periods. The harmony of their effect is therefore not due to any deliberate planning; rather it springs from the mediæval craftsman's instinctive knack of matching architectural details together, much as a

ON LEFT: A Gothic arch in which two different types of capital are satisfactorily combined.
ON RIGHT: A 'classical' porch in which the introduction of dissimilar capitals introduces a
    jarring note.

child might match a posy of wild-flowers. At the west end of the building the two towers may be of different shapes and sizes; perpendicular windows may be interspersed among Norman arches; the capital on one side of an arch may disagree with its counterpart on the other. But what matter? The result, notwithstanding, is somehow satisfactory to the eye.

With classical art it is far otherwise. Were an architect, in designing a classical porch, to place a Doric column on its right and an Ionic column on its left, the result would be nothing short of excruciating. Exact symmetry, in short, was essential. Contrast, of course, there will be. Carved ornament will be set off by the adjacent flat surfaces; and the rake of the gable will relieve the monotony of the horizontal entablature. But the whole will be knit together—by a system of geometrical balance and of proportions calculated to the fraction of an inch—into a coherent harmony of formal design.

It is the more unfortunate, therefore, that of the surviving Greek temples none have come down to us altogether intact. To suppose that they look better in ruins than they did in their original state is the merest moonshine—an insult to a great race of artists.[1] But even to conjure up an image of such temples' one-time perfection is for ourselves impossible. It is not enough to substitute with the mind's eye a marble of pearly whiteness in place of the present weather-stained gold, or to reconstruct in imagination the now chipped or crumbled mouldings in their first delicate exactitude. We must also restore the statuary that once filled the triangle of the gable, the gilded ornaments that flamed up above it in the glare of the southern sunshine, and the gaily painted designs which have long since faded from the marbles' surface. The same is true of Greek statuary. For here, too, colour was freely used to give verisimilitude of eyes or hair and to enliven the garments by a sprinkle of pattern. And, as with architecture, so with sculpture: no single work from the more famous hands has come down to us intact, not even the celebrated Hermes of Praxiteles, well-preserved though it was by its fortunate tumble into a deep bed of clay. This Hermes, moreover—probably the sole extant full figure by an acknowledged genius—was never rated very high in antiquity. We are therefore unable wholly to appreciate what consummate combination of artistry—balance of poise, rhythm of line and proportion of limb—went to create the original perfection of the greater Greek masterpieces. Even to reconstruct the missing arms of the Venus de Milo—a second-rate work—has completely baffled the ingenuity of modern imagination.

In the use of the spoken or written word, no less than in the visual arts, Unity of Form was the invariable aim. Rhetoric—that characteristic invention of an argumentative people—was studied and taught on systematic principles. Speeches were planned from prelude to peroration with an eye to their total effect. The Greek orator was a master of balance and symmetry; and he was apt to carry the trick of antithesis to an unfortunate extreme; for it led both him and still more his Roman imitators into the pitfall of forced contrasts. Latin poets, and even historians, were

[1] It is probably impossible for any but the trained eye of the architect to appreciate such a temple as the Parthenon to the full. To such lengths of subtlety has the design been carried that almost every line, which is apparently straight, has in reality a scarcely perceptible upward convex curve, thus avoiding the appearance of sagging. Some of these modulations can be detected only by the touch, not seen by the eye. No people, a modern architect has said, ever built like this; and it is in the last degree unlikely that any will build so again.

only too often guilty of falsifying truth in their desire for a telling point or a stylish phrase.

In Drama the Law of Unity was carried still further. In the construction of a Greek tragedy the scenes were as closely interrelated as the tiers of a building. Knock one away and the whole would be spoiled. Even for the audience to disperse between the acts (after the modern manner) would be scarcely less disastrous. For the plot is planned to move forward in a continuous crescendo. There are no diversions such as Shakespeare employed in his sub-plots, no comic interruptions like the drunken porter in Macbeth. So the sense of tragedy mounts and mounts; and the tension produced by this cumulative progression towards anticipated catastrophe is unique in drama. The climax once reached, however, the tension is deliberately relaxed. The Greeks preferred to end on a quiet note.

Then again the very limitations of the Greek stage itself imposed certain restrictions on the playwright's freedom. In the absence of a curtain the action of the play had perforce to take place in one setting; and for the same reason it was normally conceived as falling within the compass of a single day. Such limitations, however, were turned to positive advantage. The Unities of Place and Time (as they came to be called) served to emphasize and enhance the unity of the plot. In detail, too, many self-imposed conventions were rigidly observed, even by such a revolutionary artist as Euripides. In dialogue, for example, long set-speech was answered by long set-speech, usually with a comment by the chorus-leader at the close of each. Variation of tempo, when required, was produced by a more rapid interchange, character replying to character in a series of single lines apiece. Thus a sense of formal balance was preserved throughout; and the choric interludes with their apposite themes were far better calculated to bind the play together than the less relevant interventions of a modern orchestra.

Thus the technique of the playwright was reduced almost to a formula; and, as with the other arts, the author of one generation could learn it from his predecessor and then, not without improvements of his own, hand it on to his successor of the next. Indeed, classical formalism lends itself to imitation far more readily than does the looser technique of our own Romantic poets and artists. No one can to-day recapture the spirit of the Old English ballad; and modern mimicry of mediæval Gothic has seldom been much better than a travesty. For in a Romantic art, where taste and instinct are everything and the heart counts for more than the

PLATE XIII
Head of a Greek statue in bronze.

PLATE XIII

PLATE XIV

head, even the most faithful of copyists may well miss the whole secret of its mysterious charm. On the other hand, in classical poetry and classical architecture there are hard-and-fast rules based on rational principles or on mathematical formulæ; and these the mind can apprehend and so pen or hand reproduce. That is why so many playwrights in France and Germany have looked back for their model to the formal unity of the Greek drama, and why the best building since the Renaissance has been done in the classical style.

Here then lies the final answer to our original question. Unity in one shape or another is the ultimate goal of all human thought or endeavour. To live completely in the moment is the mark of the animal. Man for his part is bound, whether he likes it or not, to co-ordinate what he thinks, says or does. In his daily behaviour he must in some degree be true to himself or else be locked up as a lunatic. His sense of Beauty finds satisfaction in harmony and is offended by discord. He must think consistently or abandon all care for the truth. An unco-ordinated life, in fact, would not be human at all. This the Greeks understood more clearly than any people in history; and it is because they themselves sought with such diligence and so much penetration after intellectual, æsthetic and even (within certain limits) after ethical unity that their example has inspired in others the desire to continue the quest and their methods have furnished the classical model how best to conduct it. So the spirit of Hellas lives on.

3

Of the intellectual and æsthetic sides of the Greek Genius enough has already been said; the third and more important side remains still to be discussed. It has sometimes been held against the Greeks that they lacked a moral sense and that ethically they were somehow inferior to the Romans. This ill reputation is an unfortunate legacy of the worst period of their decline; for in the time of the Roman Empire the charge of shallowness and instability of character was certainly not unmerited. But at their best the Greeks would have had little enough to learn from a people whose favourite form of punishment was crucifixion and whose idea of spreading culture was to erect provincial amphitheatres for repulsive scenes of carnage. When Greek comedies came to be adapted to the taste of Roman audiences, it was even thought necessary to spice

---

PLATE XIV
(From Rodenwaldt's "Acropolis," p. 33)
Part of the Parthenon Frieze, designed by Phidias and carried out by one of his pupils or assistants. Though this frieze was placed as high above the spectator as a third floor window the detail was of the most exquisite finish.

them up with sadistic jokes about the chastisement of slaves. On the other hand, about tolerance and humanity and the minor decencies of life, there was little the Romans knew which the Greeks had not taught them. No people ever thought more about morality or discussed its problems more earnestly. Even an Athenian comedy-writer, as we have already seen, could make his championship of the old-fashioned virtues the theme of a play. If the Greeks fell short of their ideals in practice, the same is true of us all; and, to do them justice, they lived up more closely to their own limited code than does the modern man to the precepts of the Sermon on the Mount. Nor should we apply to their case any other criterion than we apply, let us say, to the Jews. We must judge them by their best products, not by their worst, by the Athenians rather than by the Spartans, and by the Athenians of the fifth century rather than of the fourth.

Direct literary evidence about private ways and personal character during the Periclean epoch is unhappily scanty. Thucydides tells little of everyday life. Aristophanes belonged rather to the beginning of the decline; and in any case comedy by its very nature tends to lay exaggerated emphasis on men's foibles and vices. Yet, if we must allow some basis of fact for the satirist's caricatures, so equally must we allow the same for the idealization of poets and artists. The personalities of Sophoclean drama reflected, we may be sure, the best Athenian type, just as the characters of Tennyson's Morte d'Arthur reflected the ideals of the mid-Victorian gentleman. Similar evidence may be gleaned from the sculptured figures to be found on tomb-stones or in the Parthenon Frieze. And to these may be added the testimony of numberless vase-paintings.[1] The impression thus to be gathered is of men who first and foremost have looked life and suffering in the face and have triumphed over them, men of strong character, dignified, free from meanness or pettiness, superb in their physical development and highly self-controlled in their actions, courteous, thoughtfully grave, and, according to their lights, humane. By comparison with such men the upper-class Old Testament Jew, whatever his virtues, might have seemed luxury-loving, obsequious, intellectually null, and physically flabby; and his Roman counterpart over-drilled, insensitive, unmannerly and brutal. The lot of a slave under Athenian masters—by no means an irrelevant test—must have been vastly preferable to service in the household of an Augustan nobleman. It might even have compared favourably with the lot of some female drudge in a mid-Victorian basement, to say nothing of the child-sweep who was set to scale the chimneys of our great-great-grandfathers' mansions.

[1] It must be remembered, however, that as many of these were employed in decorating drinking-cups or wine-jars, they tend to emphasize the worst side of Greek character—its prevalency to drunkenness.

The character of the Greeks none the less had many serious limitations; and these, as was but natural, arose from their historical background. Their moral sense had originally grown (as among all early peoples) out of the primitive tribal code. Deeply-rooted in their minds was a sense of Propriety or Good Form. They themselves called it "Shame," an instinct bred by long social habit, which told them to be courteous towards strangers and respectful towards the old, to keep their bodies fit, to behave demurely in public, and, in general, to do as their fellows did. This sense of "shame" represented in fact the germ of a conscience, but no more than a germ. For "Sin" the Greeks had no word; for they lacked any real sense of contrition. Its nearest verbal equivalent (used in Biblical Greek) meant literally a "mis-hit," a blunder or false step which might expose them to Divine Wrath or Nemesis. The idea was given a more rational and precise definition by the poets and thinkers who preached the need for moderation and self-mastery, the doctrine of "Mêden Agân." It told of a straight path to be followed, any deviation from which into violent extremes would inevitably lead to disaster [1]; and not even Socrates and Plato could altogether rid their minds of the belief that, if only men *knew* the path, they would automatically follow it. The same idea was somewhat differently expressed in the Greeks' conception of Justice—a conception symptomatic of the advance from a tribal to a more strictly political society. The original meaning of the word Justice or "Dikê" was a "Way"—the way, that is, hallowed by established custom. But it signified something more than judicial or constitutional correctness. It might also be applied to personal rectitude; so that Plato could define Justice as the condition of mind which creates harmony both in the State and within the individual soul. St. Paul was later to use it of Righteousness in the sight of God.

Meanwhile "Virtue" or "Aretê," as we have pointed out above, was more narrowly identified with the ideal of good citizenship; and despite philosophic attempts to widen its scope, the original significance clung— the perfect pattern of what a man should be as member of a community. This close identification of civic and personal virtue reached its climax under the intense communal life of the Polis. Psychologically it may be said to correspond with the adolescent phase in the life of an individual, during which he will accept almost unquestioningly the code of his fellows and be content simply to become a good member of the team.

[1] By comparison the path sometimes followed in the name of conscience would have appeared to the Greeks somewhat devious. They would have been puzzled by the cruelties of the Inquisition or the fanaticism and eccentricities of some Puritan sects. The complacency and sense of infallibility which over-conscientiousness sometimes breeds might even have struck them as a challenge to Nemesis.

Unhappily, before the Greeks could outgrow this phase, the stress and strain of political events distorted their whole moral outlook. If after the Persian wars Pan-Hellenic unity had been achieved, it is not impossible that the better side of their nature might have triumphed; but, as things were, the pressure of economic and other forces drove them in an opposite and fatal direction. During the fifth century—the most formative period of their history—the bitter antagonisms between State and State were progressively reproduced first as between faction and faction, and then as between man and man. Thucydides has shown how the cynicism bred of the bitter experiences of the Peloponnesian War was reflected in a complete breakdown of religious and moral codes; and in one famous passage of the Funeral Speech (not quoted above) we actually find Pericles himself giving the selfish principles of state policy a universal application to everyday life, and bluntly asserting that the primary motive of conferring a favour is to place the recipient under a debt. The individual, in short, was driven to take his cue from the State; and when the State itself began to go to pieces, the individual was left with little to fall back on beyond the evil lessons he had learned from it. Moral bankruptcy was thus the inevitable sequel to political bankruptcy.

It is not least among the miracles of history that at such a time of disillusionment and anarchy Plato was capable of rising to the sublimest heights of moral idealism. "For him," it has been said, "Love of the Divine was at once the inspiration and the reward of the moral life." The vision of a philosopher could scarcely reach further; but Plato's solitary voice could not dispel the darkness of fourth-century Greece. The harsh struggle for existence ran on; and the trend of current thought was more accurately reflected by Aristotle than by his more visionary master. From Plato's Utopian endeavour to re-establish the supremacy of Society's claims, Aristotle fell back on what in essence was an Individualist standpoint. The summit of human bliss and attainment, he held, because "desirable for its own sake alone and serving no ulterior purpose," was the life of intellectual activity which he called "Contemplation." Such emphasis on things of the mind was unexceptionable; few of us, after all, would deny the palm to a Shakespeare or a Newton. It is rather the implication of moral self-sufficiency that runs counter to the modern and Christian conception. The truth is that from first to last Greek thought was cursed with an ego-centric tendency; and at the end, as we have seen, self-realization and self-satisfaction came to be nakedly avowed as the goal of the philosopher's quest.

At the same time to imagine that there was no kindness or generosity among the ancient Greeks would be a grave injustice. No people ever set a higher value on Friendship; and family ties, especially perhaps as between father and son, were immensely strong. Such plays as the "Antigone" would have had little meaning unless acts of devotion had been greatly admired; and during the Plague, on Thucydides' own showing, many Athenians sacrificed their lives in succouring those they loved and even, we may infer, their neighbours. But such altruism had its limits. It was not extended to all and sundry. Whether an Athenian would have gone out of his way to tend a wounded Spartan on the battlefield is more than doubtful. It is very certain that for a Persian he would not have stirred a finger. There is much, in fact, to be said for the view[1] that in spite of their phenomenal cultural development the Greeks were still living ethically in the atmosphere of the tribe. Their loyalties were the tribal loyalties of kinship and common interest. "Love those," their code said, "from whom you may expect as much again." The complementary rule "Hate your enemy" was equally a survival of the old intertribal feuds, and perhaps of the vendetta. In Attic drama the prayer most constantly on the lips of both male and female characters was "Blessing to my friends and all manner of misfortune to my foes!" The average man in his daily practice made no bones about the matter. It was a positive duty to get even with his adversary; and when a litigant in Court, he would ostentatiously boast of his long-standing grudges and of his satisfaction at the chance to repay them. Like so much else in his life, Socrates' forgiveness of the jury who condemned him was wholly exceptional. So, if a Greek prided himself (as he did) on his capacity for mercy and pity, its application was reserved for a comparatively narrow circle.[2] It might extend, let us say, to a faithful slave of his household, but most certainly not to slaves in the mass. This may help to explain, though not to condone Aristotle's callous defence of the system; and his glib logic-chopping phrase about "human instruments" remains a crowning revelation of Greek limitations. Nor can we readily forget the Athenian Nicias with his thousand miserable chattels in the Laureum silver-mines and his life spent in the sterile observance of all the orthodox pieties.

Few things in antiquity are more difficult to determine than the relationship between Religion and Conduct. On one point, however, let there be no mistake. The Greeks took their worship very seriously. They believed profoundly in the ability of the Unseen Powers to help or to harm them; and in moments of distress, such as the Athenian soldiers

[1] See F. R. Earp's "The Way of the Greeks," to which this and succeeding paragraphs owes much.
[2] Till quite recent years Feudal Custom has had a similar hangover in the ethical outlook of English society. One attitude towards the rich and another towards the poor is even now by no means extinct.

experienced on the seashore at Syracuse, it was their habit to turn instinctively to prayer. But their religion was nothing if not institutional. It was rooted and grounded in the observance of a ritual, at which ancestral custom—perhaps the strongest force in their lives—made attendance well-nigh compulsory. It was as natural among the ancients as it is inconceivable among ourselves for the entire population of a city to join together in an act of worship, whether at the annual celebration of some patron god or goddess, or at the inauguration of a naval expedition. Religion even pervaded the commonest acts of life. Before drinking wine

Two women make offerings at the Shrine of the Wine-god Dionysus or Bacchus. (From a vase.) One with a ladle pours a libation from her jar into the large receptacle before the god's image.

it was the habit with the Greek of those days (as it still is with his modern descendant) to tip out a drop or two on the ground. For him it was a conscious act of reverence, an offering to some deity.

All this, however, did not necessarily imply that ritual was meaningless; but rather that what ritual should mean to the individual was left to the individual's choice. An Æschylus could read the deepest truths into the traditional myths and time-hallowed customs. The critical Sophist could pull the characters of the Olympians to pieces without giving serious offence. Strangest of all to our way of thinking, Aristophanes, a thorough-going conservative, could actually make a god the leading buffoon in one of his comedies. It all comes to this. There was no orthodox creed; nor, indeed, did there exist any authoritative voice to dictate one. Provided a man played his part in the outward observances, he was free to think of them what he liked—a fact which no doubt did much to avert the danger of religious intolerance or persecution.

At the same time we can clearly discern a gradual but steady advance towards a more spiritual interpretation of ritual. Sacrifice, it came to be thought, was more acceptable to the Deity when it was offered by worthy

Offerings to the dead, whose spirits may be seen hovering round the tomb. (From a painting on a white vase.)

hands. All the while, too, the tragedians were striving to educate their audiences. A play like the "Antigone" raised crucial religious problems: what was true piety? and what false? And its heroine appealed, as we have seen, from the ordinance of man to the "unwritten laws of God." It is unlikely that such teaching would fall on wholly deaf ears. Taken all in all, therefore, Greek religion cannot have failed to play an important part in the formation of character. To the devout, who had eyes to look below the surface, ritual might hold a genuinely moral significance. On the majority it must have exercised an unconscious but none the less a refining influence—not least because it made a strong appeal to their innate sense of the beautiful. It was not for nothing that the Greeks spent so much labour on the adornment of their temples or that the skill of their greatest artists was devoted in the main to the sculptural representation of the gods. It used to be said in antiquity that the mere sight of Phidias' famous statue of Olympian Zeus was in itself a spiritual education.[1]

On one point and an important point the Greeks were frankly puzzled. Their belief in an after-life was painfully vague. Pericles in his Funeral Speech made no allusion whatever to immortality, beyond his reference to the "memory which will live on in men's hearts." Even mythology spoke with no very certain voice. It told indeed of certain exceptional sinners who suffered picturesque torments appropriate to their crimes, and of certain exceptional heroes who enjoyed the pleasures of friendship and sport in the "asphodel meadows" of an ill-defined Elysium. But ordinary mortals, good, bad and indifferent alike, were all bundled into Hades without discrimination; and, though Socrates could quote legendary authority for a tribunal of Four Just Judges, popular belief in these remained of the shadowiest. The philosopher's sociable anticipations of the Underworld were correspondingly a triumph of optimism. To the man-in-the-street the prospect of that phantom realm was most unattractive. It suggested a tenuous and comfortless existence—no more than a pallid reflection of his life on earth—in which his dead soul would pine for the warmth and the sunlight and the full-blooded activities he had there left behind him.

There was indeed one form of Greek religion which claimed to afford a more comforting hope. Closely associated with the Orphic Movement (in which the school of Pythagoras appears to have been mixed up) there were certain Mystery Cults, the most popular of which had its seat at Eleusis near Athens. To these mysteries initiates alone were admitted, and that only after a prescribed course of purification. What secrets were witnessed by the privileged few in the darkened hall at Eleusis no one ever divulged. It is known, however, that they were somehow connected with the spirit of spring-time growth and Nature's annual resurrection; and there can be little doubt that in the ecstasy of rapture which mass-emotion induced the mystics experienced some inner assurance of a better life to come. Equally it would appear that they gained from the sacra-mental rite a sense of communion with the deity and of purgation from the stain of sin. It may well have been this aspect of the cult which led

[1] Religious values apart, it would be an instructive and not unfair analogy to consider the effect of compulsory attendance at school-chapels. The few agnostics may think their own thoughts. The devout find real opportunity for worship. The remainder will be influenced by the sermons (vaguely corresponding to the moralization of the ancient tragedians) and still more by the atmosphere of congregational fervour and the beauty of the music and the architectural surroundings.

St. Paul to employ the word "mysterion" in speaking of the Christian Faith itself. For all that, the experience can scarcely have been more than a superficial and passing mood. The cult had no deep moral influence. Even its preliminary purifications were confined to abstention from various kinds of food and other physical indulgence; and, though Aristophanes—perhaps playfully—suggests that rogues, smugglers and traitors should be banned from their company, there is no solid evidence to show that the devotees became better men than their fellows.

Such unrestrained emotionalism, in any case, ran counter to the attitude of the more thoughtful Greeks; and Socrates was probably typical in declining initiation. It was against his principles to put faith in anything so manifestly irrational. Nevertheless, if the Greeks had one fault more than another, it was, we must admit, an intellectual impatience. Among their early physicist-philosophers an eagerness to spin theories before they had fully observed proved a fatal handicap to real scientific progress; and the same overhaste to rationalize all things in heaven and earth went a long way to paralyse their religious development. Apart from one or two notable exceptions, they were unable to think deeply and feel deeply at one and the same time. Thus Homer, in his desire to clarify the character of the gods, made them so deplorably human that they could hardly command the respect of any thinking man. The subsequent efforts of poets and artists to restore the lost dignity was largely offset by the unsettling influence of speculative criticism; and finally, when the sceptical habit grew, and belief in mythology crumbled, philosophy erected in its place a conception of the Deity so abstract and impersonal that it could make no cogent appeal to more than a few rare spirits.

When all is said, however, God was not to the Greeks, as he was to the Hebrews, the main source of their idealism. It was Man that they placed at the centre of their universe; and it was their intense preoccupation with man's affairs and problems that made them what they were. Their Humanism brought to them, as it has brought to the rest of mankind, many troubles as well as many triumphs; and there is no real paradox in the fact that its greatest gift "whether for good or for evil" (as Sophocles would say) was the product not of their palmier days, but of the unhappy period of their political and moral decline. For, just when they were engaged in criticizing almost everything else out of existence, they achieved the supreme feat of their constructive faculty—they created the Individual Man.

Individualism was born, where alone perhaps it could have been born, in the narrow cradle of the diminutive republics founded by a people endowed with unique social and intellectual gifts. From these it was carried outwards, first by Alexander's conquests to the East, then to Rome and the West, till it came at last to permeate most of the civilized world. In the process the conception was doubtless enlarged and strengthened under the influence of new environments; but it is none the less difficult to resist the conclusion that the contribution of Greece remained paramount.

Christianity is so commonly thought of in relation to its Jewish origin that we are apt to forget what it owed also to the Greeks. When the Christian era began, the Jews themselves had for more than two hundred years been subjected to Hellenistic influences. Their Alexandrian theologians, such as Philo, the contemporary of Christ, were steeped in Platonic and Aristotelian philosophy. But the Jews were not primarily thinkers. Rather it was a profound religious experience that shaped their ideas; and these had undergone what was probably a quite independent development. Their earlier prophets, even when preaching the social virtues of mercy and justice, had always spoken in terms of the race: "Israel" was to be punished for her sins or rewarded for her piety. It was not till Ezekiel that the idea of *personal* responsibility for guilt emerged. Thenceforward and particularly during the Hellenistic period (though how far as a result of Greek influence is very difficult to say) greater and greater emphasis was laid on personal behaviour. In the writings of that period, notably Wisdom, Ecclesiastes, and parts of Proverbs, their precepts are addressed no longer to "Israel," but to the individual man. Hope of a personal immortality correspondingly gained ground; and in our Lord's day the Pharisees were zealously preoccupied with the salvation of their own souls.

But the conviction that a man is responsible for his actions is only one aspect of Individualism. A sense of *personal status*, derived from the Deity, was a Greek rather than a Jewish idea. It may be said to have originated with Plato; but the Stoics carried it further, holding that all members of the human race were of equal status, Hellenes and barbarians, freemen and slaves. In the third century A.D., if not before, this Greek intellectual conception, merging with the Jewish religious conception, served to crystallize the specifically Christian doctrine that every individual has a supreme and equal value in the eyes of God. With these two strands was probably interwoven a third, the conception drawn from the political institutions of the Roman Empire which is expressed in St. Paul's well-known saying, "Our *citizenship* is in Heaven."

As himself a freeborn "citizen" of the Roman Empire, Paul was immensely proud of the privilege; but in the development of his mind, by far the more important influence was Hellenism; and this it was that very largely served to control and clarify the somewhat diffuse and turgid flow of his Hebraic thought and so make possible his supreme contribution towards building the foundations of the Christian Faith. He had been brought up as a boy in the semi-Greek city of Tarsus, a University town; and he was able, we know, to quote from the works of a Greek Stoic poet. Throughout his missionary life he was in almost daily contact with Greeks or Hellenized Jews; and in his correspondence he was for ever engaged in answering the difficulties raised by their inquisitive and critical minds. Thus the interplay of the two currents of thought, Hebrew and Greek, is manifest in nearly all that he wrote, and not least in his final solution of the problem with which he had wrestled so long. The watchword of Hellenism, it has been said, was Liberty, and of the Jews Obedience; but Paul found a synthesis of the two when he proclaimed the "service which is perfect freedom."

On the Greeks of the best period the religious implications of the Apostle's words would, of course, have been utterly lost; but at the same the significance of his paradox is by no means lessened if we remember how these Greeks themselves conceived of liberty. Liberty to them did not mean licence. Control by irresponsible or irrational authority they consistently repudiated, but never the need for discipline voluntarily accepted, or, better still, self-imposed. Every civilization is based upon disciplines of one sort or another; but, on a broad view, none were ever more rigorous than theirs; and of this their very habits of mind—an indication of character which we tend often to underestimate—were a most revealing evidence. It was an intellectual discipline, uniquely strict in the use of language and logic, which gave them their extraordinary philosophic pre-eminence. And their æsthetic standards—the constraint which art sets on emotion—were at least equally severe. No poets have ever laid on themselves the shackles of such exacting metrical forms; no dramatists have obeyed such a rigid convention; and the technical methods of their sculptors and builders called for a combination of mental and manual precision which has no parallel. People of such a temper were little likely to shirk difficulties or refuse to face issues squarely.

Then again, politically, socially and even, from certain aspects, morally, too, the Greeks were, next to the Romans, the most disciplined race in antiquity. Their democratic type of government would never have worked for a day without a close regard for constitutional rules; and, turbulent as their assemblies must often have been (for they were an excitable people) there is nothing to show that debates ever got out of hand. Their military tactics demanded strenuous and accurate practice in concerted movement; and it was this superior discipline which won them their wars against Persia. Physical training was a national institution; and much of their dancing, a national pastime, was a species of musical drill. They enjoyed the ordered dignity of ceremonial; and their manners, if we except a blatancy about sex, showed a strong sense of decorum. They lived hard, energetic lives, holding effeminacy and indolence in special scorn; nor despite occasional orgies can they be considered by habit a self-indulgent race. Whatever their ethical shortcomings, they had their own peculiar virtues—the disciplined virtues of Restraint, Reason and Justice which their moralists so insistently preached. Thus they were free from the Jews' fanaticism and intolerance. They were not, like the Egyptians, the priest-ridden victims of gross superstition; and among them, take it all in all, the average citizen received a far fairer deal than at Rome.

Even when the spirit of Individualism grew, all was not immediately lost. A Plato's idealism could still attract a steady flow of pupils; and many of the finer spirits saw with the Stoics that Individualism was a challenge to greater self-mastery and not less. But logic and precept are not, in the long run, enough. Once the stimulus of patriotism was gone, man found themselves left, as we have seen, without a compelling motive; and in default of this the soul of Greece turned inwards upon itself. Art and literature increasingly echoed the past. The schools of philosophy lapsed, as Paul in his day discovered, into an academic sterility. Cynicism spread among the more thoughtful, and libertinism among the less. So character deteriorated till when Trajan the Emperor (like Juvenal the satirist) wrote about these incorrigible "Greeklings," he was voicing the sentiment almost universal among Romans—a half-pitiful contempt.

Individualism clearly is a dangerous adventure, as indeed for that matter are most good things in life. Nevertheless, without that heritage modern civilization would be something quite other than what it is. The whole fabric of our European and Christian tradition is rooted in the doctrine—so rudely challenged by Totalitarian creeds—that the State exists for the Individual, not the Individual for the State. And Toleration, that hall-mark of a truly civilized society, implies the threefold right of the Individual, to think his own thoughts, to utter them in public, and, so far as the welfare of his fellows will permit, to act in accordance with his own private conscience. This conception we owe to the Greeks; and, if Greece herself, as a political entity, was doomed to perish in bringing it to birth, that would not be a solitary example in history of the "seed which cannot be quickened except it die." To wish that her historic development had followed different lines would be not merely futile, but wrong-headed. "Individualism," it has been said, "may have destroyed many empires, but it is still the most precious thing the human race possesses." Zîto Hellas!

INDEX

BEACON PAPERBACKS